Body Dressing

Dress, Body, Culture

Series Editor **Joanne B. Eicher**, *Regents' Professor, University of Minnesota*

Books in this provocative series seek to articulate the connections between culture and dress which is defined here in its broadest possible sense as any modification or supplement to the body. Interdisciplinary in approach, the series highlights the dialogue between identity and dress, cosmetics, coiffure, and body alterations as manifested in practices as varied as plastic surgery, tattooing, and ritual scarification. The series aims, in particular, to analyze the meaning of dress in relation to popular culture and gender issues and will include works grounded in anthropology, sociology, history, art history, literature, and folklore.

ISSN: 1360-466X

Previously published titles in the Series

Helen Bradley Foster, *"New Raiments of Self": African American Clothing in the Antebellum South*

Claudine Griggs, *S/he: Changing Sex and Changing Clothes*

Michaele Thurgood Haynes, *Dressing Up Debutantes: Pageantry and Glitz in Texas*

Anne Brydon and Sandra Niesson, *Consuming Fashion: Adorning the Transnational Body*

Dani Cavallaro and Alexandra Warwick, *Fashioning the Frame: Boundaries, Dress and the Body*

Judith Perani and Norma H. Wolff, *Cloth, Dress and Art Patronage in Africa*

Linda B. Arthur, *Religion, Dress and the Body*

Paul Jobling, *Fashion Spreads: Word and Image in Fashion Photography*

Fadwa El-Guindi, *Veil: Modesty, Privacy and Resistance*

Thomas S. Abler, *Hinterland Warriors and Military Dress: European Empires and Exotic Uniforms*

Linda Welters, *Folk Dress in Europe and Anatolia: Beliefs about Protection and Fertility*

Kim K.P. Johnson and Sharron J. Lennon, *Appearance and Power*

Barbara Burman, *The Culture of Sewing*

Annette Lynch, *Dress, Gender and Cultural Change*

Antonia Young, *Women Who Become Men*

David Muggleton, *Inside Subculture: The Postmodern Meaning of Style*

Nicola White, *Reconstructing Italian Fashion: America and the Development of the Italian Fashion Industry*

Brian J. McVeigh, *Wearing Ideology: The Uniformity of Self-Presentation in Japan*

Shaun Cole, *Don We Now Our Gay Apparel: Gay Men's Dress in the Twentieth Century*

Kate Ince, *Orlan: Millennial Female*

Nicola White and Ian Griffiths, *The Fashion Business: Theory, Practice, Image*

Ali Guy, Eileen Green and Maura Banim, *Through the Wardrobe: Women's Relationships with their Clothes*

Linda B. Arthur, *Undressing Religion: Commitment and Conversion from a Cross-Cultural Perspective*

DRESS, BODY, CULTURE

Body Dressing

Edited by

Joanne Entwistle and Elizabeth Wilson

Oxford • New York

First published in 2001 by
Berg
Editorial offices:
150 Cowley Road, Oxford, OX4 1JJ, UK
838 Broadway, Third Floor, New York, NY 10003-4812, USA

Berg is an imprint of Oxford International Publishers Ltd.

Library of Congress Cataloging-in-Publication Data
A catalogue record for this book is available from the Library of Congress.

British Library Cataloguing-in-Publication Data
A catalogue record for this book is available from the British Library.

ISBN   1 85973 439 1 (Cloth)
       1 85973 444 8 (Paper)

Typeset by JS Typesetting, Wellingborough, Northants.
Printed in the United Kingdom by Biddles Ltd, Guildford and King's Lynn.

Contents

Contents

Introduction: Body Dressing

Joanne Entwistle and Elizabeth Wilson

In the last fifteen years the study of fashion and dress has been transformed. Interdisciplinarity has gained ground across the humanities and social sciences and scholars have approached fashion and dress from a number of perspectives that have challenged the marginal place of fashion within traditional academic scholarship. Within philosophy and sociology, for example, fashion has long been largely neglected or been considered as a frivolous endeavour not worthy of serious analysis.

In the same period there has been an explosion of interest in the body within a number of disciplines and it would seem that this should have provided the incentive to analyze fashion and dress more closely. However, academic interest in the body has not generally focused attention on fashion and dress. The need to address fashion from the point of view of its relationship to the body is therefore one of the aims of this book as is, we hope, demonstrating the value of such an engagement. *Body Dressing* aims also to capture some of the vitality of current research in the area. Further, it illustrates how the study of fashion and dress has become detached from its location within costume history and anthropology respectively, to flourish within social history, philosophy, sociology, social psychology and cultural studies. The links between and across these discipline boundaries then become clear.

In Britain, costume history originally emerged as a subset of art history, evolving from the dating of paintings; it was garment based and strongly empirical. Work on nineteenth- and twentieth- century fashion consisted largely of descriptive works on haute couture, although efforts were made by some historians to include a social and critical dimension. Serious disciplines, such as philosophy and sociology, neglected fashion and dress, unless to consider them from a moralistic point of view. One of the most influential, Thorstein Veblen, whose *Theory of the Leisure Class* was published in 1899, was still being quoted as an authority on dress in the 1960s and 1970s – and by writers on fashion, although he utterly rejected fashionable dress as not only wasteful, a form of 'conspicuous consumption', but also as irredeemably ugly. This view was replicated by Jean Baudrillard in the 1960s (Baudrillard, 1981). As Llewellyn Negrin has pointed out (Negrin, 1999), Baudrillard (1981) has since shifted his position (although in a different controversial direction). But in any case Veblen, Baudrillard, and for that matter the psychoanalytic writer, J. C. Flugel (1930), did little more than reiterate objections based on the idea of fashion as unnecessary, trivial and worldly – negative criticisms that had been around since the Christian divines of the sixteenth century fulminated against luxury and female sinfulness.

Dress *was* studied by anthropologists, but their work usually concentrated on 'traditional' and/or non-Western societies. Jennifer Craik (1993) has criticized the way in which fashion has been equated with Western dress. She argues that this is Eurocentric and fails to acknowledge the processes of change in dress practices throughout the world. However, even she admits that there is something special about Western dress in a consumer society in which a cycle of changing styles is deliberately fostered by the economic system.

It was for this reason that Veblen and sociologists such as Georg Simmel (1971), when they did analyze fashion, could perceive only its wastefulness. Simmel was able to see little point to it other than the search for distinction by the upper classes, a one-dimensional point of view that has, however, continued to dominate left-wing thinking on fashion until very recently.

The development of cultural studies in the late 1960s caused a gradual change in the way in which dress practices were perceived. Now, however, there was a move to the opposite end of the spectrum as authors interested themselves in sub-cultural style, with the publication of several influential studies such as those by Phil Cohen (1997 [1972]), Dick Hebdige (1979), Angela McRobbie (1989) and Paul Willis (1978, 1990). This was part of a commitment to the study of youth culture and radical groups in society. Hippies, punks and others signalled their dissidence forcefully in their modes of dress, which provided fruitful opportunities for the semiotic analysis of both overt and hidden meanings.

A number of theorists saw the manner in which dress communicated as a kind of language. This may have been partly because it had become somewhat commonplace to assert the idea that fashion and dress are ubiquitous to culture, a fundamental feature which defines humanity. This apparent universality is one of the reasons why fashion and dress are often compared to language. Moreover, it would seem that dress and language are part of the same fundamental human concern, namely to communicate. It is not surprising therefore to find the idea of language appropriated to explain dress and fashion (see, for example, Barnard 1996; Barthes 1985; Eco 1979; Lurie 1981). However, attempts such as Lurie's to demonstrate the language-like nature of fashion and dress are riddled with problems, not least of which is the problem of communication itself which is far less clear in the realm of clothing than it is with spoken language. Recognizing this problem, Fred Davis (1992) argues that dress is more like music than speech, suggestive and ambiguous rather than bound by the precise grammatical rules Lurie tried to apply.

Semiology is better able to deal with sign systems, linguistic and non-linguistic, but it too is problematic when applied to fashion and dress. Barthes' (1985) attempt to understand fashion discourse within fashion journalism illustrates how, in order to work, semiotics has to narrow its focus considerably. Barthes himself recognizes this in his study of the 'fashion system'. He notes how dress in everyday life is far more complex and messy than fashion discourse as laid out within the magazine and this is precisely the reason for his choice of the latter: it is, he says, the 'methodological purity' of fashion writing that makes it so accessible to analyse as opposed to the heterogeneity of everyday dress practice. In appropriating language to the realm of clothing both Lurie and Barthes (along with other semioticians such as Hebdige and Eco) approach fashion/dress as an abstract symbolic system. In this way, these structuralist approaches tend to be reductive, failing to take into account the many complex social dimensions of fashion as it is practiced in everyday life.

A further development in the 'culturalisation' of the social sciences was a growing interest in the study of the body in the last fifteen to twenty years. Yet between these two growing areas of interdisciplinary work – fashion/dress and the body – there has been relatively little cross fertilization. This is especially strange given the obvious relationship between them. It is also a striking omission given current fashion trends: while Western dress has become more androgynous and more casual, there has been an increased emphasis on the decoration of the body itself. Practices such as tattooing and piercing, once confined to marginal and deviant sections of society, have become widespread and there has been an ever increasing emphasis on fitness, the care of the body and beauty culture. A growing literature is emerging on these practices but there is a real absence of research on the more mundane and ordinary practices of dress and body decoration that have still be to examined. Conventions in the dress of, for example, professional figure skating and ballroom dancing (subcultures whose fashions have been little studied if at all) have shifted so that more and more of the body, particularly the bodies of women participants, have been revealed. Also, as Joanne Eicher points out in this book, celebrity events such as the annual Hollywood Oscar ceremony require female stars to bear ever more daring expanses of flesh.

Yet despite a steady stream of books on fashion and dress, as well as a more recent surge of interest in the body, there are few examples of research on fashion/dress which deal directly with the body (although see Entwistle 2000; Gaines and Herzog 1990; Wilson 1992). For the most part, fashion theorists have failed to give due recognition to the way in which dress is a fleshy practice involving the body. In other words, they disembody fashion and in doing so fail to consider the way in which fashion and dress are not merely textual or discursive but embodied practices. The dominance of linguistic explanations of fashion and dress has therefore led to rather narrow accounts, which neglect the place and significance of the body.

In fact, in the process of adding to, embellishing, covering or adorning, the body is shaped by culture and rendered meaningful. With its changing styles and constant innovation fashion is always reinventing the body, finding new ways of concealing and revealing body parts and thus new ways of making the body visible and interesting to look at. In addition, dress and fashion mark out particular kinds of bodies, drawing distinctions in terms of class and status, gender, age, sub-cultural affiliations that would otherwise not be so visible or significant. In this way, fashion can tell us a lot about the body in culture – throwing light on the ways in which bodies are made meaningful to us, as well as lending insight into the way in which the body enters into the realm of aesthetics.

Body Dressing addresses this relationship between fashion/dress and the body, suggesting new ways of thinking about this relationship and addressing the absence of scholarly work bridging the two. It draws on scholarship in a wide range of disciplines (sociology, cultural studies, anthropology, history, social psychology) in order to explore ways of understanding fashion and dress which acknowledge how they operate on the body. In this respect, the book demonstrates the diversity of approaches to fashion and dress and how, in recent years, this area has been liberated from traditional disciplinary domains.

The chapters in this book attend to the social and cultural context of dress, which were largely neglected by semioticians such as Barthes, and from a variety of perspectives to examine the way in which dress is integral to our relationship with the body. With the exception of Joanne Eicher, the authors deal with fashion, i.e. Western dress. However, what is interesting about this collection is that the fashionable dress they analyse is not haute couture. Here again, the book illustrates an important shift in scholarship on fashion, which, as we noted earlier, traditionally addressed haute couture almost exclusively. Only Caroline Evans' chapter on Alexander McQueen's collections deals with couture dress. She however, does not attempt to privilege him as genius creator but interprets the representations of the feminine in his shows. Most of the chapters thus deal with fashion from the perspective of daily practice rather than as a privileged artist practice. This is clear, for example, in Ruth Holliday's chapter on the way in which dress forms part of the routine experience of the self and body in everyday life.

It would do a disservice to the diversity of the perspectives presented here to suggest that the authors all share a similar theoretical and/or methodological approach. On the contrary, the papers presented in this book present a variety of perspectives and are suggestive of many different approaches to the study of fashion/dress. Indeed, they do not all share the same basic objective: some of the authors are concerned to address absences or failings within their own subjects areas and develop new ways of thinking about fashion and dress. Others are more concerned to illuminate particular practices, either historically or within contemporary culture.

Part One, 'Theoretical Approaches' groups together those authors concerned to address either the various problems with current theoretical work in the area and/or suggest new theoretical or methodological approaches. Thus, this section illustrates the very diverse nature of approaches within the field: the authors work within, and sometimes across, various disciplines – sociology, cultural studies, philosophy and social psychology. Kate Soper's chapter examines the relative neglect or repression of a philosophy of dress within the Western tradition. She suggests that perhaps 'repression' is more apt than 'neglect', since it might owe something to the Platonist emphasis on abstraction and the 'prioritisation of the mental, the rational and the spiritual over the corporeal, the material, and the sensual'. This tradition, which tended to define human identity by reference to mind rather than body, does amount to a repression of the body, anticipating the binary division fostered by Christianity between the 'nobility' of mind and spirit by contrast with the bodily 'low'. Joanne Entwistle's chapter also begins by acknowledging the absence of the body in studies of fashion and dress and indeed, the absence of dress in the current explosion of research on the body. She explores the various theoretical traditions within social theory, particularly post-structuralism and phenomen-ology, that can be drawn on to understand the way in which dress works on the body in a given context. She argues that dress is best understood as a 'situated bodily practice'. In a similar vein, Paul Sweetman's paper addresses the neglect of the corporeal in his discussion of classic and recent sociological and subcultural studies of dress, and focuses in particular on the work of Maffesoli and Bourdieu. He is critical of their work, as well as other scholarly research on fashion, which has neglected the phenomenological aspects of dress – the way in which dress is embodied. Studies of fashion have, he argues, treated the body as 'simply a mannequin or shop-window dummy – it is the clothing, rather than the wearing of it, that is regarded as significant'.

Susan Kaiser's concern is to find a framework for understanding the relation-ship between style, truth and subjectivity. This linkage is one that is pertinent within everyday life, where we want to 'express ourselves' and read others' dress as expressive of their identity, and is also important within academic literature which attempts to tease out the way in which dress is connected to, and expressive of some 'true' identity. Kaiser poses the idea of 'minding appearances' as one theoretical way of linking these three things – identity, truth and our appearance or style. Similarly, Efrat Tseëlon attempts to resolve another central problem within thinking of dress and in theories of fashion, namely how to understand gender difference in dress without essentializing it. Gender is probably the most crucial feature of dress, the aspect of identity most clearly and consistently articulated by clothes, and in this chapter Tseëlon proposes the idea of masquerade as a way to understand the gendering of the body through dress.

The idea of masquerade is taken up in Christoph Heyl's chapter, although his emphasis is not so much theoretical as concerned to understand the practices of masking and how they impacted upon the behaviour of the wearer. His chapter explores a variety of masks in non-masquerade contexts – in the seventeenth century as punishments and later, in the eighteenth century as accessories worn in the daytime. The wearing of such masks in public illustrates the ways in which outer bodily accoutrements are related both to the wearer's own body and sense of self in public and to the social context itself so as to effect patterns of behaviour in public. Heyl's chapter opens Part Two, 'Historical Case Studies' which explores specific practices of dress within the West. All these case studies trace the various ways in which practices of dress have marked, managed or displayed the body in particular ways. Ronnie Mirkin examines the costumed body in the English Renaissance through the concept of a 'prism' where ideologies, practices and the aesthetics of contemporary culture could converge. In contrast to costume historians who analyze dress but ignore or diminish the importance of the body, Mirkin's idea of the 'costumed body' acts to unify dress/body and how both are tied to performances of the self.

The remaining two chapters in this section tease out some of the ways in which dress forms part of our understanding of the gendered body. Drawing on a range of historical documents, especially those produced by the tailoring industry, Chris Breward examines how concerns about 'manliness' at the turn of the nineteenth century are stitched into the 'very seams and tucks of the modern man's wardrobe'. He examines the relationship between tailoring practice and discourse and the male body as a site for exploring the sartorial shift in men's relationship to dress at this time. As his examples show, the male body was perceived in this context as active, vigorous, even erotic, but also increasingly commodified in ways which had the potential to threaten its masculinity. The final historical chapter by Hilary Radner, which also deals with the representation of gender, moving us further into the twentieth century to explore the new feminine body as represented in 1960s magazine and photographic representation. Radner examines how the female body depicted in these representations defies a singular reading. Instead, they illustrate both a potentially democratic shift towards new forms of representing woman as autonomous but in ways which define this 'new woman' in terms of a style of body that is adolescent, requiring a rigorous regime of diet and exercise for the modern adult woman to maintain.

Part Three, 'Contemporary Case Studies' examines three very different contemporary practices around fashion, dress and the body. Caroline Evans' chapter explores the meanings of the feminine in Alexander McQueen's collections in the early 1990s. Like Radner, Evans is keen to eschew simplistic readings of McQueen's work, many of which have condemned it as misogynistic. She by contrast, argues that his 'theatre of cruelty' constructs a contemporary femme fatale whose appearance is one of aggressive and powerful sexuality rather than victim. Holliday and Eicher's chapters deal with issues of gender and sexuality at work in practices of dress. Holliday examines how dress forms the basis of identity construction, drawing on empirical data collected in the form of video diaries. She is concerned to explore how the idea of 'comfort', often used by her respondents, is used to explain and justify particular ways of dressing and presenting the self. Eicher likewise uses visual data, drawn from two very different cultural contexts – the dress of Euro-Americans and that of the Kalabari people of Nigeria – to illustrate how dress and the exposure of flesh is gendered. In both contexts, gender difference is marked out by how much flesh men and women show, particularly at formal occasions such as weddings and ceremonies, with women exposing more flesh than men in both examples. Both chapters illustrate the way in which gender and sexuality are not self-evidently given properties but ones in which dress plays a significant role.

Collectively, these papers represent the 'work in progress' of evolving disciplines. Naturally, they do not and cannot deal with all aspects of fashion and dress. Nor do they deal with the changing face of the physical performance that is embodied dress, although Evans' study of McQueen does indicate the way in which fashion has, at one level, become an aspect of popular culture, and at another approximates to performance art.

We hope that these chapters will be fruitful in suggesting further avenues for the development of studies of dress in relation to the body. There is much further work that could be explored, for example, non-Western dress within 'global' culture and how it is increasingly appropriated by western fashion. Kimonos and saris now travel the globe as 'fashion' whereas they were once seen as 'traditional', competing with jeans as part of daily dress in many Western wardrobes, indeed, are sometimes now worn *over* jeans. Other research could investigate specialized forms of dress in sports, dance and music video.

Further research could examine the relationship between textiles and the body: for example, developments in the manufacture of textiles that may in the future (and in some cases already do in the present) change the relationship between body and garment. Just as lycra since the 1980s has improved the fit of clothes and made new types of clothing possible, so now new 'intelligent' fibres that respond to changing temperatures have begun to appear. Tights that massage and moisturize the legs can be purchased in major department stores and we have other fabrics which work to keep us warm when it's cold and cool when it's hot. Changing social situations also create new forms of dress for different bodies, from the shields and headgear of the riot police to the face paint of the eco warriors. We should also not neglect the very divergent attitudes to the body and its display demonstrated by Western dress which reveals the body, on the one hand, and the veil (a term that stands for a number of different garments and practices) worn by some women which intends to obscure it on the other. Thus there is a real sense in which the chapters in this book represent less a definitive word on the subject than contributions to an ongoing dialogue. We hope they are useful and constructive and look forward to future conversations.

References

Barnard, M. (1996), *Fashion as Communication*, London: Routledge.

Barthes, R. (1985), *The Fashion System*, London: Cape.

Baudrillard, J. (1981), *For a Critique of the Political Economy of the Sign*, St Louis, MO: Telos.

Cohen, P. (1997 [1972]), 'Subcultural Conflict and Working-Class Community', in K. Gelder and S. Thornton (eds), *The Subcultures Reader*, London: Routledge.

Craik, J. (1993), *The Face of Fashion*, London: Routledge.

Davis, F. (1992), *Fashion, Culture and Identity*, Chicago: Chicago University Press.

Eco, U. (1979), *Travels in Hyper Reality*.

Eco, U. (1979), *A Theory of Semiotics*, Bloomington: Indiana University Press.

Entwistle, J. (2000), *The Fashioned Body: theorizing fashion and dress in modern society*, Cambridge: Polity.

Flügel, J.C. (1930), *The Psychology of Clothes*, London: The Hogarth Press.

Gaines, J. and Herzog, C. (eds) (1990), *Fabrications: Costume and the Female Body*, London: Routledge.

Hebdige, D. (1979), *Subculture: The Meaning of Style*, London: Methuen.

Lurie, A. (1981), *The Language of Clothes*, New York: Random House.

McRobbie, A. (1989), *Zoot Suits and Secondhand Dresses*, Macmillan.

Negrin, L. (1999), 'The Self as Image: A Critical Appraisal', in *Theory, Culture and Society*, 16 (3): 99–118.

Simmel, G. (1971), 'Fashion', in D. Levine, N. (ed.), *On Individuality and Social Forms*, London: University of Chicago Press.

Sweetman, (1999), 'Anchoring the (Postmodern) Self? Body Modification, Fashion and Identity', *Body & Society*, 5 (2–3): 51-76.

Veblen, T. (1953 [1899]), *The Theory of the Leisure Class: An Economic Study of Institutions*, New York: Mentor.

Willis, P. (1978), *Profane Culture*, London: Routledge & Kegan Paul.

Willis, P. (1990), *Common Culture: Symbolic Work at Play in the Everyday Cultures of the Young*, Milton Keynes: Open University Press.

Wilson, E. (1992), 'The Postmodern Body', in J. Ash and E. Wilson (eds), *Chic Thrills: A Fashion Reader*, London: Pandora.

Part One

Theoretical Approaches

Dress Needs: Reflections on the Clothed Body, Selfhood and Consumption

Kate Soper

Thomas Carlyle (1888: 1–2) opens his work, *Sartor Resartus,* by remarking that

> We have disquisitions on the Social Contract, on the Standard of Taste, on the Migration of the Herring . . . Philosophies of Language, of History, of Pottery, of Apparitions, of Intoxicating Liquors . . . . The whole life of humanity has been elucidated: scarcely a fragment or fibre of his Soul, Body, and Possessions – not a cellular, vascular, muscular Tissue – but has been probed, dissected, distilled desiccated and scientifically decomposed . . . How then comes it that the grand Tissue of all Tissues, the only real Tissue, should have been quite overlooked – the vestural Tissue, namely, or woollen or other cloth; which Man's Soul wears as its outmost wrappage and overall; wherein his whole other Tissues are included and screened, his whole Faculties work, his whole Self lives, moves, and has its being?

In other words, how come we have no Philosophy of Clothes?

The question, of course, is not intended very seriously, and the voluminous 'Philosophy of Clothes' offered by the fictional Professor Teufelsdröckh, whose life and career form the subject matter of *Sartor Resartus* is, in fact, the vehicle for Carlyle's idiosyncratic engagement with the speculative German philosophy of the day. Yet the point about the relative absence of philosophical engagement with dress could well be taken more seriously. For when we consider the role of clothing and bodily adornment in the lives of human beings, and how complex our attitudes to dress are, its seems remarkable how little philosophers (as opposed to sociologists, cultural historians or anthropologists) have had to say about the 'clothed body'.

There are, of course, some qualifications to be made here. In the first place, philosophy does, like other modes of discursive reasoning, draw quite extensively on clothing simile and metaphor in its references to veils and embroideries, folds and pleated arguments, on the one hand, bare facts and naked givens, on the other. There are also some disputes – notably those associated with the Enlightenment in the late eighteenth century – which very consciously invoke the clothing metaphor. Consider, for example, the terms in which Mary Wollstonecraft and Edmund Burke express their differences over Enlightenment humanism. While Wollstonecraft complains against the 'gorgeous drapery' in which Burke has 'enwrapped his tyrannic principles' (Wollstonecraft 1989: 25), Burke himself charges Wollstonecraft with seeking to denude society of all the 'decent drapery of human life'. Is all this, he asks, to be rudely torn away? Are 'all the super-added ideas, furnished from the wardrobe of moral imagination, which the heart owns and the understanding ratifies, as necessary to cover the defects of our naked shivering nature, and to raise it to dignity in our own estimation, to be exploded as ridiculous, absurd, and antiquated fashion?' (Burke 1961: 90; cf.19). To defend the idea of a commonly shared human nature is indeed, according to Burke, to strip us of all the protective clothing of custom without which we reduce to the level of beast, an animal literally without clothing.

We are referred to clothing, then, in the rhetoric of philosophical exchanges; and there are also occasions when items of clothing get caught up in philo-sophical debates. One example, well known to Continental philosophers, is the long-running preoccupation, sparked by Heidegger in his essay on 'The Origin of the Work of Art' (Heidegger 1971; Shapiro 1968), and latterly given a new lease of life by Derrida in his *The Truth in Painting*, with a pair (or is it, as Derrida queries, merely a couple?) of old boots in a painting by Van Gogh (Derrida 1987: 255–382). The debate is a complex one: in part it is about who owned the real boots depicted in the picture, a peasant, as Heidegger claims, or the painter, Van Gogh, himself, and how far Heidegger in his sympathy in 1935-6 with the *Volk* pathos and its 'call to the earth', has sought to appropriate them for his own philosophical feet; but it is in part also about whether this question of the ownership of the represented boots has any real bearing on the understanding of Heidegger's aesthetic argument, or of what is going on in painting generally and how, if at all, it may be said to register truth. I do not intend to discuss its ramifications any further here, but simply cite it as an instance of the kind of way philosophers have at times related to matters of dress, and even developed their own shoe fetishes.

All the same, neither in the recourse to clothing metaphors, nor in such cases as the Van Gogh boots can we be said to be offered any but a rather oblique set of references to the questions about human needs for dress upon which I want to focus here, and which I have in mind in speaking of the relative philosophical neglect of clothing. Or perhaps repression is the apter term: for I think we have to relate this neglect ultimately to the Platonist emphasis in the Western philosophical tradition – that is, to its abstraction and prioritisation of the mental, the rational and the spiritual over the corporeal, the material, and the sensual, and the related tendency to define what is distinctive to human being in terms of the possession of mind or soul rather than by reference to embodied existence. In the words of Nietzsche's challenge to this tradition, 'philosophy says away with the body, this wretched idée fixe of the senses, infected with all the faults of logic that exist, refuted, even impossible, although it be impudent enough to pose as if it were real'. (Nietzsche 1974: 34–5; cf.18). Nor is it any accident that this type of critique of the philosophical distrust of the flesh has been subsequently deepened and elaborated in the feminist attack on philosophy's repudiation of the body as the intellectual form of its repudiation of the feminine. For when philosophy said 'away with the body' it always also, in effect, said 'away with the female'. In this sense, the philosophical disengagement from the sartorial can be viewed as the most readily disregarded 'outmost wrappage' (to invoke Carlyle's phrase) of a stance that has typically been at once both anti-corporeal and androcentric.

This is a stance which also lends itself to a more general cultural process of gender stereotyping and masculine disassociation in Western culture, according to which it is women who are the vainer sex and the more concerned with what they wear while men are largely indifferent to questions of attire. Yet showiness in dress is quite compatible with, even a mark of, manliness in certain contexts such as the military parade;[1] and as Virginia Woolf (1992) pointed out some time ago in her *Three Guineas*, male attitudes to dress have been just as concerned and, if anything, even more complicated than those of women – and especially on the part of those in the academy and other areas of public life. Whereas dress for women, she claims (1992: 179), is a comparatively simple matter, having only two functions additional to covering the body – those of creating beauty for the eye and attracting the admiration of the male sex; for men themselves it is altogether more significant:

> your dress in its immense elaboration has obviously another function. It not only covers nakedness, gratifies vanity, and creates pleasure for the eye, but serves to advertise the social, professional, or intellectual standing of the wearer. If you will excuse the humble illustration, your [male] dress fulfils the same function as the tickets in a grocer's shop. But here instead of saying 'This is margarine; this pure butter; this is the finest butter in the market,' it says, 'This man is a clever man – he is Master of Arts; this man is a very clever man – he is Doctor of Letters; this man is a most clever man – he is Member of the Order of Merit.'

And she goes on to point out that a woman 'who advertised her motherhood by a tuft of horsehair on the left shoulder would scarcely be considered
a very venerable object' (Woolf 1992: 176–80). We might want to claim, in
fact, that if there are, or have been, significant differences between the sexes
in respect of their attitudes to dress they have been less to do with the degree
of experienced vanity than with the extent to which the feeling has been openly
acknowledged. Men, perhaps, have been inclined to disavow an interest to
which women have more readily admitted. However, all such claims are to
some extent speculative and need to be scrutinized in the light of the historical
evidence. The point here, surely, is that any comparative history, whether
for Europe or anywhere else, of the differences between men and women in
the type and level of their interest in clothing would prove an immensely
complex affair reflecting huge disparities in terms of class and other social
stratifications, but also, of course, amounting to little less than a history
itself of shifting patterns of genderization (Ash and Wilson 1997; Barnes
and Eicher 1993; Breward 1995; Bullough & Bullough 1993; Cavallaro and
Warwick, 1998; Evans and Thornton 1989; Finkelstein 1991; Flugel 1950;
Garber 1992; Laver 1966; Silverman 1986; Wilson 1985).

I am not in a position to offer any contribution to that kind of history here.
Nor shall I be engaging in an explicitly feminist theorisation of dress and the
body. My argument in what follows, however, is offered in awareness of the
complex interconnection between the Platonising repudiation of the body
and its post-de Beauvoirean feminist critique.[2] It is also offered, more
generally, with an eye to the need to qualify and rethink some of the more
conventional assumptions about dress, including those – often associated
with the gender stereotyping I have noted – which invite us to think of it, and
our attitudes to it, as a less complex matter than they truly are. In an overall
way, I shall be drawing on philosophy and literature to explore aspects of
these attitudes in a way that I hope can supplement while in no way vying
with their extensive treatment in sociology and cultural theory.

The question of the human 'need' for dress is interestingly posed – but
not entirely satisfactorily answered – by King Lear in his well-known response
to his daughters' queries as to why he needs the company of such an extensive
retinue of men:

> O, reason not the need ! Our basest beggars
> Are in the poorest things superfluous.
> Allow not nature more than nature needs
> Man's life is cheap as beast's. Thou art a lady;
> If only to go warm were gorgeous,
> Why, nature needs not what thou gorgeous wear'st
> Which scarcely keeps thee warm.
>
> (Act II, scene 4, ll.263–9)

The need for clothing as providing warmth or protection is one thing, suggests Lear, the need we have for it as 'gorgeous apparel' yet another; the one is natural or that which 'nature needs', the other: what? A luxury? Well, yes and no. Yes in the sense that it is not an exigence of nature; no in the sense that it is nonetheless a *human* need, and in being such, as opposed to a want, on a par with the need for clothing as warmth and protection. Dress, Lear seems to imply, is both essential to survival in certain climes and conditions, or while undertaking certain activities; but also wholly 'unneeded', except as decoration or mode of expression – but therefore also, in another sense, entirely essential (cf. Flugel 1950, Chap.1). And maybe, therefore, also 'natural' too, despite what Lear says? At any rate, since some form of decoration of the body and its use as signifier has been a feature of human societies from earliest times, we are not talking here of a need that is any more obviously 'cultural' in status than that for clothing as protection. Nor it would seem, are we talking of a need that is 'cultural' or 'non-natural' in the sense of being entirely exclusive to human beings, at least not if we allow some analogy of function here with that of fur and feather, which also serve other animals both as protection and as display.

All the same, if clothing may, indeed, be said to satisfy needs that are 'natural' in the sense of being held in common with other creatures, we should recognize that it also serves needs of a more strictly aesthetic and semiotic kind which *are* exclusive to human beings. In Christian mythology, we acquire our clothes in losing our 'natural' innocence and coming into knowledge of good and evil. Clothes are in this sense definitively cultural objects closely bound up with a sense of shame, and their primary purpose is to conceal the organs of those functions (sexual intercourse, lactation, excretion) which have been deemed to degrade us by tying us too closely to a bestial nature. Clothes, in short, serve us as a cardinal marker of the *divide* between ourselves and the rest of the animal world. By this I do not mean that the donning of clothes is essential to being human, which it obviously is not. Clothes wearing does not present itself as a possible candidate for defining humanity in the way that language or tool use or the capacity to laugh have been thought to do. The point, rather, is that clothes have been very extensively used to assert the cultural status of human beings, to police the border between humans and animals, to deny or cover over our animality and thereby preserve a seemly distance from the beast. Where other animals go about unclad, or clad only in the garments bestowed on them by their human owners or protectors, only in privacy or in very exceptional social circumstances are human beings found without at least some garments, if only the fig leaf equivalent.

Pondering in his second *Meditation* on how to overcome his doubts about the existence of the so-called external world, Descartes takes the example of a piece of wax: how does he acquire his knowledge that the molten wax is the same as the wax solidified despite the multiple changes it undergoes? Descartes argues that he would be disposed to conclude that this knowledge were acquired through the act of sight and not by intuition of the mind, were it not, as he puts it,

> for the analogous instance of human beings passing in the street below, as observed from a window. In this case I do not fail to say that I see the men themselves, just as I see the wax; and yet what do I see from the window beyond hats and cloaks that might cover artificial machines, whose motions might be determined by springs? But I judge that there are human beings from these appearances, and thus I comprehend by the faculty of judgement alone which is in the mind, what I believed I saw with my eyes.

Being clothed, Descartes presumes, is the mark of a distinctively human form of consciousness, of being a 'person' (Descartes, 1924: 92–3).[3] One is not suggesting here that Descartes thinks a person to be a person must be clothed. It is true that he mistakenly implies that the hats and cloaks form an irremovable surface to their human wearers analogously to the way in which its surface appearances are an inseparable feature of the wax. All the same, it seems fair to suppose that had his window looked onto a nudist camp Descartes would still have posed essentially the same question as to how he knew these naked bodies were not the surface appearance of automata. The point is not that clothing is essential to being a person, but only that, once clothed, the presumption of personhood is overriding – and that in picking out hatted and coated entities as the appropriate beings for his judgement, Descartes had already in effect acknowledged their human status.

Clothing, then, signals a human wearer, and in doing so is tied into our conceptions of dignity, personhood and bodily integrity. But the linkage is complex and overdetermined since it reflects both the instrumental interest in clothing as bodily protection, and our sense of self as seen by others, and this latter may take a variety of forms, ranging from extreme diffidence and discretion, on the one hand, to blatant self-assertion and ostentation, on the other. Some of this complexity is registered in the distinction which Rousseau draws in his *Discourse on Inequality* (1973: 64–75) between *amour de soi* and *amour propre*, the former being the mode of self-love associated with instincts for self-preservation (and which Rousseau thinks we share with other animals); the latter being the self-esteem or vanity which he presents as a distinctive feature of being human, and which is essentially social and other-dependent in origin (and hence, he argues, emulative and factitious in tendency).[4]

Sometimes, no doubt, we do literally just dress in the mode of *amour de soi*: as we say, to please ourselves, but this tends to happen only where there is no one to appear to; and for the most part, clothing or adornment is about satisfaction of *amour propre*, where the aim is indeed other directed: the point is to dress in the manner in which we are happy for others to see us. This may be either with a view to their barely noticing us (or noticing us only for our discretion), or with the more extrovert end of focusing their attention on us.

Where the latter form of vanity is more to the fore, it is either in respect of what Virginia Woolf calls the advertisement function (where the robes, and garters and wigs and insignia pronounce upon the professional or intellectual achievements of the wearer (Woolf 1992: 176)); or it is to signal the wearer's identification with a particular clique or constituency; or it is with an eye to the sexual attraction we want to exert. (The designer, Vivienne Westwood, may here be right in her suggestion that fashion in dress is about eventually being naked. We dress at least in part in order to entice others into wanting us undressed. Carlyle's Professor Teufelsdröckh offers a comparable insight: 'The beginning of all Wisdom,' he remarks, ' is to look fixedly on clothes . . . until they become transparent' (1888: 45)).

But in its less extrovert and sexually directed mode, vanity or *amour propre* in dress, is about *not* being noticed or not being noticed *as* someone demanding attention, sexual or otherwise. If the first step to this kind of self-effacement is not to go naked, the second is to adhere to the ramifying and complex dress codes which obtain in one's culture. It is in this sense – as Umberto Eco suggested in a talk to a 1970s conference on structuralism – that dress is most comparable to language:

> I am speaking through my clothes. If I were wearing a Mao suit, if I were without a tie, the ideological connotations of my speech would be changed. Obviously fashion codes are less articulate, more subject to historical fluctuations than linguistic codes are. But a code is no less a code for the fact that it is weaker than the stronger ones. Gentlemen button suit jackets shirts and coats from left to right, ladies from right to left. Suppose I were speaking of semiotics standing in front of you buttoned from right to left: it would be very difficult for you to eliminate a subtle connotation of effeminacy, in spite of my beard. (Eco 1973: 59)[5]

But we should note here, too, that even when clothing is selected with a view to discretion, or in maximum conformity to an existing protocol or 'language' of dress, it is still functioning as a form of self-expression and rooted in a certain aesthetic sensibility. Of some relevance here is Kant's claim in his *Critique of Judgement* that looking upon a human being as a person is at odds with looking upon him or her *purely* aesthetically. Essentially Kant's point is that judgement of aesthetic beauty in a person is intimately bound up with the conception of that person as determining his or her ends by reason – with the idea of his or her moral and intellectual being – and thus we cannot regard a human person in the way we would an entity of a purely ornamental kind. When, therefore, we judge a human being beautiful, we do so by reference to an *ideal* of Beauty, by reference, that is, to a conception of how what is outward and visibly manifest about the person accords with the notion of 'inner' humanity defined as a set of intellectual purposes.

We arrive at this ideal in part, Kant says, upon the basis of what is normal to the figure of a human being as a member of a particular animal species; but, more importantly, on the basis of a 'rational idea' of what outward forms or bodily manifestations are most appropriate to the revelation of the moral being of the person (Kant 1952: 72–80). Kant is thinking more in terms of physiognomy here, and does not actually say much about how clothing figures in this. On the one hand it might be argued that his position is quite consistent with dismissing dress as either pure instrument (of warmth, etc.) or else mere ornament distracting from the 'true' beauty of the human being. But it is also, I think, consistent with his position, and maybe is even an impli-cation of it, that insofar as we view the clothing as chosen by or voluntarily donned by a *person* in the normal course of life, we are committed to viewing it as something more than either mere instrumental source of protection, on the one hand, or as *purely* aesthetic addendum, on the other. We are committed, that is, to regarding it as aesthetic index or expression of the moral self, and would have to judge the extent of its 'seemliness' or 'beauty' accordingly. Clothing, we might say, from such a Kantian perspective is 'beautiful' only when it is not designed to be simply beautiful, only insofar as it is the phenomenal – and almost unconsciously chosen – effect of the ends of personhood.

It is arguably some such Kantian commitment which underlies the view that to care too much for one's clothing, or to display too much conscious-ness of it, is to reveal a failure of moral worth. Kant is justly criticized for the historical abstraction and culture-bound assumptions he makes about what it is to be 'human'; but he does, I think, also point to a relatively persistent rationale of our sense that clothes do not – or ought not – to matter very much.[6] To put it more paradoxically, he implies that clothes *do* have an aesthetic importance for us, but it lies precisely in conveying the sense that they are *not* mere adornment but 'seemly' signs of our rationality. Conversely, to delight in someone as mere 'doll' or clothes-horse is precisely – as the common parlance implies – to treat him or her as aestheticized objects rather than as fully human persons.

But if this is right, and our clothes do have this type of connection to a distinctively human sense of dignity and moral personhood, then by the same token they can also be used to mark out differing degrees of access to it, to undermine or deny it altogether. In the emphasis on the need for clothing as personal self-expression, we should not overlook the recourse to regulations on dress and the wearing of uniform as a means of excluding, oppressing and condemning. Nor should we forget the extent to which restrictions on human dress are used to distinguish and police social and sexual hierarchies. The extensive sumptuary laws on dress and other modes of consumption, which persisted until the nineteenth century, were expressly designed to preserve a supposedly natural and divinely ordained difference of class and rank, and to prevent upward mobility (Bell 1976; Sekora 1977: 60–80; Slater 1997: 68–9). Women have frequently in the past been the victims of rules on clothing which have denied them freedom of movement, sensory experience and expression, and which have sometimes directly led to irreparable physical damage. So, too, have many infants and children; and this is not even to begin to speak of the multiple cultural uses in our own times of dress or insignia to ostracize or humiliate particular classes and groups of individuals. If it is true that the preservation of human dignity and autonomy is closely bound up with the wearing of clothes and the choice of what one wears, it is also precisely because of this that one, very insidious, way of exercising power over others is by means of control over their mode of dress.

Nowhere is this more cruelly exemplified than in the denial of clothing altogether. To take away a person's clothing is to put him or her 'out on the heath', to snatch away the clutched straw of human dignity. As all prison camp guards and torturers have always been well aware, to force strip the victim is to initiate the process of dehumanisation, to signal contempt for personal identity by playing with or mocking at the aspiration to preserve it. The power of denuding the other in these contexts is also the power to de-personalise the other's clothing or adornment: to treat it as mere use-value without ulterior significance: as so much anonymous stuff for others to use, gold and silver to be melted down. Behind the horror of the holocaust images of piled-up clothing and jewellery is the sense of a world from which all person-alizing sentiment has been deliberately eliminated or, worse, preserved, but only in an involuted mode in which it is made an object of derision. This is the world within which the torturer knows so well how to move about. One of the most abhorrent narratives in Neil Belton's recent book on Helen Bamber, the founder of the Medical Foundation for the Care of the Victims of Torture, is that of the pain inflicted on the Chilean, Luis Munos, whose tormentors under Pinochet took his clothes and wore them themselves while they were torturing him. As Munos himself put it, speaking to Bamber on a 134 bus in North London:

> It's as though they want you to feel you are torturing yourself; something that you've honoured and bought and worn, your leather jacket, your jeans, your shirt; they are suggesting to you that they have completely removed your personality, and it reverses everything, takes a personality and destroys everything a person loves, like playing music while torturing. (Belton 1999: 226)

These are extreme and abnormal contexts from whose atrocities most of us are mercifully spared. But the qualities of clothing reflected here – its protective role as a 'bandage' or 'dressing' against the pain of involuntary exposure of nudity (Scarry, 1985, pp. 281–2); its figuring of the human; its linkage in a special intimacy with its owner – all these have other repercussions of a kind which *are* more generally experienced. Even as it signifies our cultural status and raises us above other animality, clothing can also bear melancholic witness to the mortality and subjection to biological process which we share with the rest of nature. Much of our clothing and bodily adornment will outlast us, sometimes by many years, thus escaping the relatively speedy post mortem decomposition of our fleshly selves; and it is arguably this combination of proximity with the organic body and alterity from it that is responsible for the poignancy of lost or no longer needed clothing. The pathos or morbid quality of garments bereaved of their owners has frequently been commented on in cultural works, and was a reference point for several of the exhibits at the recently staged Hayward Gallery exhibition, 'Addressing the Century: 100 Years of Art and Fashion'. Lun'aa Menoh's spectral dresses chart the history of changing modes of dress by means of a ghostly fashion parade. Emily Bates' disturbing *Depilator* dress is itself woven from hair; and Mona Hatoum's *Hair Necklace* also plays on a similar ambiguity between adornment and relic.

Figure 1.1 Lun⋆a Menoh *Spring and Summer Collections 1770–1998* (1998) Lun⋆a Menoh. © Lun⋆a Menoh. Photo: Relah Eckstein.

Figure 1.2 Emily Bates *Depilator* (1994). Spun and knitted human hair
260 × 75 × 20 cm. © Emily Bates (1998). Contemporary Arts Society,
London. Photo: Shirley Tipping.

But there are poignant registers in literature too. Take Pip's reaction on first perceiving Miss Havisham in her withered bridal attire:

> Once, I had been taken to see some ghastly waxwork at the Fair, representing I know not what impossible personage lying in state. Once, I had been taken to one of our old march churches to see a skeleton in the ashes of a rich dress, that had been dug out of a vault under the church pavement. Now, waxwork and skeleton seemed to have dark eyes that moved and looked at me. I should have cried out, if I could. (Dickens 1965: 87).

Or Thomas Mann's arresting description in *The Magic Mountain* of Hans Castorp's experience of looking at the x-ray of his beringed hand:

> Hans Castorp saw precisely what he must have expected, but what is hardly permitted man to see, and what he had never thought it would be vouchsafed him to see: he looked into his own grave. The process of decay was forestalled by the powers of the light-ray, the flesh in which he walked disintegrated, annihilated, dissolved in vacant mist, and there within it was the finely turned skeleton of his own hand, the seal ring he had inherited from his grandfather hanging loose and black on the joint of his ring-finger – a hard, material object, with which man adorns the body that is fated to melt away beneath it, when it passes on to another flesh that can wear it for yet a little while. With the eyes of his Tienappel ancestress, penetrating, prophetic eyes, he gazed at this familiar part of his body, and for the first time in his life he understood that he would die. (Mann 1960: 218–19).

Clothing or jewellery, then, in being destined to become a residue of the living person, can also figure as memento mori.

What seems, in virtue of our mortality, to be foregrounded about clothing is its separable and even alien quality. We are struck by the anomaly of our condition as biological creatures who live our lives so 'unnaturally' bedecked. But if it is the uncannily artificial quality of clothing and adornment that post-humously asserts itself and causes a tremor of angst, this is no more than the antithesis we would expect to the intimacy of the connection in life between the human body and its garb. Indeed, so close is this intimacy that we may well wonder quite where to draw the line between nature and artifice. It is this question which is wittily raised by several of Magritte's paintings, or by Elsa Schiaparelli's and Meret Oppenheims's glove-hands or Pierre Cardin's shoe-feet: what exactly counts as clothing – where does the body end and the accoutrement or decoration begin? Is there, indeed, a way in which garments, as we say, 'become' the wearer? – meaning by this, of course, not that they literally mutate into their owners, but that they express, or assume, or even form an emanation of their personality.

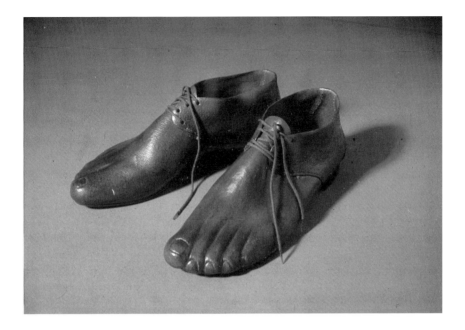

Figure 1.3 Pierre Cardin. *Men's shoes with toes* (1986). Brown leather
11 × 24.5 × 29.4 cm. Museum of the Fashion Institute of Technology,
New York. Gift of Richard Martin. Photo: Irving Solero.

Proust captures something of this quandary in a satirical passage in *Recherche du Temps Perdu* where the item of adornment – in this case the monocle – is presented as metonymic of the wearer.

The Marquis de Forestell's monocle was minute and rimless, and, by enforcing an incessant and painful contraction of the eye over which it was incrusted like a superfluous cartilage, the presence of which there was inexplicable and its substance unimaginable, it gave to his face a melancholy refinement, and led women to suppose him capable of suffering terribly when in love. But that of M. de Saint-Candé girdled, like Saturn, with an enormous ring, was the centre of gravity of a face which composed itself afresh every moment in relation to the glass, while his thrusting red nose and swollen sarcastic lips endeavoured by their grimaces to rise to the level of the steady flame of wit that sparkled in the polished disc, and saw itself preferred to the most ravishing eyes in the world by the smart, depraved young women whom it set dreaming of artificial charms and a refinement of sensual bliss; and then, behind him, M. de Palancy, who with his huge carp's head and goggling eyes moved slowly up and down the stream of festive gatherings, unlocking his great mandibles at every moment as though in search of his orientation, had the air of carrying upon his person only an accidental and perhaps purely symbolical fragment of the glass wall of his aquarium . . . . (Proust 1966: 152–3).[7]

Figure 1.4 Elsa Schiaparelli, *Pair of Gloves*, (1938). Black suede, red snakeskin cording. Philadelphia Museum of Art. Gift of Elsa Schiaparelli. Photo: Lynn Rosenthal (1998).

In this rather astonishing confounding of the biological eye and its glassy accountrement, it is as if we have an analogue for the superficial and vacuous being of the monocle wearers themselves – a being which has no deeper level of existence than the artificial tropes and conventions through which it makes its social appearance.

Indeed, even as the passage charts the idiosyncratic modes wherein the monocle wearers have 'become' their monocle (or their monocle has become a part of them . . .), it portrays them also as mere followers of fashion who have collectively lent themselves to a passing vogue in eye-wear. It thus points to the equivocations of fashion itself (to turn now briefly to this, in conclusion . . .) since fashion seems to deny personal distinction even as it promises to secure it. Dressing in fashion is in this respect quite distinct from using one's clothing as a form of individual expression. One can be very concerned, for what might be called 'Kantian' reasons, with what one wears without caring a fig-leaf about what is in fashion or whether one's clothing conforms to that.

Fashion certainly offers the individual some novelty, the escape from repetition and the cyclical mode of being. But it does so only in a rather ironical and self-subverting mode. Oscar Wilde famously described high fashion as 'a form of ugliness so unbearable that we are compelled to alter it every six

26

months'. In Elizabeth Wilson's more nuanced account: 'a new fashion starts from rejection of the old and often an eager embracing of what was previously considered ugly; it therefore subtly undercuts its own assertion that the latest thing is somehow the final solution to the problem of how to look'. (Wilson 1985: 9). The paradox of fashion, moreover, is that it presents itself as a means of self-realization, but only on condition you submit to the dictate of a collectivity you have neither willed nor authored.

In this respect its ontology is what Sartre (in his *Critique of Dialectical Reason*) terms 'serial': a series (as opposed to a 'group') being comprised of a plurality of isolations and lacking any concerted project of social transformation (Sartre 1976: 256–69). A serial formation is one brought into being through the passive agreement of separate individuals to live their interiority as exteriority; and its existence is inherently centrifugal and dispersing, or, as Sartre puts it, 'in flight'.

Individuals are thus linked in following a fashion but only impersonally and always dispensably as individuals. It is collectivity without solidarity. To the existence of a fashion, whatever kind it be, it matters not who follows it, provided only that sufficient number do so. In the context of capitalism, high-street fashion may offer the individual a kind of way of belonging, but only in the pseudo-mode of the serial collective – in the mode of the market

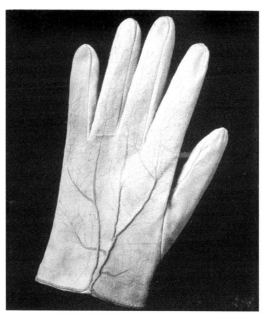

Figure 1.5 Meret Oppenheim, *Project for Parkett No. 4* (1985). Goat suede with silk-screen, hand-stitched, one of an edition of 50, h. 20 cm. © DACS (1998). Private collection, Matthias Beltz, Frankfurt am Main, Germany.

itself, which flourishes on constantly renewed ways of providing essentially homogeneous forms of consumption rather than on promoting genuine difference and eccentricity. Moreover, as profits have come to derive increasingly from quick turnover and style innovation rather than from sheer volume production, this market dynamic has become ever more insistent in our lives.[8] In this respect, clothing fashion is exemplary of the way in which consumerist culture plays on (and enables huge profits to be gained from) the anxieties about individuation and self-expression it both stimulates and condemns. It provides

Figure 1.6 *Philosophy in the Boudouir* 1966. Magritte. Gouache 74 × 65 cm. Private Collection.

a way of accommodating the contradictory injunction that the individual should both stand out from the crowd and merge with it. It promises a certain 'distinction' while sparing the person from the social stigma of really exceptional or non-conformist behaviour.

Marx, as is known, viewed the establishment of the capitalist mode of production and its generalized system of exchange-relations as having a double-edged impact on individual needs and forms of self-realization (Marx 1973: 471–514; Soper 1981: 125–42). On the one hand, in severing the personal ties and localised dependencies of the feudal order, it destroyed the erstwhile bases of self-making and reproduction, thus denying individuals a mode of self-extension or objective dimension of being in their relationship to the land, or in their particular tasks and fixed role in their community; and in being deprived of these inorganic conditions of self-extension, individuals are rendered, as Marx puts it, 'objectless' or 'naked in their subjectivity'. On the other hand, Marx also presents this very deprivation or loss of the objective presuppositions of self-reproduction as the essential precondition of a much richer – all-round – development of the self, because it frees the individual from (in his words) 'all traditional, confined, complacent, encrusted satis-factions of present needs, and reproductions of old ways of life' (Marx 1973: 409–10). (Although, as he also emphasized, this was a potentiality for self-realization that could never be realized so long as it was confined within the contradictory structure of capitalist relations of ownership, exchange and distribution).

Looked at from the perspective of this double but unresolved dynamic of capitalist commodification, we might see the seriality of fashion as both com-pensating, if only in a very partial and ultimately unsatisfactory way, for the loss of more traditional forms of self-extension and collective belonging; but also, and conversely, as offering a mode of consumption which gratifies, if again only very partially, the urge to escape from any fixed and presupposed existence and sense of self. Some of the seduction of high-street fashion, one might say, lies precisely in its combination of social seriality and personal alienation: in the fact that one can join in a kind of collective project, but entirely anonymously and without any commitment to its continuity. Fashion attracts, paradoxically, even perversely, because it seems to solve the problem of how to belong without having to belong – without any real personal investment or self-exposure.

But if it would be a mistake to deny or overlook the seduction of this form of alterity, it would also be a mistake to deny the displaced, compensatory and superficial aspects of market-driven fashion consumption; and also very wrong to condone a form of affluent gratification so dependent on deprivation and exploitation of the poorer areas of the globe.

There will always be a human need for clothing both as a protection against the elements and as self-display. But fashion-following, although interesting in what it reveals about the resistance to fixed conceptions of selfhood, and the complexity of modern forms of narcissism and *amour propre*, would seem to offer to 'naked subjectivity' only a very inadequate and threadbare mode of self-extension.

In this sense, like so many other aspects of modern consumption, it invites us to think about how we might secure innovation and a non-cyclical mode of existence without social and ecological exploitation; and thus to consider what alternative sources of self-realization and collective belonging might substitute for those currently so reliant upon the acquisition of new style commodities.

Notes

1. Bell has noted the 'eminent place' of war in the sartorial history of men, and calls attention to the role of military dress in arousing sexual admiration (1976: p. 43 and pp. 148–51). Cf. also Silverman on the ostentation of male dress and the possible reasons for it (1986: pp. 139ff).

2. Clearly there are precursors in earlier feminist argument to de Beauvoir's argument in *The Second Sex*, but I would nonetheless treat this as the founding text of feminist *philosophy* in virtue of its sustained analysis of the relationship between the 'secondary' status of women and the philosophical idealization of a supposedly intrinsically masculine, and mentalistic, power of transcendence. It is no accident that *The Second Sex* is the first philosophical work to deal at length with embodiment, reproduction, narcissism and vanity. Any extended bibliography of post de Beauvoirean feminist critiques of the philosophical treatment of the body would be inappropriate in this context, but some of the more influential discussion is to be found in the work of Monique Wittig, Luce Irigaray, Elizabeth Grotz, Susan Bordo, Michelle le Doeuf, Rosi Braidotti and Judith Butler.

3. Certainly the judgement is analogous, but clothes are not analogous to the surface of the wax since they are, of course, removable.

4. In a footnote on the distinction, Rousseau writes, '*Amour propre* must not be confused with *amour de soi* ; for they differ both in themselves and in their effects. *Amour de soi* is a natural feeling which leads every animal to look to its own preservation, and which guided in man by reason and modified by compassion, creates humanity and virtue. *Amour propre* is a purely relative and factitious feeling, which arises in the state of society, leads each individual to make more of himself than of any other, causes all mutual damage men inflict one on another, and is the real source of the "sense of honour"' (p. 66).

5. Cf. Barthes 1983; Lurie 1992.

6. In concluding her major work on clothes and art (1993: p. 450), Hollander writes, 'Serious people, aspirers to unworldliness, devotees of the importance of things-not-seen, are particularly unhappy with the idea of clothes and especially with the phenomenon of fashion – the thing (. . .) that makes clothing resist any universal idealization of use or aspect.'

7. Cf. the citations of Proust on fashion in Silverman (1986: p. 146), and McDowell (1995: pp. 255–8).

8. Between 1971 and 1989, to cite but one example, the average life of Nike shoes designs decreased from seven years to ten months. (Skoggard 1998: p. 59).

References

Ash, J. and Wilson, E. (eds) (1997), *Chic Thrills: a Fashion Reader*, London, Harper Collins (Pandora).

Barnes, R. and Eicher, J.B. (1993), *Dress and Gender: Making and Meaning*, Oxford, Berg.

Barthes, R. (1983), *The Fashion System*, trans. Ward, M. and Howard, R., New York, Hill and Wang.

Bell, Q. (1976), *On Human Finery*, rev. edn., London, Hogarth.

Belton,N (1999), *The Good Listener: Helen Bamber, a Life Against Cruelty*, London: Weidenfeld and Nicolson.

Breward, C. (1995), *The Culture of Fashion: a new History of Fashionable Dress*, Manchester and New York, Manchester University Press.

Bullough, B. and V.L. (1993), *Cross Dressing, Sex and Gender*, Philadelphia: University of Pennsylvania.

Burke, E. (1961), *Reflections on the Revolution in France*, London, Doubleday.

Carlyle, T. (1888), *Sartor Resartus*, London, Chapman and Hall.

Cavallaro, D. and Warwick, A. (1998), *Fashioning the Frame: Boundaries, Dress and the Body*, Oxford, Berg.

Derrida, J. (1987), *The Truth in Painting*, Chicago, Chicago University.

Descartes, R. (1924), *A Discourse on Method etc.*, London, Dent.

Dickens, C. (1965), *Great Expectations, Harmondsworth*, Penguin English Library.

Eco, U. (1973), 'Social Life as Sign System' in Robey, D. (ed.), *Structuralism, an Introduction*, Oxford, Oxford University.

Evans, W.C. and Thornton, M. (1989), *Women and Fashion: a new look*, London, Quartet Books.

Finkelstein, J. (1991), *The Fashioned Self*, Cambridge, Polity.

Flugel, J.C. (1950), *The Psychology of Clothes*, London, Hogarth.

Garber, M. (1992), *Vested Interests: Cross-Dressing and Cultural Anxiety*, London, Penguin Books.

Laver, J. (1966), *Dress* 2nd ed., London, John Murray.

Heidegger, M. (1971),'The Origin of the Work of Art' in *Poetry, Language, Thought*, trans. Hofstadter, A., New York, Harper Row.

Hollander, A. (1993), *Seeing Through Clothes*, Berkeley and Los Angeles, University of California.

Kant, I. (1952), *Critique of Pure Judgement*, trans. James Creed Meredith, Oxford, Clarendon.

Lurie, A. (1992), *The Language of Clothes*, revised edn., London, Bloomsbury.

Mann, T. (1960), *The Magic Mountain*, Harmondsworth, Penguin Modern Classic.

Marx, K. (1973), *Grundrisse*, Harmondsworth, Penguin.

McDowell, C. (1995), *The Literary Companion to Fashion*, London, Sinclair and Stevenson.

Nietzsche, F. (1974), *The Gay Science*, trans. Kaufmann, K., New York, Vintage.

Proust, M. (1966), *A la Recherhe du Temps Perdu*, Vol. 2, trans C.K. Scott Moncrieff, London, Chatto and Windus.

Rousseau, J.-J. (1973), *The Social Contract and Discourses*, London, Dent.

Sartre, J.-P. (1976), *Critique of Dialectical Reason*, London, Verso, 1976.

Scarry, E. (1985), *The Body in Pain*, Oxford, Oxford University.

Sekora, J. (1977), *Luxury: the Concept in Western Thought, Eden to Smollett*, Baltimore, MA, John Hopkins University Press.

Shapiro, M. (1968), 'The Still Life as a Personal Object' in *The Reach of the Mind: essays in Memory of Kurt Goldstein*, New York, Springer Publishing Co.

Silverman, K. (1986), 'Fragments of a Fashionable Discourse' in Modleski, T. (ed.), *Studies in Entertainment*, Bloomington, Indiana University, pp. 139–52.

Skoggard, I. (1998), 'Transnational Commodity Flows and the Global Phenomenon of the Brand' in Brydon, A. and Niessen, S. (eds), *Consuming Fashion: Adorning the Transnational Body*, Oxford and New York, Berg.

Slater, D. (1997), *Consumer Culture and Modernity*, Cambridge, Polity.

Soper, K. (1981), *On Human Needs*, Brighton, Harvester.

Wilson, E. (1985), *Adorned in Dreams: Fashion and Modernity*, London, Virago.

Wollstonecraft, M. (1989), 'Vindication of the Rights of Man, in a Letter to the Right Honourable Edmund Burke', Vol. 5, 2nd edn. of Todd, J. and Butler, M. (eds), *The Works of Mary Wollstonecraft*, New York, New York University.

Woolf, V. (1992), *Three Guineas*, London, World's Classics.

The Dressed Body

Joanne Entwistle

Introduction

'There is an obvious and prominent fact about human beings,' notes Turner (1985: 1) at the start of *The Body and Society*, 'they have bodies and they are bodies.' However, what Turner omits in his analysis is another obvious and prominent fact: that human bodies are *dressed* bodies. Dress is a basic fact of social life and this, according to anthropologists, is true of all human cultures that we know about: all cultures 'dress' the body in some way, be it through clothing, tattooing, cosmetics or other forms of body painting (Polhemus 1988, Polhemus and Proctor 1978). Conventions of dress transform flesh into something recognizable and meaningful to a culture and are also the means by which bodies are made 'decent', appropriate and acceptable within specific contexts. Dress does not simply merely serve to protect our modesty and does not simply *reflect* a natural body or, for that matter, a given identity; it *embellishes* the body, the materials commonly used adding a whole array of meanings to the body that would otherwise not be there. While the social world normally demands that we appear dressed, what constitutes 'dress' varies from culture to culture and also within a culture since what is considered appropriate dress will vary according to the situation or occasion. The few mere scraps of fabric that make up a bikini are enough to ensure the female body is 'decent' on beaches in the West but would be entirely inappropriate in the boardroom. Bodies which do not conform, bodies which flout the conventions of their culture and go without the appropriate clothes are subversive of the most basic social codes and risk exclusion, scorn or ridicule. The 'streaker' who strips off and runs across a cricket pitch or soccer stadium draws attention to these conventions in the act of breaking them: indeed, female streaking is defined as a 'public order offence' while the 'flasher' by comparison, can be punished for 'indecent exposure'. As these examples illustrate, dress is fundamental to micro social order and the exposure of naked flesh is, potentially at least, disruptive of that order. Indeed, nakedness in those exceptional situations where it is deemed appropriate, has to be carefully managed (nude bathing in the UK and other Western countries is regulated and restricted; doctors must pay close attention to ethical codes of practice and so on). So fundamental is dress to the social presentation of the body and the social order that it governs even our ways of seeing the naked body. According to Hollander (1993) dress is crucial to our understanding of the body to the extent that our ways of seeing and representing the naked body are dominated by conventions of dress. As she (1993: xiii) argues,

> art proves that nakedness is not universally experienced and perceived any more than clothes are. At any time, the unadorned self has more kinship with its own usual *dressed* aspect than it has with any undressed human selves in other times and other places.

Hollander points to the ways in which depictions of the nude in art and sculpture correspond to the dominant fashions of the day. Thus the nude is never naked but 'clothed' by contemporary conventions of dress. Naked or semi-naked bodies that break with cultural conventions, especially conventions of gender, are potentially subversive and treated with horror or derision. Competitive female body builders, such as those documented in the 1984 semi-documentary film *Pumping Iron II: The Women*, are frequently seen as 'monstrous' (Kuhn 1988: 16, see also Schulze 1990, and St. Martin and Gavey 1996).

However, while dress cannot be understood without reference to the body and while body has always and everywhere to be dressed, there has been a surprising lack of concrete analysis of the relationship between them. In this chapter, I want to flesh out a study of the dressed body which attempts to bridge the gap that exists between theories of the body, which often overlook dress and theories of fashion and dress, which too frequently leave out the body. I want to suggest some of the connections that can be made between the various theorists in these related areas, suggesting how one might do a study of the dressed body. In doing so, I sketch out a theoretical framework which takes as its starting point the idea that dress is an embodied practice, a *situated bodily practice* which is embedded within the social world and fundamental to micro social order (Entwistle 2000a). While emphasizing the social nature of dress, this framework also asserts the idea that individuals/ subjects are active in their engagement with the social and that dress is thus actively produced through routine practices directed towards the body. In order to capture this sense of dress as both socially structured and embodied and practical, I will draw on a wide range of theoretical resources.

The main discussion will focus on the uses and limitations both the structuralist/post-structuralist approaches since these has been influential in recent years in the sociological study of the body. In particular, the work of Mary Douglas (1973, 1984), Michel Foucault (1977, 1986) and Marcel Mauss (1973) offer fruitful insights into the way in which the body is rendered meaningful by culture. However, such approaches are limited when it comes to acknowledging the 'fleshy' body and its experiential dimensions. They also neglect to account for how structures and rules result in actual embodied practices, sometimes with the effect of reducing individuals to puppet-like actors. In contrast, the phenomenology Maurice Merleau-Ponty (1976, 1981), which begins with the idea of the body as the 'existential ground of culture' (Csordas 1993) is suggestive of the ways in which dress can be understood as an *embodied practice.* These theoretical traditions may seem at odds with one another and indeed, according to Crossley (1996), they have been considered incommensurable by some. However, as he argues, they offer different and complimentary insights into the body and embodiment in society. Following Crossley (1995a, 1995b, 1996) and also Csordas (1993, 1996) I will argue that an account of dress as a situated bodily practice can draw on the insights of these two different traditions, structuralism and phenomenology and indeed must do so. Dress, as both a social and personal experience, is a discursive and practical phenomenon. A study of the dressed body thus requires understanding of both the socially processed body which discourses on dress and fashion shape, as well as the experiential dimensions of embodiment wherein dress is translated into actual bodily presentation. In addition to these two paradigms, Bourdieu (1984, 1989, 1994) and Goffman (1971, 1972) are particularly useful in that they both bridge the gap between these traditions and acknowledge how social structures are reproduced at the level of bodily practices.

Ad-dressing the Literature

If nakedness is unruly and disruptive, this would seem to indicate that dress is a fundamental aspect of microsocial order. When we dress we do so to make our bodies acceptable to a social situation. Given this issue of social order it seems strange to find little discussion of dress within sociology and other disciplines which have been concerned with this issue on both a macro and microlevel (for example, in the work of Parsons and Goffman). This would seem strange given that the force of pressure on the body to conform has a moral imperative to it as well. Dressed inappropriately we are uncomfortable, we feel ourselves open to social condemnation. According to Bell (1976), wearing the right clothes is so very important that even people not interested in their appearance will dress well enough to avoid social censure. In this sense, he argues, we enter into the realm of feelings 'prudential, ethical and aesthetic, and the workings of what one might call sartorial conscience' (1976: 18–19). Classical social theory failed to acknowledge the significance of dress, largely because it neglected the body and the things that bodies do (Turner 1985). The emergence of a sociology of the body in the last twenty years would seem an obvious place to look for literature on dress and fashion, but, as with mainstream sociology, it too has also tended not to examine dress (as noted above, Turner does not discuss dress in his account of bodily order). Moreover, the literature on fashion and dress, coming out of history, cultural studies and other fields, has paid little attention to the body, focusing instead on the communicative aspects of adornment (often adopting the rather abstract, and disembodied linguistic model from Saussure) and examining the spectacular, creative and expressive aspects of dress, rather than the mundane and routine part it plays in reproducing social order (Barthes 1985, Hebdige 1979, Lurie 1981, Polhemus 1994).

Between these bodies of literature, between the theorists of the classical tradition and those theorists of the body who tend to overlook dress, and those theorists of fashion and dress who have focused rather too much attention on the articles of clothing, the *dressed body* as a discursive and phenomeno-logical field vanishes. Either the body is thought to be self-evidently dressed (and therefore beyond discussion) or the clothes are assumed to stand up on their own, possibly even speaking for themselves without the aid of the body. And yet, the importance of the body to dress is such that encounters with dress divorced from the body are strangely alienating. Wilson (1985) grasps this when she describes the unease one feels in the presence of mannequins in the costume museum. The eeriness of the encounter comes from the 'dusty silence' and stillness of the costumes and from a sense that the museum is 'haunted' by the spirits of the living, breathing humans whose bodies these gowns once adorned. Our experience of the costume museum, along with our sadness when confronted with the clothes of dead relatives, points to the ways in which we 'normally' experience dress as alive and 'fleshy': once removed from the body, dress lacks fullness and seems strange, almost alien, and all the more poignant to us if we can remember the person who once breathed life into the fabric. The body and dress operate dialectically: dress works on the body, imbuing it with social meaning while the body is a dynamic field which gives life and fullness to dress (Entwistle and Wilson 1998). Thus the dressed body is a fleshy, phenomenological entity that is so much a part of our experience of the social world, so thoroughly embedded within the micro-dynamics of social order, as to be entirely taken for granted.

With a growing literature emerging on fashion, dress, the body, embodiment, performativity, it seems almost a cliché to insist that fashion and dress operate on the body and that, by implication, the body and dress are now a crucial arena for the performance and articulation of identities. And yet, the precise relationship of the body to dress and dress to the body remains unclear and under-theorized. In the discussion that follows, I want to suggest the theoretical resources that can be brought to bear on the analysis of the dressed body as situated practice.

Situating the Dressed Body in the Social World

Dress lies at the margins of the body and marks the boundary between self and other, individual and society. This boundary is intimate and personal since our dress forms the visible envelope of the self and, as Davis argues, serves as a visual metaphor for identity; it is also social since our dress is structured by social forces and subject to social and moral pressures. If, as Mary Douglas (1973, 1984) has so forcefully demonstrated, the boundaries of the body are dangerous, it is therefore no surprise that clothing and other forms of adornment, which operate at these 'leaky' margins, are subject to social regulation and moral pronouncements. It is no surprise either to find individuals concerned with what to hang at these margins. Douglas articulates this relationship between the individual body and the social forces pressing on it, arguing that there are 'two bodies': the physical body and the social body. She summarizes (1973: 93) the relationship between them in *Natural Symbols*:

> the social body constrains the way the physical body is perceived. The physical experience of the body, always modified by the social categories through which it is known, sustains a particular view of society. There is a continual exchange of meanings between the two kinds of bodily experience so that each reinforces the categories of the other.

According to Douglas, 'the body is capable of furnishing a natural system of symbols' (1973: 12). This means that the body is a highly restricted medium of expression since it is heavily mediated by culture and expresses the social pressure brought to bear on it. Indeed, the body becomes a symbol of its cultural location. She gives the example of laughter arguing that the social situation determines the degree to which the body can laugh: the looser the social constraints, the more free the body is to laugh out loud. In this way, the body and its functions and boundaries symbolically articulate the concerns of the particular group in which it is found. Her analysis (1973) of shaggy and smooth hair also illustrates this relationship between the body and the situation. Shaggy hair, once a symbol of rebellion, can be found among those professionals who are in a position to critique society, in particular, academics and artists. Smooth hair, however, is likely to be found among those who conform, such as lawyers and bankers. This analysis can of course be extended to the analysis of dress and adornment. The dressed body is always situated within a particular context which often sets constraints as to what is, and what is not, appropriate to wear. The degree to which the dressed body can express itself can therefore be symbolic of this location: for example, the more formal and conservative the occupation, the more constraints set around the body and thus on dress. Therefore traditional or conservative occupations are likely to have stricter codes of dress and necessitate the wearing of a suit, while more 'creative' professions will set few restrictions on the body and dress.

Mauss (1973) has likewise discussed the way in which the physical body is shaped by culture when he elaborates on mundane 'techniques of the body' and these have some potential for understanding the situated nature of the dressed body. The techniques he outlines are not 'natural' but the product of particular ways of being in the body which are embedded within culture and his examples also point to the ways in which these are gendered. Ways of walking, moving, making a fist, and so on, are different for men and women because, in the making of 'masculine' and 'feminine', culture inscribes the bodies of men and women with different physical capacities. Mauss's 'techniques of the body' has obvious application to dress and the way in which dress modifies the body, embellishing it and inflecting it with meanings which, in the first instance, are gendered. Although he says little about dress, he does note how women learn to walk in high heels which would be difficult and uncomfortable for men who are generally unaccustomed to such shoes. Illustrative of this particular technique in her exaggeration of it is Marilyn Monroe's sashaying gait in *Some Like It Hot* which was apparently the product of high heels cut diagonally at each side. These lopsided shoes enabled her to generate the wiggle that constituted part of her performance as the sexually provocative Sugar Cane.

Although they don't acknowledge Mauss's work, Haug (1987) provide ample evidence of the ways in which femininity is reproduced through various techniques, bodily and sartorial. They argue that the female body and its ways of being and adorning are the product of particular discourses of the body which are inherently gendered. These discourses are explored through the work of Foucault and I want to suggest some of the ways in which his concept of discourse, with its emphasis on the body, could be utilized for analysis of the situated nature of the body.

In *Discipline and Punish* Foucault (1977) argues that bodily practices are part of the capillary like operations of power which work to render bodies docile, obedient. While feminists such as Diamond and Quinby (1988) and McNay (1992) argue that Foucault ignores the issue of gender, they also point out that his theoretical concepts can provide feminists with a framework for understanding the ways in which the body is acted on by power/knowledge. Indeed, Foucault's notion of discourse can enable the analysis of fashion as a discursive domain which sets significant parameters around the body and its presentation. Fashion (defined here as a system of continual changing styles) which sets out an array of competing discourses on image and is the dominant system governing dress in the West has been linked to the operations of power, initially marking out class divisions, but more recently playing a crucial role in policing the boundaries of sexual difference.

Although utilized by Wilson (1992), Foucault's work on the body has not been usefully employed in the analysis of fashion as a textual site for the construction of the body although it would seem that it would have some application. Fashion, particularly as it is laid out in the fashion magazine, is 'obsessed with gender' (Wilson 1985: 117) and constantly shifts the boundary between the genders. This preoccupation with gender starts with babies and is played out through the life cycle so that styles of dress at significant moments are very clearly gendered (weddings and other formal occasions are the most obvious examples). Such styles enable the repetitious production of gender, even when gender appears to break down as with androgynous fashion, and are aided in part by the repetition of gendered styles of bodily posture routinely reproduced in fashion magazines. While these styles of being reproduce gender as a body style, they are also open to subversion through exaggeration and parody, as Butler (1990, 1993) has forcefully suggested, although some of the most exaggerated performances, such as drag, could be said to reinforce rather than undermine conventions of gender (Gamman and Makinen 1994).

In addition, Foucault's insights into the ways in which bodies are subject to power and are discursively constituted can be utilized to show how institutional and discursive practices of dress act upon the body, marking it and rendering it meaningful and productive. For example, styles of dress are regularly employed in the workplace as part of institutional and corporate strategies of management. This is explored by Freeman (1993) who draws on Foucault's notion of power, particularly his idea about the panoptican, to consider how dress is used in one particular context, a data-processing corporation, *Data Air,* as a strategy of corporate discipline and control over the female workforce. In this corporation a strict dress code insisted that the predominantly female workers dress 'smartly' in order to project a 'modern' and 'professional' image of the corporation. If their dress does not meet this standard they are subject to disciplinary techniques by their managers and could even be sent home to change their clothes. The enforcement of this dress code is facilitated by the open-plan office which keep the women under constant surveillance from the gaze of managers.

Such practices are familiar to many offices, although the mechanisms for enforcing dress codes vary enormously. Particular discourses of dress, such as 'smart' or 'professional' dress, and particular strategies of dress, such as the imposition of uniforms and dress codes at work, are utilized by corporations to exercise control over the bodies of the workers within. This is true of men's dress for work as much as it is of women's. The male suit is perhaps the most formally coded dress for men today, exerting itself with considerable force over the bodies of men in a wide range of occupational settings. Looser codes of bodily presentation are often set over the bodies of 'professionals' who, rather than be told what to wear, are expected to have internalized the codes of the profession. For example, the discourse of power dressing, which I have analysed elsewhere (Entwistle 1997, 2000a, 2000b), sets out clear codes of dressing for success but its adoption by professionals is largely dependent upon them having internalized a particular notion of themselves as 'enterprising' subjects. The discourse on power dressing called upon career women to think about and act upon their bodies in particular ways as part of an overall 'project of the self' (Giddens 1991) in order to maximize one's chances of career success. The rules of such dressing as delineated in dress manuals and magazine articles set out a strategy of dressing for work which relies on technical knowledge of dress and its 'effects' (the term 'wardrobe engineering', devised by the most famous exponent of power dressing, John T. Molloy (1980) captures this technical and instrumental concern).

As I have demonstrated, Foucault's framework is quite useful for analysing the discursive aspects of dress. In particular, his notion of discourse is a good starting point for analysing the relations between discourses on dress and gender as they are constituted in fashion texts and organizational strategies of management and are suggestive of particular forms of discipline of the body. However, there are problems with Foucault's notion of discourse as well as problems stemming from his conceptualization of the body and of power, in particular his failure to acknowledge embodiment and agency. These problems stem from Foucault's post-structuralist philosophy and these I now want to summarize in order to suggest how his theoretical perspective, while useful in some respects, particularly for textual analysis, is problematic for a study of dress as a situated bodily practice. In other words, his theoretical concepts do not stretch to the analysis of dress as an embodied practice.

Foucault's account of the socially processed body and provides for analysis of the way in which the body is talked about and acted on but it does not provide an account of dress as it is lived, experienced and embodied by individuals. For example, the existence of the corset in the nineteenth century and the discourses about the supposed morality of wearing one (the terms 'loose' and 'straightlaced' used to describe a woman refer to the wearing of a corset and illustrate, if metaphorically, the link between this article of clothing and morality) tell us little or nothing about how Victorian women experienced the corset, how tightly they chose to lace it, and what bodily sensations it produced. However, it would seem that by investing importance in the body, dress opens up the potential for women to use this for their own purposes and experience pleasures that are perhaps the 'reverse' of dominant ones. However, as Ramazanoglu (1993) argues, while the notion of reverse discourse is potentially very useful to feminists, it is not developed fully in Foucault's analysis. So while the corset is seen by some feminists (Roberts 1977) as a garment setting out to discipline the female body and make her 'docile' and subservient, an 'exquisite slave', Kunzle (1982) has argued in relation to female tight lacers that these women were not passive or masochistic victims of patriarchy, but socially and sexually assertive. Kunzle's suggestion is that women more than men have used their sexuality to climb the social ladder and that tight lacers experienced sexual pleasures from the tightly laced corset which went against the dominant norm of the Victorian woman as asexual. If his analysis is accepted, these particular Victorian women could be said to illustrate the ways in which power, once invested in the female body, results in 'the responding claims and affirmations, those of one's own body against power... of pleasure against the moral norms of sexuality, marriage, decency...' (Foucault 1980: 56). In other words, illustrative of 'reverse discourse'.

However, this issue lies dormant in Foucault's own analysis, partly because Foucault's particular form of post-structuralism is not sensitive to *practice*. Instead it *presumes* effects, at the level of individual practice, from the existence of discourse alone. He thus 'reads' texts *as if* they were practice rather than a possible structuring influence on practice that might, or might not, be implemented. In assuming that discourse automatically has social effects, Foucault's method, as Turner (1985: 175) notes, 'reduce(s) the individual agent to a socialised parrot which must speak/perform in a determinate manner in accordance with the rules of language'. In failing to produce any account of how discourses get taken up in practice, Foucault also fails to give an adequate explanation as to how resistance to discourse is possible. Moreover, his analysis lacks sensitivity to the body as the environment of the self and tends to assume a notion of the 'passive body' thereby failing to explain how individuals may act in an autonomous fashion. If bodies are produced and manipulated by power, then this would seem to contradict

Foucault's concern to see power as force relations which are never simply oppressive. Such an account might lead to the discussion of fashion and dress as merely constraining social forces and thus neglect the way individuals can be active in their selective choices from fashion discourse in their everyday experience of dress.

The extreme anti-humanism of Foucault's work, most notably in *Discipline and Punish*, is questioned by McNay (1992) because it does not allow for notions of subjectivity and experience and she proposes that his later work on 'technologies of the self' offers a more useful theoretical framework. However, as she herself later acknowledges (McNay 1999) Foucault's notion of subjectivity as developed in his 'technologies of self' is disconnected from his earlier work on the body and is thus, strangely disembodied. In terms of producing an account of embodiment and of agency, McNay suggests that Bourdieu's notion of the *habitus* and *the field* are more productive. If the dressed body is to be understood as always situated in culture and as an embodied activity located within specific temporal and spatial relations then these concepts from Bourdieu offer much potential. I will discuss Bourdieu's work in more detail below.

Further problems arise from Foucault's rather ambivalent notion of the body: on the one hand, his bio-politics would appear to construct the body as a concrete, material entity, manipulated by institutions and practices; on the other hand, his focus on discourse seems to produce a notion of the body which has no materiality outside of the representation. Such a vacillation is problematic since the question of what constitutes a body is one that cannot be avoided – does the body have a materiality outside of language and representation? The body cannot be at one and the same time both a material object outside of language and a solely linguistic construction. This refusal to develop an ontology of the body fits with Foucault's general refusal of all essence, as Turner (1985) notes. However, Terence Turner (1996: 37) goes as far as to suggest that Foucault's body is more contradictory and problematic in terms of his own claim to critique essences: it is 'a featureless *tabula rasa* awaiting the animating disciplines of discourse . . . an a priori individual unity disarmingly reminiscent of its arch-rival, the transcendental subject'. If, as it seems, Foucault errs on the side of the body as a discursive construct this would appear to undermine his aim to produce a 'history of bodies' and the invesments and operations of power on them. What is most material and most vital about a body if not its flesh and bones? What is power doing if not operating on, controlling or dominating the material body?

However, if the body has its own physical reality outside or beyond discourse, how can we theorize this experience? How can one begin to understand the experience of choosing and wearing clothes that forms so significant a part of our experience of our body/self? With these issues in mind, Csordas (1993, 1996) details the way forward for what he calls a 'paradigm of embodiment' which he poses as an alternative to the 'paradigm of the body' that characterizes the structuralist approach. This methodological shift 'requires that the body be understood as the existential ground of culture – not an object that is "good to think with" but as a subject that is "necessary to be"' (1993: 135). The body, in phenomenological terms, is the environment of the self and therefore something acted upon as part of the experience of selfhood. This is in contrast to the semiotic model which considers the body as a symbolic and discursive object worked on by culture. Csordas's express aim is therefore to counter-balance the 'strong representational bias' of the semiotic/textual paradigm found in works such as that of Derrida (1976), Douglas (1973, 1979) and Foucault (1977). Csordas calls for a shift away from a semiotic/textualist framework to a notion of embodiment and 'being in the world' drawn from phenomenology.

He notes how, 'of all the formal definitions of culture that have been proposed by anthropology, none have taken seriously the idea that culture is grounded in the human body' (Csordas 1996: 6). Thus, the phenomenological concern with embodiment starts from a different premise to structuralist and post-structuralist accounts of the social world, positioning the body as 'the existential ground of culture and self' (Csordas 1993). He argues for a study of embodiment that draws on the phenomenology of Merleau-Ponty (1976, 1981) as well as Bourdieu's (1989) 'theory of practice'. His paradigm of embodiment thus marks a methodological shift away from a concern with texts to a concern with *bodily experience* and *social practice*. According to Csordas, both Bourdieu (1989, 1994) and Merleau-Ponty (1976, 1981) shift the concern away from the body as an inert object to an idea of the body as implicated in everyday perception and practices. A similar distinction is drawn by Crossley (1995a, 1995b, 1996) who argues that the 'sociology of the body' is concerned with 'what is done to the body', while 'carnal sociology' examines 'what the body does' (1995b: 43). He too identifies this latter tradition with the work of Merleau-Ponty but looks also to Goffman whose account of microsocial interactions positions the body as the central vehicle of the 'self'. In the following section, I want to detail the theoretical and methodological assumptions underlying a 'paradigm of embodiment', drawing on the work of Merleau-Ponty, and suggest how phenomenology might enable a study of dress as situated practice. I want also to suggest how the work of Bourdieu and Goffman may be applied to the study of the dressed body and how their insights bridge the gap between structuralist and phenomenological concepts. In both their work, the body is a socially constituted object, determined by social structures, and also the site of social and personal identity.

Dress and Embodiment

Merleau-Ponty (1976, 1981) places the body at the centre of his analysis of perception, arguing that the world comes to us via perceptive awareness, i.e. from the place of our body in the world. Merleau-Ponty stresses the simple fact that the mind is situated in the body and comes to know the world through what he calls 'corporeal or postural schema': in other words we grasp external space, relationships between objects and our relationship to them through our position in, and movement through, the world. Thus the aim of his work on perception, as he (1976: 3–4) points out in *The Primacy of Perception,* is to

> re-establish the roots of the mind in its body and in its world, going against doctrines which treat perception as a simple result of the action of external things on our body as well as against those which insist on the autonomy of consciousness.

As a result of his emphasis on perception and experience, subjects are reinstated as temporal and spatial beings. Rather than being 'an object in the world' the body forms our 'point of view on the world' (1976: 5). In this way, Merleau-Ponty counteracts the tendency in Foucault to see the body as a passive object. According to Merleau-Ponty, we come to understand our relation in the world via the positioning of our body physically and historically in space. 'Far from being merely an instrument or object in the world our bodies are what give us our expression in the world' (1976: 5). In other words, our body is not just the place from which we come to experience the world, but it is through our bodies that we come to see and be seen in the world. The body forms the envelope of our being in the world and our selfhood comes from this location in our body and our experience of this. In terms of dress, approaching it from a phenomenological framework means acknowledging the way in which dress works on the body which in turn works on and mediates the experience of self. Eco (1986) captures this very well when he describes wearing jeans which are still too tight after losing some weight. He (1986: 192–4) describes how the jeans feel on his body, how they pinch and how they restrict his movement, how they make him aware of the lower half of his body; indeed, how they come to constitute an 'epidermic self-awareness' which he had not felt before:

> As a result, I lived in the knowledge that I had jeans on, whereas normally we live forgetting that we're wearing undershorts or trousers. I lived for my jeans and as a result I assumed an exterior behaviour of one who wears jeans. In any case, I assumed a demeanour . . . Not only did the garment impose a demeanour on me; by focusing my attention on demeanour it obliged me to live towards the exterior world.

If for the most part, we don't experience our jeans (or any other item of clothing for that matter) in this way then this hints at our 'normal' experience of dress and its relationship to the body; namely that it becomes an extension of the body which is like a second skin. Dressed uncomfortably, on the other hand, we may develop the 'epidermic self-awareness' Eco refers to since the garment/s impinge upon our experience of the body and make us aware of the 'edges', the limits and boundaries of our body. This body/dress awareness is gendered: as Tseëlon (1997: 61) notes, women's sense of self (and self worth) is frequently a 'fragile' one and dress can either bolster confidence or make one acutely self-conscious and uncomfortable.

Merleau-Ponty's notion of subjectivity is neither essential nor transcendental: the self is located in a body, which in turn is located in time and space. The notion of space is for Merleau-Ponty crucial to the phenomenology of lived experience since the movement of bodies through space is an important feature of their perception of the world and their relationship to others and objects in the world. This concern with space is apparent in Foucault's (1977) work on the institutions of modernity but while his account of space acknowledges its disciplinary and political dimensions, it lacks any sense of how people experience space. Foucault's analysis looks at space in relation to social order and, ultimately, power, a phenomenological analysis of space such as that offered by Merleau-Ponty, considers how we grasp external space via our bodily situation or 'corporeal or postural schema' (1976: 5). Thus, 'our body is not in space like things; it inhabits or haunts space' (1976: 5). For Merleau-Ponty, body/subjects are always subjects in space but our experience of it comes from our movement around the world and our grasping of objects in that space through perceptual awareness. Space is grasped actively by individuals through their embodied encounter with it. Of course, space is a crucial aspect of our experience of the dressed body since when we get dressed we do so with implicit understanding of the rules and norms of particular social spaces. A formal dinner, a job interview, a shopping expedition, a walk in the park, to name a few situations, demand different styles of dress and require us to be more or less aware of our dress, make it more or less an object of our consciousness.

In bringing embodiment to the fore of his analysis and emphasizing that all human experience comes out of our bodily position, Merleau-Ponty's analysis offers a fruitful starting point for the analysis of dress as situated bodily practice. Dress is always located spatially and temporally: when getting dressed one orientates oneself/body to the situation, acting in particular ways upon the surfaces of the body which are likely to fit within the established norms of that situation. Thus the dressed body is not a passive object, acted upon by social forces, but actively produced through particular, routine and mundane practices. Moreover, our experience of the body is not as inert object but the envelope of our being, the site for our articulation of self. Merleau-Ponty's insistence on the embodied nature of subjectivity means that it is crucial to the experience and expression of self and what could be more visible an aspect of the body than dress? This relationship between the body and identity and between identity and dress has been the subject of many discussions within fashion theory as well as some accounts of the body (Davis 1992, Finkelstein 1991, Synnott 1993, Wilson 1985, 1992). However, these accounts have tended not to talk of embodiment and of the ways in which dress constitutes part of the experience of the body and identity. In unifying body/self and in focusing on the experiential dimensions of being located in a body, Merleau-Ponty's work demonstrates how the body is not merely a textual entity produced by discursive practices but is the active and perceptive vehicle of being.

There are, however, a number of problems with Merleau-Ponty's phenomenology. Firstly, he neglects to consider the body as gendered when in everyday life gender plays a significant part in the way in which individuals, male and female, experience embodiment and come to live in their bodies. Not only is gender in part the product of 'techniques of the body' as discussed by Mauss above, the body itself moves through time and space with a sense of itself as gendered. This is illustrated by the ways in which men and women experience the spaces of the public realm differently. As I have discussed elsewhere (Entwistle 1997, 2000b) the spaces of work are experienced differently by women and men and impacts upon the ways in which the body is dressed and presented. Furthermore, as argued by numerous theorists (Berger 1972; McNay 1992; Mulvey 1989, Wolf 1990), women are more likely to be identified with the body than men and this may generate differential experiences of embodiment. It could be argued that women are more likely to develop greater body consciousness and greater awareness of themselves *as* embodied than men whose identity is less situated in the body. Tseëlon's (1997) work in this area would seem to testify to this. Secondly, Merleau-Ponty's approach remains philosophical: as a method, it cannot be easily applied to the analysis of the social world. However, Crossley (1995a) and Csordas (1993) see much potential in the works of Goffman and Bourdieu respectively, since both draw some inspiration from phenomenology but develop approaches to embodiment which are sociological rather than philosophical and substantiate their accounts with empirical evidence of actual social practices. I want to explore what each has to say about Goffman and Bourdieu as well as suggest the ways in which these two theorists could be applied to the study of the dressed body.

Dress and Embodied Subjectivity

Crossley (1995a) suggests that there are many other fruitful connections to be made between Goffman (1971, 1972) and Merleau-Ponty (1976, 1981), particularly their insistence on subjectivity as embodied. Furthermore, Goffman's concern with the temporality and spatiality of interaction provides another point of contact with Merleau-Ponty's whose work is concerned with these aspects of perception. In terms of providing an account of embodied subjectivity as experienced within the flow of everyday life, Goffman's concepts have some considerable potential for understanding the dressed body. It enables description and analysis of the way in which individuals, or social actors, come to orientate themselves to the social world and learn to perform in it and recognizes how the body is central to this experience. In Goffman's work, the body is both the property of the individual and the social world: it is the vehicle of identity but this identity has to be 'managed' in terms of the definitions of the social situation which impose particular ways of being on the body. Thus the individual feels a social and moral imperative to perform their identity in particular ways and this includes learning appropriate ways of dressing. Like so much bodily behaviour, codes of dress come to be taken for granted and are routinely and unreflexively employed, although some occasions, generally formal ones (like weddings and funerals) which set tighter constraints around the body, lend themselves to more conscious reflection on dress. Goffman's work thus adds to Douglas's account of the 'two bodies' by bringing embodiment and actual bodily practices into the frame.

In considering the body as central to interaction, his analysis also lends itself to the understanding of the dressed body and thus an account of dress in terms of situated bodily practice. Not only does dress form the key link between individual identity and the body, providing the means, or 'raw material' for performing identity, dress is fundamentally an inter-subjective and social phenomenon, an important link between individual identity and social belonging. Davis (1992: 25) argues that dress frames our embodied self, serving as 'a kind of visual metaphor for identity and, as pertains in particular to the open society of the West, for registering the culturally anchored ambivalence that resonates within and among identities'. In other words, not only is our dress the visible form of our intentions, but in everyday life dress is the insignia by which we are read and come to read others, however unstable and ambivalent these readings may be (Campbell 1997). Dress works to 'glue' identities in a world where they are uncertain: as Wilson (1985: 12) puts it, 'the way in which we dress may assuage that fear by stabilizing our individual identity'. This idea is the basis of much subcultural theory on the symbolic work performed by members of subcultures who, it is argued, deploy cultural artefacts such as dress to mark out the boundaries of their group and register their belonging (Hall and Jefferson 1976; Hebdige 1979; Luck 1992; Willis 1975, 1978).

While Goffman does not discuss the ways dress and its role in the 'presentation of self in everyday life', his ideas could be elaborated to discuss the way in which dress is routinely attended to as part of the 'presentation of self in everyday life'. Most situations, even the most informal, have a code of dress and these impose particular ways of being on bodies in such a way as to have a social and moral imperative to them. Bell (1976) gives the example of a five-day-old beard which could not be worn to the theatre without censure and disapproval 'exactly comparable to that occasioned by dishonourable conduct'. Indeed, clothes are often spoken of in moral terms, using words like 'faultless', 'good', 'correct'. Few are immune to this social pressure and most people are embarrassed by certain mistakes of dress, such as finding one's flies undone or discovering a stain on a jacket. Thus, as Bell (1976: 19) puts it, 'our clothes are too much a part of us for most of us to be entirely indifferent to their condition: it is as though the fabric were indeed a natural extension of the body, or even of the soul'.

Thus in the presentation of self in social interaction, ideas of embarrassment and stigma play a crucial role and are managed, in part, through dress. Dressed inappropriately for a situation we feel vulnerable and embarrassed and so too when our dress 'fails' us, when in public we find we've lost a button, stained our clothes or find our flies undone. However, the embarrassment of such mistakes of dress is not simply that of personal *faux pas,* but the shame of failing to meet the standards required of one by the moral order of the social space. When we talk of someone's 'slip showing' we are, according to Wilson (1985: 8) speaking of something 'more than slight sartorial sloppiness' but 'the exposure of something much more profoundly ambiguous and disturbing . . . the naked body underneath the clothes'. A commonly cited dream for many people is the experience of suddenly finding oneself naked in a public place: dress, or the lack of it in this case, serves as a metaphor for feelings of shame, embarrassment and vulnerability in our culture as well as indicating the way in which the moral order demands that the body be covered in some way. These examples illustrate the way in which dress is part of the micro-order of social interaction and intimately connected to our (rather fragile) sense of self which is, in turn, threatened if we fail to conform to the standards governing a particular social situation. Dress is therefore a crucial dimension in the articulation of personal identity but not in the sense, as is sometimes argued by theorists (for example, Finkelstein (1991) and Polhemus (1994)) who err too much on the side of voluntarism, seeing dress as freely willed, 'expressive' and creative. On the contrary, identity is managed through dress in rather more mundane and routine ways because social pressure encourages us to stay within the bounds of what is defined in a situation as a 'normal' body and 'appropriate' dress. This is not to say that dress has no 'creative' or expressive qualities to it, but rather that too much attention and weight has been given to this and too little to the way in which strategies of dress have a strong social and moral dimension to them which serve to constrain the choices people make about what to wear. Tseëlon (1997) has argued that dress choices are made within specific contexts and provides good examples of the ways in which occasions such as job interviews, weddings, etc. constrain dress choices. Her work therefore points to an important aspect of dress which requires that it be studied as a situated bodily practice. Different occasions, different situations, operate with different codes of dress and bodily demeanour so that while we may dress unreflexively some of the time (to do the grocery shopping or take the kids to school), at other times we are thoughtful, deliberate and calculating in our dress (I must not wear that white dress to the wedding; I must buy a new suit/jacket/tie for that job interview). Furthermore, dress is also structured in the West (and increasingly beyond) by the fashion system which, in defining the latest aesthetic, helps to shape trends and tastes which structure our experience of dress in daily life.

Crossley (1995a) suggests another point of contact between Goffman and Merleau-Ponty is that both take account of space in their analysis. He argues that while Merleau-Ponty is good at articulating spatiality and the perception of it, Goffman provides us with concrete accounts of how this occurs in the social world. Goffman's (1972) sense of space is both social and perceptual, and provides a link between the structuralist/post-structuralist analysis of space delineated by Douglas (1973, 1979) and Foucault (1977) in terms of social order and regulation, and the phenomenological analysis of space as experiential. Moreover, according to Crossley, Goffman takes the analysis of bodily demeanour in social situations further than either Merleau-Ponty indeed Mauss. Goffman elaborates on Mauss's 'techniques of the body' not only recognizing that such things as walking are socially structured, but considering also how walking is not only a part of the interaction order, but serves also to reproduce it. For Goffman, the spaces of the street, the office, the shopping mall, operate with different rules and determine how we present ourselves and how we interact with others. He reminds us of the territorial nature of space and describes how, when we use space, we have to negotiate crowds, dark quiet spaces, etc. In other words, he articulates the way in which action transforms space. This acknowledgement of space can illuminate the situated nature of dress. If, as I have argued, dress forms part of the microsocial order of most social spaces, when we dress we attend to the norms of particular spatial situations: is there a code of dress we have to abide by? who are we likely to meet? what activities are we likely to perform? how visible do we want to be (do we want to stand out in the crowd or blend in?) etc. While we may not always be aware of all these issues we internalize particular rules or norms of dress which we routinely employ unconsciously. I have argued elsewhere (Entwistle 2000b) that the professional woman is more likely to be conscious of her body and dress in public spaces of work than at home or even in her private office. Space is experienced territorially by professional women who routinely talk of putting on their jacket to go to meetings and when walking around their workplace (taking it off when in the privacy of their office) to cover their breasts so as to avoid unsolicited sexual glances from men. Thus spaces impose different ways of being on gendered bodies: women may have to think more carefully about how they appear in public than men, at least in some situations, and how they experience public spaces such as offices, boardrooms, quiet streets at night, is likely to be different to how men experience such spaces. The spaces at work carry different meanings for women and as a consequence they have developed particular strategies of dress for managing the gaze of others, especially men, in public spaces at work. Their strategies of dress both reflect the gendered nature of the work-place and represent an adaptation to this space in terms of their experience of it. In a similar way, women dressing up for a night out might wear a coat to cover up an outfit, such as a short skirt and skimpy top which might feel comfortable when worn in a night club but which would otherwise make them feel vulnerable when walking down a quiet street late at night. In this respect, the spaces of the night club and street impose their own structures onto the individual and her sense of her body and she may in turn employ strategies of dress aimed at managing her body in these spaces.

Dress and Habitus

Bourdieu's (1984, 1989, 1994) work offers another potentially useful socio-logical analysis of embodiment and his analysis, which builds a bridge between approaches to the world that prioritize either objective structures or subjective meanings, provides a way of thinking through dress as a situated bodily practice. His notion of the habitus marks an attempt to overcome the either/or of objectivism and subjectivism. As 'a system of durable, transposable dispositions' that are produced by the particular conditions of a class grouping, the habitus enables the reproduction of class (and gender) through the active embodiment of individuals who are *structured* by it, as opposed to the passive inscription of power relations onto the body. Thus, the notion of lived practice is not individualistic, it is more than 'simply the aggregate of individual behaviour' (Jenkins 1992). In this respect, Bourdieu's work elaborates in concrete ways Merleau-Ponty's philosophical approach to embodiment. As Csordas (1993: 137) argues,

> to conjoin Bourdieu's understanding of 'habitus' as an unselfconscious orchestration of practices with MP notion of the 'pre-objective' suggests that embodiment need not be restricted to the personally or diadic micro-analysis customarily associated with phenomenology but is relevant as well to social collectivities.

In this way, the habitus is the objective outcome of particular social conditions, 'structured structures', but these structures cannot be known in advance of their lived practice. The individual social agent develops a 'feel for the game', and in the process, comes to interpret, consciously or unconsciously, the 'rules' and improvise around them.

According to McNay (1999) in foregrounding embodiment in his concept of the habitus and in arguing that power is actively reproduced through it, Bourdieu provides for a more complex and nuanced analysis of the body than Foucault whose 'passive body' is inscribed with power and the effects of it. The potential of the habitus as a concept for thinking through embodiment is that it provides a link between the individual and the social: the way we come to live in our bodies is structured by our social position in the world but these structures are only reproduced through the embodied actions of individuals. Once acquired, the habitus enables the generation of practices that are constantly adaptable to the conditions it meets. In terms of dress, the habitus predisposes individuals to particular ways of dressing: for example, the middle-class notion of 'quality not quantity' generally translates into a concern with quality fabrics such as cashmere, leather, silk which, due to cost, may mean buying fewer garments. However while social collectivities, class and gender for example, and social situations structure the codes of dress, these are relatively open to interpretation and are only realized through the embodied practice of dress itself. Thus, dress is the result of a complex negotiation between the individual and the social and, while it is generally predictable, it cannot be known in advance of the game since the structures and rules of a situation only set the parameters of dress, but cannot entirely determine it.

Bourdieu's habitus and his theory of practice is useful for overcoming the bias towards texts and towards the discursive body and has much potential for understanding the dressed body as the outcome of situated bodily practices. The strength of Bourdieu's account applied to dress is that it is not reductive: dress as lived practice is not the outcome of either oppressive social forces on the one hand, or agency on the other. As McNay (1999: 95) argues, 'it yields a more dynamic theory of embodiment than Foucault's work which fails to think through the materiality of the body and thus vacillates between determinism and voluntarism'. Bourdieu provides an account of subjectivity which is both embodied, unlike Foucault's passive body and his 'technologies of the self', and which is active in its adaptation of the habitus. As such, it enables an account of dress which does not fall into voluntarism and assume that one is free to self-fashion autonomously. Polhumus's (1994) analysis of 'streetstyle' is illustrative of such an approach to fashion and dress which has tended to define recent work in this area. In his idea of the 'supermarket of style' Polhemus argues that the mixing the youth culture 'tribes' in recent years has meant less clearly differentiated boundaries between groups while the metaphor suggests that young people are now free to choice from a range of styles at will as if they were choices on display in a supermarket. However, such emphasis on free and creative expression glosses over the structural constraints of class, gender, location, income, etc., which set material boundaries around young people, as well as the constraints at work in a variety of situations that serve to set parameters around dress choice. As McNay (1999: 97) argues, Foucault's later work on technologies of the self rather assumes that identity is open to self-fashioning, thus failing 'to consider fully the recalcitrance of embodied existence to self-fashioning'.

However, the notion of the habitus as a dynamic, durable and transposable set of dispositions does allow some sense of agency on the part of individuals. Dress in everyday life cannot be known in advance of practice by examination of the fashion industry or fashion texts. It is a practical negotiation between the fashion system as a structured system, the social conditions of everyday life such as class, gender and the like, as well as the 'rules' or norms governing particular social situations. Choices over dress are always defined within a particular context: the fashion system provides the 'raw material' of our choices but these are adapted within the context of the lived experience of the woman, her class, race and ethnicity, age, occupation and so on. The outcome of this complex interaction cannot be known in advance precisely because the habitus enables improvization and adaption to these conditions. It thus enables one to talk about dress as an individual attempt to orientate oneself to particular circumstances and recognizes the structuring influences of the social world on the one hand, and the agency of individuals who make choices as to what to wear on the other.

The habitus is also useful for understanding how dress styles are gendered and how gender is actively reproduced through dress. However much gendered identity has been problematized of late and however much gender roles may have changed, gender is still entrenched within the body styles of men and women or, as McNay (1999: 98) puts it, 'embedded in inculcated, bodily dispositions' which are 'relatively involuntary, pre-reflexive'.

To give a concrete analysis of a particular *field* and return to the example of dress at work, it is apparent that there are gendered styles of dress within the workplace, especially the white collar and professional workplace. Here we find that the suit is the standard 'masculine' dress and, while women have adopted suits in recent years, theirs differ in many respects from men's. Women have more choices in terms of dress in that they can, in most workplaces, wear skirts or trousers with their jacket; they have wider choice in terms of colour than the usual black, grey, navy of most male suits for the conventional office and can decorate it more elaborately with jewellery and other accessories (Entwistle 1997, 2000b; Molloy 1980) However, in order to understand this field one must take account of the historical modes of being in the workplace as well as the nature of the habitus of this particular field. Significantly, women's adoption of tailored clothes has to do with the orientation of women's bodies to the context of the male workplace and its habitus. In this field, sexuality is deemed inappropriate (it is distracting from production) and the suit, which covers all the male body, except for the neck and hands, has become the standard style of dress by men. The meanings of the suit are complex and nuanced and, while it does not obliterate the sexuality of the male body, it works to obscure, blur or reduce it as Collier (1998) has argued. In addition, it has come to connote 'professional'. By examining different styles of dress and corporeality at work, Collier (1998: 34) argues that male body at work attempts to distance itself from connotations of the body and eroticism: the suit serves the purpose of de-sexualizing the male body, 'not in the sense of rendering men in suits beyond erotic attachment (far from it) but rather in terms of erasing the sexed specificity of the individual male body'. In other words, by rendering 'invisible' the male body, the suit hides sexed characteristics, but more importantly, as the standard of dress long established, 'this body is normative within the public sphere, it has come to represent neutrality and *dis*embodiment' (Thornton in Collier 1998: 34).

Women's movement into this sphere, as secretaries and later as professionals, required them to adopt a similar uniform to designate them as workers and thus as public as opposed to private figures. However, the feminine body, as Berger, (1972), McNay (1992), Mulvey (1989), Wolf (1990) have argued is always, potentially at least, a sexual body and women have not entirely been able to escape this association despite their challenge to tradition and the acquisition, in part, of sexual equality. In other words, women are still seen as located in the body whereas men are seen as transcending it. Thus, while women can wear a tailored suit much the same as a man, her identity will always be as a 'female professional', her body, her gender being outside the norm 'masculine' (Entwistle 2000b; Sheppard 1989). While her suit may work to cover her body and reduce its sexual associations (the jacket is the most crucial aspect of female professional dress, covering the most sexualized zone, the breasts as noted above) as I have argued it can never entirely succeed since a woman brings to her dress the baggage of sexual meanings which are entrenched within the culturally established definitions of 'femininity'. This is not to say that women are embodied and men are not, but that cultural associations do not see men embodied in the way that women are. In his analysis Collier (1998: 32) argues for consideration of male corporeality at work, suggesting that different styles of masculinity operate in legal practice but that the '*sexed* specificity of this style has, in contrast to the growing literature on the corporeality of women in the profession, remained largely unexplored'. In other words, men's bodies are taken for granted or rendered invisible, in contrast to the attention paid to female bodies at work and in other public arenas. Thus, as he argues, men are embodied but the experience of embodiment is often left out of accounts of masculinity. He (1998: 32) suggests that this 'de-sexing' of men has been dependent 'on certain deeply problematic assumptions' and asks, 'does this mean that a courtroom consisting solely of men is without, or beyond the erotic? Such an argument would presume, first, that intra-male relations are asexual . . . and secondly, that as sexed beings, men's eroticism is confined to the private, affective sphere.'

However, while the male suit can, at least superficially efface the male body, it cannot obliterate the female body which is always 'feminine' and by association, 'sexual'. Thus, while more women work and increasingly in male-defined arenas, breaking with more traditional images of femininity, 'the transformatory impact upon embodied feminine identity and upon the collective subordination of women in society is far from certain' (McNay 1999: 106). McNay (1999: 106) therefore argues, 'in pointing to the rootedness of gender divisions in social forms, the concepts of the habitus and "le sens pratique" serve as a corrective to sociologically naïve claims about the transformation of social and sexual identities'. This is due, in part, to the largely unreflexive nature of gender which, if we draw again on Mauss (1973), is reproduced through 'techniques of the body' that come to feel 'natural'. Bourdieu's notion of the habitus allows for the analysis of such differences in gender in terms of how it is socially reproduced through bodily styles. It enables consideration of how gender is embodied through various techniques, practices, styles and how these are repetitive and deeply embedded within unreflective practice. Changes in the social world, such as the changing status of women, are, according to Bourdieu, slow to find their way into the habitus. However, he does also recognize that the habitus is a *relatively* open structure and one that is constantly, if slowly, modified. Thus, according to (McNay 1999: 105), he produces an account of gender identity which is 'not a mechanistically determining structure but an open system of dispositions'. These dispositions are 'durable but not eternal' Bourdieu quoted in McNay (1999: 105).

Conclusion

This chapter has set out the theoretical framework for a sociology of the dressed body as a situated bodily practice. I have argued that to understand dress requires adopting an approach which acknowledges the body as a social entity and dress as the outcome of both social factors and individual actions. Foucault's work may contribute to a sociology of the body as discursively constituted but is limited by its inattention to the lived body and its practices, and to the body as the site of the 'self'. Understanding dress in everyday life requires understanding not just how the body is represented within the fashion system and its discourses on dress, but also how the body is experienced and lived and the role dress plays in the presentation of the body/self. Abandoning Foucault's discursive model of the body does not, however, mean abandoning his entire thesis. This framework, as I have shown, is useful for understanding the structuring influences on the body and the way in which bodies acquire meaning in particular contexts. However, the study of dress as situated practice requires moving between, on the one hand, the discursive and representational aspects of dress and the way the body/dress is caught up in relations of power, and on the other hand, the embodied experience of dress and the use of dress as one means by which individuals orientate themselves to the social world. Dress involves practical actions directed by the body upon the body which result in ways of being and ways of dressing, such as ways of walking to accommodate high heels, ways of breathing to accommodate a corset, ways of bending in a short skirt and so on. A sociological account of dress as an embodied and situated practice needs to acknowledge the ways in which both the experience of the body and the various practices of dress are socially structured.

References

Barthes, R. (1985), *The Fashion System*, London: Cape.
Bell, Q. (1976), *On Human Finery*, London: Hogarth Press.
Berger, J. (1972), *Ways of Seeing*, Harmondsworth: Penguin.
Bourdieu, P. (1984), *Distinction: A Social Critique of the Judgement of Taste*, Cambridge, MA: Harvard University Press.

Bourdieu, P. (1989), *Outline of a Theory of Practice*, Cambridge: Cambridge University Press.

Bourdieu, P. (1994), 'Structures, Habitus and Practices', in P. Press (ed.), *The Polity Reader in Social Theory*, Cambridge: Polity Press.

Butler, J. (1990), *Gender Trouble: Feminism and the Subversion of Identity*, London: Routledge.

Butler, J. (1993), *Bodies That Matter*, London: Routledge.

Campbell, C. (1997), 'When the Meaning is not a Message: A Critique of the Consumption as Communication Thesis', in M. Nava, A. Blake, I. MacRury, and B. Richards (eds), *Buy this Book: Studies in Advertising and Consumption*, London: Routledge.

Collier, R. (1998), '"Nutty Professors", "Men in Suits" and "New Entrepreneurs": Corporeality, Subjectivity and Change in the Law School and Legal Practice', *Social and Legal Studies* 7 (1): 27–53.

Crossley, N. (1995a), 'Body techniques, agency and inter-corporality: on Goffman's relations in public', *Sociology* 129 (1): 133–49.

Crossley, N. (1995b), 'Merleau-Ponty, the Elusive Body and Carnal Sociology', *Body and Society* 1 (1): 43–63.

Crossley, N. (1996), 'Body/Subject, Body/Power: Agency, Inscription and Control in Foucault and Merleau-Ponty', *Body and Society* 2 (2): 99–116.

Csordas, T.J. (1993), 'Somatic modes of attention', *Cultural Anthropology* 8 (2): 135–56.

Csordas, T.J. (1996), 'Introduction: the body as representation and being-in-the-world', in T.J. Csordas (ed.), *Embodiment and Experience: The Existential Ground of Culture and Self*, Cambridge: Cambridge University Press.

Davis, F. (1992), *Fashion, Culture and Identity*, Chicago: Chicago University Press.

Derrida, J. (1976), *Of Grammatology*, Baltamore: John Hopkins University Press.

Diamond, I. and Quinby, L. (eds) (1988), *Feminism and Foucault: Reflections on Resitance*, Boston: Northeastern University Press.

Douglas, M. (1973), *Natural Symbols*. Explorations in Cosmology, London: Barrie and Rockcliff/Cresset Press.

Douglas, M. (1979), *Implicit Meanings: Essays in Anthropology*, London: Routledge.

Douglas, M. (1984), *Purity and Danger: An Analysis of the concept of pollution and taboo*, London: Routledge and Kegan Paul.

Eco, U. (1986), 'Lumbar Thought', *Travels in Hyperreality*, Orlando, Fl: Jarcourt Brace Jovanovich.

Entwistle, J. (1997), 'Power dressing and the Fashioning of the Career Woman', in M. Nava, I. MacRury, A. Blake, and B. Richards (eds), *Buy this Book: Studies in Advertising and Consumption*, London: Routledge.

Entwistle, J. (2000a), *The Fashioned Body: theorizing fashion and dress in modern society*, Cambridge: Polity.

Entwistle, J. (2000b), 'Fashioning the career woman: power dressing as a strategy of consumption', in M. Talbot and M. Andrews (eds), *All the World and Her Husband: Women and Consumption in the Twentieth Century*, London: Cassell.

Entwistle, J. and Wilson, E. (1998), 'The Body Clothed', Catalogue *100 years of Art and Fashion,* London: Hayward Gallery.

Finkelstein, J. (1991), *The Fashioned Self*, Cambridge: Polity.

Foucault, M. (1977), *Discipline and Punish*, Harmondsworth: Penguin.

Foucault, M. (1980), 'Body/Power', in C. Gordon (ed.), *Power/Knowledge: Selected Interviews and Other Writings 1972–77*, New York: Pantheon Books.

Foucault, M. (1986), *The History of Sexuality: Volume Three, The Care of the Self*, London: Penguin.

Freeman, C. (1993), 'Designing women: Corporate discipline and Barbados's off-shore Pink Collar Sector', *Cultural Anthropology* 8 (2): 169–86.

Gamman, L. and Makinen, M. (1994), *Female Fetishism: A New Look*, London: Lawrence and Wishart.

Giddens, A. (1991), *Modernity and Self-Identity: Self and Society in the Late Modern Age*, Cambridge: Polity.

Goffman, E. (1971), *The Presentation of Self in Everyday Life*, London: The Penguin Press.

Goffman, E. (1972), *Relations in Public*, Harmondworth: Pelican Books.

Hall, S. and Jefferson, T. (et al.) (eds) (1976), *Resistance Through Rituals: Youth Subcultures in Post-war Britain*, London: Hutchinson.

Haug, F. (ed.) (1987), *Female Sexualization*, first ed., London: Verso.

Hebdige, D. (1979), *Subculture: The Meaning of Style*, London: Methuen.

Hollander, A. (1993), *Seeing Through Clothes*, Berkeley: University of California Press.

Jenkins, R. (1992), *Pierre Bourdieu*, London: Routledge.

Kuhn, A. (1988), 'The Body and Cinema: Some Problems for Feminism', in S. Sheridan (ed.), *Grafts: Feminist Cultural Criticism*, London: Verso.

Kunzle, D. (1982), *Fashion and Fetishism: A Social History of the Corset, Tight-lacing and other Forms of Body-Sculpture in the West*, Totowa, N.J.: Rowan and Littlefield.

Luck, K. (1992), 'Trouble in Eden, Trouble with Eve: Women, Trousers and Utopian Socialism in Nineteenth Century America', in J. Ash and E. Wilson (eds), *Chic Thrills: A Fashion Reader*, London: Pandora.

Lurie, A. (1981), *The Language of Clothes*, New York: Random House.

Mauss, M. (1973), 'Techniques of the Body', *Economy and Society* 2 (1): 70–89.

McNay, L. (1992), *Foucault and Feminism: Power, Gender and the Self*, Cambridge: Polity Press.

McNay, L. (1999), 'Gender, Habitus and the Field: Pierre Bourdieu and the Limits of Reflexivity', *Theory, Culture and Society* 16 (1): 95–117.

Merleau-Ponty, M. (1976), *The Primacy of Perception*, USA: Northwestern University Press.

Merleau-Ponty, M. (1981), *The Phenomenology of Perception*, London: Routledge and Kegan.

Molloy, J.T. (1980), *Women: Dress for Success*, New York: Peter H. Wyden.

Mulvey, L. (1989), *Visual and Other Pleasures*, London: Macmillan.

Polhemus, T. (1988), *Bodystyles*, Luton: Lennard.

Polhemus, T. (1994), *Streetstyle*, London: Thames and Hudson.

Polhemus, T. and Proctor, L. (1978), *Fashion and Anti-fashion: An Anthology of Clothing and Adornment*, London: Cox & Wyman.

Ramazanoglu, C. (ed.) (1993), *Up Against Foucault: Explorations of some Tensions between Foucault and Feminism*, London: Routledge.

Roberts, H. (1977), 'The Exquisite Slave: The Role of Clothes in the Making of the Victorian Woman', *Signs* 2 (3): 554–569.

Schulze, L. (1990), 'On the muscle', in J. Gaines and C. Herzog (eds), *Fabrications: Costume and the Female Body*, London: Routledge.

Sheppard, D.L. (1993), 'Women Managers' Perceptions of Gender and Organizational Life', in A. Mills, J. and P. Tancred (eds), *Gendering Organizational Analysis*, London: Sage Publications.

Sheppard, D.L. (1989), 'Organisations, Power and Sexuality: The Image and Self-Image of Women Managers', in J. Hearn (ed.), *The Sexuality of the Organisation*, London: Sage Publications;

St. Martin, L. and Gavey, N. (1996), 'Women Body Building: Feminist Resistance and/or Femininity's Recuperation', *Body and Society* 2 (4): 45–57.

Synnott, A. (1993), *The Body Social: Symbolism, Self and Society*, London: Routledge.

Tseëlon, E. (1997), *The Masque of Femininity*, London: Sage.

Turner, B. (1985), *The Body and Society: Explorations in Social Theory*, Oxford: Basil Blackwell.

Turner, T. (1996), 'Bodies and anti-bodies: flesh and fetish in contemporary social theory', in T. Csordas (ed.), *Embodiment and Experience: The existential ground of culture and self*, Cambridge: Cambridge University Press.

Willis, P. (1975), 'The expressive style of a motor-bike culture', in J. Benthall and T. Polhemus (eds), *The Body as a Medium of Expression*, London: Allen Lane.

Willis, P. (1978), *Profane Culture*, London: Routledge & Kegan Paul.

Wilson, E. (1985), *Adorned in Dreams: Fashion and Modernity*, London: Virago.

Wilson, E. (1992), 'The Postmodern Body', in J. Ash and E. Wilson (eds), *Chic Thrills: A Fashion Reader*, London: Pandora.

Wolf, N. (1990), *The Beauty Myth: How Images of Beauty are Used Against Women*, London: Vintage.

Shop-Window Dummies? Fashion, the Body, and Emergent Socialities

Paul Sweetman

I developed blisters just trotting around my apartment. I couldn't wear the shoes out of the house, because my feet hurt too much. I couldn't move quickly or take big steps, the heels were so high. Sometimes, I'd put them on just to sit on the couch and look at my feet as I gossiped over the phone. (Jenkins 1999: 62)

Introduction

It was, until recently, commonplace for studies within the sociology of the body to begin by noting the overall neglect of the body within sociology as a whole (Morgan and Scott 1993: 1). The same might still be said of the sociology of fashion. By this I mean not only that fashion and related issues have received insufficient attention within social and cultural theory (Edwards 1997: 1), but also that work in this area has – like mainstream sociology as a whole – neglected to afford sufficient attention to the body and issues of embodiment. This is not true of all the work in this field. Recent feminist writing, in particular, has had a good deal to say about the relationship between fashion, the media, and hegemonic forms of embodied subjectivity (see, for example, Bartky 1988; Bordo 1993). In the main, however, writing on fashion has neglected the body – and more particularly the lived-body – treating the fashionable social actor as a 'disembodied consciousness' (Turner 1992: 7), whose corporeality comes into play only implicitly, as an inert or unfeeling frame to be decorated and adorned. The body in fashion is simply a mannequin or shop-window dummy – it is the clothing, rather than the wearing of it, that is regarded as significant.

Similar points can be made about related fields. As I have argued elsewhere, for example, the classic subcultural studies of the 1970s singularly neglected the phenomenological and/or affectual aspects of subcultural involvement, adopting a predominantly textual or semiotic approach, and reducing sub-cultural activity – by and large – to the symbolic manipulation of codes (Sweetman 2001). In spite of Cohen's insistence that there are three levels to subcultural analysis – historical, structural or semiotic – and 'the phenomeno-logical analysis of the way the subculture is actually 'lived out' by those who are its bearers and supports' (1997: 95), little of this 'third level' analysis actually appears in the classic accounts (see also Gelder 1997a, 1997b, 1997c; Muggleton 1997). Just as one cannot hope to fully comprehend the meaning and significance of subcultural activity without attending to 'the intricacies of its "lived sensuality"' (Katz, in Ferrell 1993: 167), however, the same is true of fashion. Fashionable behaviour involves far more than simply the symbolic manipulation of one's appearance, and if we are to provide a more than partial analysis of fashion as a social process it is to the 'phenomenological foreground' (Katz, in Ferrell, 1993: 167) of such behaviour that we need to turn.

The following, then, looks first at some of the more influential approaches to fashion within social and cultural theory before suggesting that, despite their considerable differences, what such approaches share is a failure to adequately address the phenomenological and/or affectual aspects of fashion-able behaviour. The chapter then goes on to outline some of the ways in which the body is implicated in fashion, and to suggest that an understanding of the embodied reality of the fashion process is central rather than incidental to an analysis of both its practice and effects. Fashion is centrally implicated in the construction and reconstruction of individual bodies and subjectivities. At the same time, however, it can also be argued to provide an affectual rather than merely symbolic link between those involved, thereby constituting an experiential and bodily basis for the formation of 'taste-communities' and other types of informal, non-contractual social group. In the penultimate section of the chapter it is suggested that Maffesoli's (1988, 1991, 1996) exploration of neo-tribal sociality goes some way towards providing a theoretical frame-work for the analysis of this particular aspect of the fashion process. It is also argued, however, that Maffesoli's own work falls somewhat short in continuing to regard clothing and other forms of adornment as *symbolic* of affectual ties rather than as partially constitutive of such ties in and of them-selves. The concluding section of the chapter addresses some of the wider implications of the discussion as a whole.

Approaching Fashion and Consumption

Perhaps the most influential approach towards the study of fashion within the social sciences has been that associated with writers such as Veblen, Simmel and, more recently, Bourdieu. In each case, fashion is regarded as a specifically modern phenomenon that acts to express or maintain distinctions between different social groups in a situation where rigid and inflexible social hierarchies no longer apply. Veblen (1970), for example, saw fashionable dress as a form of 'conspicuous consumption', a means of demonstrating one's social status through the acquisition and display of appropriate attire. This was all the more important in a modern context, not simply because one's social position was no longer rigidly ascribed, but also because of the increasing likelihood of encounters with relative strangers, and the ensuing need to manage impressions in a situation where the other's knowledge of one's class or status could no longer be readily assumed. The fashion *cycle*, according to Veblen, reflected a more or less steady oscillation between the arbitrary whims of fashion and the subsequent re-assertion of good taste.

A broadly similar picture was painted by Simmel, who also linked the rise of fashion to the breakdown of rigid social hierarchies and the relative anonymity of the modern urban environment (1997). Fashion also satisfied a simultaneous desire for uniformity and difference, allowing people to express their individuality whilst remaining part of the crowd. As did Veblen, Simmel regarded fashions primarily as *class* fashions, as symbolic means of differentiating between relatively distinct social groups. Fashion was both inclusive and exclusive, marking off its followers as members of a particular status group whilst temporarily excluding the unfashionable masses, whose only hope of symbolically infiltrating the 'upper echelons' was to imitate the fashions of the social elite. In a departure from Veblen's analysis, then, Simmel (1997 [1905]: 190) famously and influentially described the fashion process as a cycle of adoption, imitation and abandonment:

> Just as soon as the lower strata begin to appropriate their style – and thereby overstep the demarcation line which the upper strata have drawn and destroy the uniformity of their coherence symbolized in this fashion – so the upper strata turn away from this fashion and adopt a new one, which in turn differentiates them from the broad masses. And thus the game goes merrily on.

While Bourdieu's concept of the habitus may allow for an approach that acknowledges the materiality of dress and the relationship between clothing and the body, his specific work on fashion reiterates Simmel's analysis, and is

thus indicative of the continuing influence of Simmel's perspective: 'Fashion is
the latest fashion, the latest difference. An emblem of class (in all senses) withers
once it loses its distinctive power. When the miniskirt reaches the mining villages
of northern France, it's time to start all over again' (Bourdieu 1993: 135). In
each case, then, fashion is understood primarily as a mark of distinction, a
signifier of class or social status which must be nominally available to all, but
which is abandoned by the 'upper echelons' as soon as it becomes so widely
adopted as to cease to refer to one's membership of the fashionable elite. The
form that fashion takes is unimportant, according to Veblen and Simmel, just
so long as what is in fashion can serve as a mark of distinction. As Simmel
puts it: 'not the slightest reason can be found for its creations from the stand-
point of an objective, aesthetic or other expediency' ([1905]: 189).

Whilst widely influential, the perspective outlined above has been roundly
criticized, not least for precisely this reason – its failure to account for or
address either the form that fashion takes or its links to wider social, cultural
and artistic movements (Wilson 1985: 52). It has also been argued that such
a 'top down' approach to the fashion process is out of date: that while it
may have accurately reflected the workings of the fashion process up to the
1950s or 1960s, such a model is no longer appropriate given the declining
influence of haute couture – and the ensuing rise of 'street-style' – since around
that period (Gronow 1997: 94). As will be expanded on below, the latter
criticism is given added weight by depictions of contemporary fashion as an
eclectic free-for-all; a postmodern 'carnival of signs' (Tseëlon 1995: 124),
where anything and everything is up for grabs in what some have described
as the 'supermarket of style' (Polhemus 1995; see also Sweetman 1999; Wilson
1990). For the purposes of the present argument though, a more significant
limitation of the approach in question is its focus on fashion almost solely as
a mechanism of social distinction, and its consequent neglect of the lived-
reality of fashionable behaviour for those involved.

The latter point is also broadly true of an alternative approach to the
fashion process – that associated with Blumer's influential paper from the
late-1960s, 'Fashion: From Class Differentiation to Collective Selection'
(1969). Where Veblen and Simmel focus solely or predominantly on fashion
as a mechanism of social distinction, adopting a 'top-down' approach that
suggests that what is in fashion at any one time is essentially arbitrary, Blumer
disagrees. Basing his argument around a detailed empirical investigation of
the Paris fashion industry, Blumer argues that fashion is not so much an
arbitrary reflection of the whims of the fashionable elite as the outcome of a
complex process of collective selection, which sees designers, buyers and other
members of the fashion *industry* attempting to anticipate and reflect emergent
trends in society and culture as a whole. Fashion can be seen as an attempt to
capture 'the proximate future' (Blumer 1969: 280), and although high-street

fashion responds to designs and trends outlined by the industry's elite, dominant groups within the industry do not so much dictate the process as themselves respond to wider trends: 'Fashion [thus] appears much more as a collective grouping for the proximate future than a channelled movement laid down by prestigeful figures' (Blumer 1969: 281). In the absence of tradition, fashion's wider function – or 'societal role' – is to allow collective adjustment to emergent trends; to introduce a semblance of 'order in a potentially anarchic and moving present' (Blumer 1969: 289).

While Veblen, Simmel and Bourdieu suggest that fashion is primarily an 'emblem of class', with the latter two authors arguing that any particular fashion is abandoned once it loses its distinctive appeal, Blumer presents a different picture, arguing that fashion is not simply an arbitrary mark of distinction, but a reflection of wider emergent trends. Despite his rejection of the view that the form of fashion is controlled or dominated by the *social* elite, however, Blumer still presents something of a 'top-down' approach in focusing on a particular section of the fashion industry and suggesting that the work of top designers and buyers is particularly influential, even if it does represent an attempt to reflect broader socio-cultural developments. Like Veblen and Simmel, Blumer also presents a picture of the fashion process as largely consensual and uni-directional, in which at any one time particular styles – however derived – can be said to dominate fashion as a whole.

As has already been briefly indicated, however, this view of fashion as a broadly homogeneous movement in a particular and approximately unified direction has been problematized by the declining influence of high-fashion and the increasing eclecticism and fragmentation of the fashion scene since the 1960s. Indeed, according to certain commentators we are now in an era of 'post-fashion', where not only does no single style dominate, but where the freedom to wear what we like means that 'fashion' has become entirely free-floating, and no longer refers to anything other than fashion itself (Tseëlon 1995: 124). Clothing or dress no longer indexes an external social reality, and particular items, whether fashionable or otherwise, can no longer be said to signify either class, status, or other conventional social attributes.

The Baudrillardian view of postmodern fashion as utterly free-floating – 'a carnival of signs with no meanings attached' (Tseëlon 1995: 124) – has itself been criticized. Just because contemporary fashion has accelerated and fragmented, for instance, such increased complexity does not necessarily indicate the *absolute* self-referentiality that Baudrillard's position implies (Tseëlon 1995: 134). It is generally accepted, however, that contemporary fashion has become increasingly eclectic and fragmented, that we are witnessing 'a blurring between mainstream and countercultural fashions [and that] all fashion has become 'stagey', self-conscious about its own status as discourse' (Wilson 1990: 222).

This accords with characterizations of contemporary consumption as increasingly individualized. While concerned with consumption in a wider sense rather than with fashion per se, proponents of the 'reflexive modernization thesis' (Hetherington 1998: 47) argue that with the declining influence of once stable 'ideological identities' (Maffesoli 1991: 15), consumption is increasingly divorced from factors such as class or status and that individuals increasingly 'consume in ways which articulate to themselves and to others a sense of identity which may be autonomous from [their membership of] traditional status groups' (Bocock 1992: 153). In late-, high-, or reflexive-modernity, 'ascriptive elements in modern societies – such as those associated with social class and gender relations – [are] disappearing as a source of identity and life-style, making us truly modern individuals able to choose identities increasingly free from the constraints of class, gender roles, locality, religion and occupation' (Hetherington 1998: 47).

According to writers such as Giddens (1991), Beck (1992) and Bauman (1992), then, identity has become increasingly reflexive and is now actively constructed through privatized patterns of consumption (see Lash 1993; Warde 1994). In pre-modern social contexts identity was taken as given, and even in simple- or organised-modernity identity was relatively stable – a fairly unambiguous reflection of factors such as occupation or familial status. In late-, high- or *reflexive*-modernity, however, identity is increasingly ambiguous, and has to be individually worked at in the context of more or less freely chosen possibilities. Accounts differ, but the essential argument is that in simple or organized modernity, identities were 'comparatively stable', because they were 'firmly bound into coherent and integrative social practices' (Wagner 1994: 170). With the continued 'decline of traditional ties' (Warde 1994: 881), however, identity has increasingly become a matter of choice. 'De-traditionalization' means that 'the monitoring by the other of traditional conventions' has been 'replaced by the necessary self-monitoring, or reflexivity' of late- or high-modernity (Lash 1993: 5) and individuals must now 'choose their identities' (Warde 1994: 878) from the range of possibilities offered in the marketplace.

Whilst associated with writers who stress the continuities between simple- or organised-modernity and what is variously termed late-, high- or reflexive-modernity, this analysis shares considerable affinities with work on identity in *postmodernity*. Much of this latter body of work similarly stresses the increasingly flexible nature of contemporary identities and the ways in which identities are increasingly forged through consumption and lifestyle choices. While certain theorists of post- rather than late-, high-, or reflexive-modernity have adopted a rather pessimistic tone, however – questioning the possibility of stable or ontologically secure identities forged through consumption (Angus 1989)

– and others have been more ambivalent (Kellner 1992), many such theorists have been more optimistic, stressing the playful and creative freedoms that such a situation of flexibility might be said to afford (see, for example, McRobbie 1994).

Aside from differences in terminology then, perhaps the key difference between proponents of the 'reflexive-modernization thesis' and their post-modern counterparts lies in their respective interpretations of the consequences and effects of the flexibility and ambiguity that both identify. For the latter group this may be seen as cause for celebration, and the implication is that at least some individuals revel in the creative and/or resistant opportunities afforded by the new-found freedoms on offer. While proponents of reflexive modernization also emphasize the choices and potential freedoms available to contemporary individuals, however, these are also seen to entail new risks and responsibilities. The implication here is that consumption practices are less geared towards creative play, and more towards an attempt to ground one's identity in a coherent lifestyle that accords with the reflexive narrative one has chosen to adopt.

From Text to Affect

The above has briefly outlined three different approaches to fashion and consumption. From the first perspective, fashion is seen primarily as a mechanism of social distinction, with particular fashions abandoned as soon as they cease to refer unambiguously to one's position in the social hierarchy. From the second, fashion is not so much an arbitrary reflection of existing patterns of social stratification as a collective attempt to anticipate and adjust to emergent social trends. In both cases, however, fashion is seen as broadly coherent and uni-directional, with particular styles regarded as dominant – or in their ascendancy – at any particular time. In line with the increasing eclecticism of fashion since the 1960s, however, writers representative of the third perspective regard contemporary fashion and consumption as increasingly individualized – a reflection of one's reflexively chosen narrative of self-identity rather than an index of one's existing position within an already established social hierarchy.

Despite these differences, however, all three approaches are united in their neglect of the phenomenological and/or affectual aspects of fashionable behaviour. From all three perspectives, fashion is regarded as primarily *symbolic*, and in this sense as an essentially cognitive exercise. It is either a signifier of class or social status, a symbolic reflection of wider socio-cultural trends, or an attempt to communicate to oneself and others an elective rather than ascribed narrative of the reflexively constructed self. Despite their differences, then, all three perspectives can be said to be overly textual in their approach: like much other recent work in social and cultural theory, all three approaches can be said to neglect 'the experiential and affective dimensions of social practice and social relations' (Turner 1996: 28). Even in some of the recent work that ostensibly brings the body into centre stage – suggesting that work on the 'outer body' (Featherstone 1991: 171) is central to contemporary projects of individualized identity-construction – the body itself is regarded not so much in terms of its lived-sensuality as a 'topic of reflexivity' (Turner 1992: 7): a cognitively apprehended phenomenon that is worked *on* as part of a wider project of the self (see, for example, Giddens 1991; Shilling 1993). While acknowledged as a central 'feature of the modern lifestyle' (Turner 1992: 87), such work also regards the body primarily as a malleable *resource*, not as an indivisible component of *embodied* social action. Indeed, as one of the key exponents of this position, this is also true of Giddens' work as a whole, which adopts a Weberian model of the social actor, as 'an implicitly disembodied consciousness' (Turner 1992: 7; see also Hetherington 1998: 53).

Fashion, as a means of clothing, adorning, and otherwise decorating the body, involves far more, however, than simply the symbolic manipulation of codes. When I wear a suit, I walk, feel, and *act* differently, and not simply because of the garment's cultural connotations, or the fact that – as a sociologist – dressing smartly is something of a novelty, but also because of the way the suit is cut, and the way its sheer materiality both enables and constrains, encouraging or demanding a certain gait, posture and demeanour, whilst simultaneously denying me the full range of bodily movement that would be available were I dressed in jogging-pants and a loose-fitting t-shirt. And this is – crucially – far from simply a matter of my own individual experience of the body: it is socially significant in a number of ways. On the one hand, the continued existence of uniforms, professional dress codes, and other more or less formal sanctions and prohibitions means that what I wear in any particular context is not solely a matter of individual choice, but is socially governed to a greater or lesser degree. On the other, whether individually chosen or otherwise, the clothing I wear significantly affects not just the way I feel but also my presentation of self.

We can talk, then, of fashion and adornment as 'techniques of the body' (Mauss 1992) which impact not only on our *appearance*, but also on our experience of the body and the ways in which the body can be used. And despite the increasing eclecticism of contemporary fashion, our clothing choices are still partially structured by gender, age and occupation, not to mention a range of other sociological variables such as sexuality, ethnicity, and class. In this sense, fashions, uniforms, age-related modes of dress and subcultural styles all effect not simply a symbolic connection between the actors concerned, but also an affectual or experiential one: a form of identification based not only on appearance but also upon the way in which the body is lived, experienced and used. Soldiers or cabin-attendants, schoolchildren or clubbers, fashion-victims or accountants: such groups are linked not only through their shared adoption of particular signifiers, but also through their shared experience of the feel of the garments in question and the restrictions and possibilities that their materiality entails.

This can in turn be argued to structure subjectivities in particular ways, helping to ensure that values and norms are embodied through a mnemonics of shared physicality. Bodies and selves are made and remade in part through the ways in which they are adorned, and this is a process that involves 'carnal knowing' as well as 'cognitive apprehension' (Mellor and Shilling 1997). As was indicated above, Bourdieu's concept of the habitus may be helpful here, in thinking through the ways in which clothing choices both reflect and impact upon this embodied set of predispositions and ways of orientating oneself to the world (Bourdieu 1984).[1] There is also a significant temporal dimension to the process that operates on a number of related levels. First, fashion, style and adornment change over time, reflecting issues such as gendered standards of deportment and bodily control. Second, the contextuality of appropriate dress operates temporally as well as spatially, changing according to such factors as the time of day and the day of the week. Third, fashions and standards of appropriate attire are age-related, and we can thus talk of the restructuring of embodied subjectivities over the life-course as a process that is centred in part around transitional stages in dress. In relation to the first of these points – changes in fashion and style over time – the contemporary convergence between youth and adult styles might in turn suggest a less strict demarcation between age-related forms of deportment and bodily control.

Lastly – and in case the above is regarded as overly deterministic – an emphasis on the way in which clothing impacts upon the body also suggests that where choices are made, these may again be regarded as more than merely symbolic. On an individual level, my clothing choices reflect and impact upon not simply my chosen narrative of self-identity, but also the way in which I experience and use my body, and the same can be said of both subcultural styles and fashion in a wider sense. The skinheads' adoption of shorn hair, boots and braces may perhaps be interpreted as an attempt to symbolically resolve the tensions inherent in the loss of traditional working-class community (Cohen 1997), but that is not the complete story. It also reflected and helped to shape a particular habitus, allowing for and responding to a particular orientation towards the body and helping to shape both individual and group subjectivities. Similar points can be made about other subcultural styles – such as the adoption of 'baggy' clothes by early ravers – and more mainstream fashions such as the widespread adoption of sportswear during the 1990s.

As has already been noted, the affectual or experiential aspects of fashionable behaviour have not been entirely neglected by contemporary theorists. Bartky (1988), for instance notes that the variety of disciplinary practices dedicated towards producing 'a body which in gesture and appearance is recognizably feminine' can be grouped into three types: 'those that aim to produce a body of a certain size and general configuration; *those that bring forth from this body a specific repertoire of gestures, postures and movements*; and those that are directed towards the display of the body as an ornamented surface' (Bartky 1988: 64, emphasis added). In considering the second of these areas, however, Bartky is concerned primarily with 'gestures, postures and movements' per se, not with the relationship between fashion and the body as experienced and used: 'makeup and the selection of clothes' (Bartky 1988: 68) are considered to impact primarily upon 'the body as an ornamented surface', not the lived-body or the body-in-use. In her consideration of dieting, 'makeup' and exercise as *disciplinary* practices, Bartky can also be argued to neglect other aspects of the relationship between fashion and the body – including the possibility of pleasure, creativity and fun – and the sense in which fashionable behaviour can lead to an experiential or affectual relationship between the various actors concerned. It is to a possible framework for the analysis of this latter side to the fashion process that I shall now turn.

Fashion, Identification and Emergent Socialities

According to Maffesoli (1988, 1991, 1996), we are currently witnessing a resurgence of basic forms of community, a move away from rational, contractual social relationships towards an *empathetic* form of sociality, where what is important is not some abstract, idealized goal, but rather the feeling of togetherness engendered by one's direct involvement with the small-scale social group. Where modernity was characterized by the proliferation of associational forms of social relationship – which were 'drained . . . of any real content' – 'postmodernity has tended to favour . . . [a] withdrawal into the group as well as a deepening of relationships within these groups' (Maffesoli 1996: 89).

This move towards *neo-tribal* patterns of solidarity represents a shift from *society*, which is 'governed by an instrumental, rationalising logic of "performativity"', to a 'form of *sociality*, governed by an empathetic logic of emotional renewal' (Evans 1997: 225, emphasis added). It can be seen, in Durkheimian terms, as representing a shift from 'an essentially *mechanical* social order towards a complex, predominantly *organic* structure' (Maffesoli 1996: 3, original emphasis).[2] Alternatively, one can argue that it represents the re-emergence of *Gemeinschaft*-like patterns of sociality, or of Weber's 'communal relationships' (Maffesoli 1996: 60).

The new tribes are informal, dynamic, and frequently temporary alliances, centred around 'their members' shared lifestyles and tastes' (Shields 1996: x): around *feelings* rather than a commitment to particular ideologies or beliefs. Built around tactility and proxemics, these are non-instrumental, apolitical allegiances – forms of 'extra-logical communality' (Maffesoli 1991: 17) – 'whose sole raison d'être is a preoccupation with the collective present' (Maffesoli 1996: 75). Tribal collectivities may have an ostensible goal, but 'this is not essential; what is important is the energy expended on constituting the group *as such*' (Maffesoli 1996: 96, original emphasis). They represent, in other words, a form of 'undirected being-together' (Maffesoli 1996: 81), or 'sociality-for-sociality's-sake', and it is this that allows them to generate a certain puissance or 'affective warmth'. Such 'affective warmth' in turn allows for that 'loss of self in the group' or 'ex-static attitude', that sense of 'collective effervescence', 'immanent transcendence' or 'shared sentiment' which 'is the true social bond' (Maffesoli 1996: 43).

The 'saturation of the political' for Maffesoli, thus corresponds with 'the saturation of individualism' (Maffesoli 1996: 64), and in this sense Maffesoli's work links to some of the literature examined above in referring to the loss of once secure forms of identity: 'It is clear . . . that ideological identity, whether . . . political, sexual or professional, is now clouded with uncertainty' (Maffesoli 1991: 15). Where Giddens (1991), and other proponents of reflexive modernization regard the loss of secure and stable 'ideological identities' as having contributed to an ongoing process of *individualization*, however, Maffesoli instead argues that we are witnessing a period of '*disindividuation*', or '*indifferentiation*': 'the 'losing' of self into a collective subject' (Maffesoli 1988: 145). And where the 'reflexive modernization thesis' suggests that individuals respond to the loss of 'ideological identities' by grounding them-selves in a reflexively constructed narrative of the self, Maffesoli – like certain other theorists of *postmodernity* – argues that members of the sociality revel in the superficiality of the neo-tribal *persona*. Contemporary sociality *refuses* 'the logic of identity' (Maffesoli 1996: 38), and while the 'characteristics of the social are that the individual can have a *function* in the society, and also function within a party, an association, or a stable group':

The characteristics of the sociality are that the person (persona), plays *roles* within his [sic] professional activities, nurturing the various tribes in which he participates. His stage costume changeable, he goes out everyday according to his fancy, whether sexual, cultural, social, or religious, to take his place in the diverse games of the *theatrum mundi*. One can never overemphasize the contrast between the social and the tragic superficiality of the sociality. (Maffesoli 1988: 148, original emphasis)

Neo-tribalism can ultimately be seen as an *aesthetic* form of sociality, which favours 'appearance and form' (Maffesoli 1996: 98) – as an *expression* of shared feelings and experiences – above, for example, formalized membership criteria, or a commitment to particular (ideological) beliefs. In this context, particular places, things, or behaviours can assume iconic significance, acting as badges of recognition, confirmation of the group's existence, and strengthening communal ties. An 'elaborate hairstyle', for instance, or 'an original tattoo', acts not only as a mask, but also reinforces social cohesion, 'subordinating' the person concerned to their 'chosen affinity group' (Maffesoli 1996: 91). 'Here,' argues Maffesoli, 'we can find an example of "disindividuation", participation, in the mystical sense, in a greater whole' (Maffesoli 1996: 91).

Examples of groups displaying neo-tribal tendencies range from 'fashion victims' and 'youth subcultures' to 'hobbyists' and 'sports enthusiasts' (Shields 1996: xi). Such 'affective collectivities' (Maffesoli 1991: 13) are, as has already been noted, distinguished primarily 'by their members' shared lifestyles and tastes' (Shields 1996: x). No longer 'marginal', such tribal sociality 'is now the ordinary reality of everyday life' (Maffesoli 1996: 75). Signalling, as it does, the death of abstract rationality, of the modern individual and 'the great economic, political and ideological structures' (Maffesoli 1996: 97), neo-tribal sociality can also be argued to herald 'the end of civilized modernity' itself (Maffesoli 1996: 70). For Maffesoli, however, this is a cause for optimism rather than despair: neo-tribalism can be seen as 'a sign of renewed vitality' (Maffesoli 1996: 60), and 'one to which due attention should be paid, since it is charged with the future' (Maffesoli 1996: 110).

This work has been criticized on a number of counts. Evans (1997), for example, argues that Maffesoli underplays the continuing importance of 'work, productivity, science, technology, and so forth' (Evans 1997: 231), and in overemphasizing the shift to an empathetic and Dionysiac postmodernity, neglects the double-sided nature of modernity itself, which should not be regarded as governed solely by an instrumental rationality (Evans 1997: 240; see also Williams 1998: 760). In a related criticism, Hetherington (1998) argues that Maffesoli downplays the continuing importance of factors such as class, gender and ethnicity 'in establishing styles of life' and responding to 'the problematizing of identity' (Hetherington 1998: 53). While such structural characteristics may no longer offer a secure and stable sense of identity, 'we can still talk about class, gender and ethnicity alongside neo-tribes' (Hetherington 1998: 53). Elsewhere, Crook (1998) has criticized Maffesoli, along with numerous other contemporary theorists, for presenting us with an overly romanticised picture of 'everyday life'.

From the perspective of this chapter, however, Maffesoli's work is both significant and important in allowing us to take seriously the affectual aspects of fashion, style and consumption in a wider sense, rather than regarding such practices simply as cognitive exercises in the manipulation and presentation of codes. With his emphasis on neo-tribal sociality, Maffesoli's work also allows us to address the sense in which fashion and other lifestyle-related practices may be central to affectual forms of identification rather than geared solely towards the construction of an individualized narrative of the self. That is not to say that Maffesoli's work is unproblematic in this regard, however. As will have been noted, while Maffesoli regards clothing, hairstyles and other iconic devices as central to the expression of neo-tribal patterns of identification, such factors are still regarded primarily as symbolic devices, as indicative or *expressive* of, rather than themselves *constitutive* of, wider affectual ties. In other words, whilst Maffesoli's analysis as a whole concentrates a good deal on the affectual realm, his analysis of clothing, fashion and style remains to some extent located within the realm of the symbolic: it has been the argument of this chapter, however, that we might regard fashion, adornment and style as more than simply expressive of wider affectual ties.

In suggesting that the clothing and adornment of the body may contribute to both the construction of individual subjectivities and to wider affectual ties, this paper also problematizes another aspect of Maffesoli's argument: the idea that neo-tribal 'masks' are as easily adopted and discarded as the tribal affiliations they symbolize. Maffesoli's references to 'the tragic super-ficiality of the sociality' accord with the idea of contemporary fashion as a free-floating 'carnival of signs' (Tseëlon 1995: 124), where identities are available ready-to-wear in what others have dubbed the 'supermarket of style' (Polhemus 1995). In arguing that clothing impacts upon the body and habitus, however, the foregoing discussion suggests that such off-the-peg identities may not be as easily adopted as such commentaries imply. In this sense, the paper is perhaps more supportive of Hetherington's (1998) analysis of neo-tribal sociality, which suggests that for many, neo-tribal forms of identification represent not so much a form of playful revelling in the postmodern funhouse, as a search for 'stability [and] belonging' (Hetherington 1998: 29); 'a politi-cised quest for an authentic sense of self amidst the uncertainty that is the [contemporary] social terrain' (Hetherington 1998: 54).

As the last quote indicates, not only does Hetherington reject Maffesoli's argument regarding the superficiality of the postmodern 'mask', he also suggests that tribal affiliations may be as much geared towards the construction of an individual sense of identity as they are to the loss of self in a wider whole.

Like Bauman (1992), then, Hetherington (1998) differs from Maffesoli in viewing 'collective identification and belonging as a means of *developing individual identity*' and not simply as a process of disindividuation (Hetherington 1998: 16, emphasis added). According to Bauman, neo-tribal sociality is not 'unambiguously anti-individualistic' (1992: 25), but is key to the construction of individual self-identities, helping to sanction lifestyle choices, and thereby offering a guide through the bewildering array of consumption choices faced by the contemporary individual. As Bauman puts it: 'joining a tribe means adopting a particular lifestyle; or, rather, the road to a coherent lifestyle leads through the adoption of tribally sanctioned structures of relevances complete with a kit of totemic symbols' (1992: 25).

There are certain problems with Bauman's argument, including the difficulty of squaring his insistence on the temporary and 'superficial' nature of tribal 'membership' with his simultaneous assertion that tribes offer 'comprehensive and relatively cohesive' (1992: 25) lifestyle packages to those searching for a stable and coherent sense of identity. A further difficulty concerns Bauman's intimation that 'tribes' are always already there to be joined through the adoption of a *pre-packaged* 'kit of totemic symbols', a point which not only denies agency to those involved, but also echoes Maffesoli's suggestion that such 'totemic' or 'iconic' devices are simply expressive of, rather than partially constitutive of, wider affectual ties. Essentially, however, the argument presented here is supportive of both Hetherington (1998) and Bauman (1992) in regarding fashion, style and adornment as allowing for both the expression of individual identities and the establishment of wider identificatory ties. In emphasizing the affectual or experiential aspects of fashionable behaviour – and in concentrating in the latter part of the paper on the ways in which clothing and adornment may be said to contribute to the establishment of 'neo-tribal' forms of identification – the intention has not been to deny either the way in which fashion operates on a symbolic level, or the way in which contemporary forms of consumption may be dedicated in part towards a reflexive project of the self. Rather, it has been to indicate that to focus solely on fashion as a symbolic process – whether as a system of demarcation or distinction or as a cognitively-oriented expression of the reflexively constructed self – is to miss much of what is significant about fashion and other, related forms of behaviour.

Concluding Comments

The above has suggested that for a full analysis of fashion as a social process, we need to examine more than simply its symbolic or textual uses and effects. Fashion, as a *material* process, involves a good deal more than the symbolic manipulation of codes: as a means of clothing, adorning and otherwise decorating the body, fashion operates at an affectual as well as a symbolic level, helping to construct and reconstruct individual subjectivities, whilst simultaneously forging an affectual or experiential relationship between the various actors involved.

In emphasizing the affectual or experiential side of fashionable behaviour, this chapter can be linked to a wider body of recent sociological literature, where the emphasis lies as much with process and 'the occasionalism of action' (Hetherington 1998: 143), as it does with wider outcomes and effects. The paper also supports the view that in examining consumption and lifestyle-related practices we need to regard these as more than simply cognitive exercises in the reflexive construction of the self. This is not to deny that fashion and related practices may be partially oriented towards a reflexive project of identity construction, and in this respect be dedicated primarily towards the manipulation of one's appearance and a marketable presentation of self. Rather it is to suggest that with fashion – as with so many other social phenomena – *there is more going on than simply that which meets the eye.* I have argued elsewhere that contemporary body modification should not be regarded simply as a fashionable trend, in part because of the significance of the modificatory process to many of those involved (Sweetman 1999). Whilst I would still maintain that such is the case, however, the argument in question was based upon – or rather addressed – an everyday understanding of fashion as superficial and lacking in wider significance or depth. Although there is still more to becoming tattooed or pierced than buying a new sweater, the argument presented here has challenged the view that fashion itself should be regarded simply as a superficial exercise, in part because of issues of embodiment and affect.

As has already been noted, to regard fashion as an experiential and affectual process, which impacts significantly on the lived-body or the body-in-use, is to question the depiction of contemporary fashion as a free-floating 'carnival of signs'. It also implies that there may be limits to our ability or willingness to reflexively revise our sense of self through attention to the exterior or 'outer body' (Featherstone 1991: 171; see also Giddens 1991; Shilling 1993). While certain forms of habitus may allow for a more flexible engagement with the self, an understanding of the way in which the materiality of dress both reflects and impacts upon the habitus as a set of embodied predispositions (Bourdieu 1984: 466) suggests that whatever their semiotic status, contemporary fashions and styles may be less easily adopted and/or discarded than certain theorists of late-, high-, or postmodernity would seem to imply.[3]

Such a perspective also problematizes the representation of fashion as essentially arbitrary, in suggesting that changing fashions impact upon and reflect wider standards of bodily deportment and control. A further significant effect of regarding fashion as an affectual rather than simply a symbolic process is to allow comparison between fashion per se, and non-Western or sub-cultural styles of dress, thereby avoiding problematic distinctions between fashion and non-fashion, which may be seen as particularly acute given Craik's questioning of the widespread differentiation between Western and non-Western styles of dress (1994: 18-19), and the sense in which the difference between mainstream and countercultural styles is becoming increasingly blurred (Wilson, 1990: 222).

This chapter has not intended to offer a complete or in any way final account of the ways in which fashionable behaviour impacts on the body through the materiality of the processes involved. Rather, the intention has been to offer some preliminary thoughts on this issue as a means of generating discussion and further debate. Fashion should not be viewed as simply a symbolic process, and the fashionable body should not be read simply as a cultural text. We also need to attend to the experiential or affectual dimensions of fashionable behaviour, and the ways in which fashion as a social process impacts upon the corporeal realities of those involved.

Bearing these points in mind, questions deserving of further consideration include the ways in which fashion contributes to the individualization, rationalization and socialization of Western and non-Western bodies and selves, and the ways in which such processes are structured over the life-course as well as historically variable over time. What does the convergence between youth and adult styles of dress tell us about wider standards of deportment and bodily control? Is the casualization of contemporary dress indicative of a lessening distinction between the public and private spheres and the requirements of discipline or civility required in these increasingly convergent domains? Finally, what about the process of shopping for clothes? How is this organized, and how might an examination of consumption as an embodied process influence our understanding of the disciplines, pleasures and pains that fashionable behaviour entails?

Notes

1. While Bourdieu himself appears to regard fashion and dress in primarily symbolic terms, he does refer, for example, to youth styles as 'a refusal of the *constraints* and conventions of "dressing up"' (Bourdieu 1984: 202, emphasis added), and accepting the importance of the materiality of dress suggests that we might argue, as Bourdieu does of sport, that a particular style of dress 'is more likely to be adopted by' a particular group not simply if it accords with taste (or the 'conscious manifestation of habitus' (Shilling 1993: 129)), but 'if it does not contradict that [group's] relation to the body at its deepest and most unconscious level, i.e., the body schema, which is

the depository of a whole world view and a whole philosophy of the person and the body' (Bourdieu 1984: 218).

2. As Hetherington explains, Maffesoli performs 'a certain twist on Durkheim's ideas about the relationship between different types of society and their form of social solidarity', arguing 'that modern societies [. . .] are characterised by a mechanical solidarity, while postmodern societies become the societies organised around an organic solidarity' (Hetherington, 1998: 52). As Hetherington goes on to point out: '[t]his is in many respects quite similar to the argument that modernity has been de-traditionalised by conditions of reflexivity' (Hetherington 1998: 52).

3. As McNay (1999) has pointed out, an understanding of habitus as a relatively durable and deeply ingrained set of embodied predispositions suggests that identity may be 'less amenable to emancipatory processes of refashioning' (1999: 95) than certain advocates of reflexive modernity propose. At the same time, however, it should be recognized that while the 'schemes of the habitus' may 'function below the level of consciousness and language, beyond the reach of introspective scrutiny or control by the will' (Bourdieu, 1984: 466), this does not, in and of itself, preclude a reflexive engagement with the self. Indeed, one might argue that for some contemporary individuals such reflexivity and flexibility is itself deeply embedded, or rather that a capacity for reflexive engagement is characteristic of certain forms of contemporary habitus, and that, while a reflexive stance may be *unreflexively adopted*, this by no means rules out such a stance but simply renders it a more durable or stable characteristic of the individuals or groups concerned.

References

Angus, I. (1989), 'Circumscribing Postmodern Culture', in I. Angus and S. Jhally (eds), *Cultural Politics in Contemporary America,* London: Routledge.

Bartky, S.L. (1988), 'Foucault, Femininity and the Modernization of Patriarchal Power', in I. Diamond and L. Quinby (eds), *Feminism and Foucault: Reflections on Resistance,* Boston: Northeastern University Press.

Bauman, Z. (1992), 'Survival as a Social Construct', *Theory, Culture & Society*, 9: 1–36.

Beck, U. (1992), *Risk Society: Towards a New Modernity*, London: Sage.

Blumer, H. (1969), 'Fashion: From Class Differentiation to Collective Selection', *Sociological Quarterly*, 10 (3): 275–291.

Bocock, R. (1992), 'Consumption and Lifestyles', in R. Bocock and K. Thompson (eds), *Social and Cultural Forms of Modernity,* Cambridge: Polity Press.

Bordo, S. (1993), *Unbearable Weight: Feminism, Western Culture and the Body*, University of California Press.

Bourdieu, P. (1984), *Distinction: A Social Critique of the Judgement of Taste*, London: Routledge & Kegan Paul.

Bourdieu, P. (1993), 'Haute Couture and Haute Culture', in P. Bourdieu *Sociology in Question*, London: Sage.

Cohen, P. (1997 [1972]), 'Subcultural Conflict and Working-Class Community' in K. Gelder and S. Thornton (eds), *The Subcultures Reader*, London: Routledge.

Crook, S. (1998), 'Minotaurs and Other Monsters: "Everyday Life" in Recent Social Theory', *Sociology*, 32 (3): 523–40.

Edwards, T. (1997), *Men in the Mirror: Men's Fashion, Masculinity and Consumer Society*, London: Cassell.

Evans, D. (1997), 'Michel Maffesoli's sociology of modernity and postmodernity: an introduction and critical assessment', *The Sociological Review*, 45 (2): 221–43.

Featherstone, M. (1991) 'The Body in Consumer Culture', in M. Featherstone, M. Hepworth and B. Turner (eds), *The Body: Social Process and Cultural Theory*, London: Sage.

Ferrell, J. (1993), *Crimes of Style: Urban Graffiti and the Politics of Criminality*, New York & London: Garland Publishing.

Gelder, K. (1997a), 'Introduction to Part Two', in K. Gelder and S. Thornton (eds), *The Subcultures Reader*, London: Routledge.

Gelder, K. (1997b), 'Introduction to Part Three', in K. Gelder and S. Thornton (eds), *The Subcultures Reader*, London: Routledge.

Gelder, K. (1997c), 'Introduction to Part Seven', in K. Gelder and S. Thornton (eds), *The Subcultures Reader*, London: Routledge.

Giddens, A. (1991), *Modernity and Self-Identity: Self and Society in the Late Modern Age*, Cambridge: Polity Press.

Gronow, J. (1997), *The Sociology of Taste*, London: Routledge.

Hetherington, K. (1998), *Expressions of Identity: Space, Performance, Politics*, London: Sage.

Jenkins, E. (1999), *Tongue First: Adventures in Physical Culture*, London: Virago Press.

Kellner, D. (1992), 'Popular Culture and the construction of postmodern identities', in S. Lash and J. Friedman (eds), *Modernity and Identity*, Oxford: Blackwell.

Lash, S. (1993), 'Reflexive Modernization: The Aesthetic Dimension', *Theory, Culture & Society*, 10: 1–23.

Maffesoli, M. (1988), 'Jeux De Masques: Postmodern Tribalism', *Design Issues*, IV (1–2): 141–51.

Maffesoli, M. (1991), 'The Ethics of Aesthetics', *Theory, Culture & Society*, 8: 7–20.

Maffesoli, M. (1996), *The Time of the Tribes: The Decline of Individualism in Mass Society*, London: Sage.

Mauss, M. (1973), 'Techniques of the Body', *Economy and Society*, 2 (1): 70–89.

McNay, L. (1999), 'Gender, Habitus and the Field: Pierre Bourdieu and the Limits of Reflexivity', *Theory, Culture & Society*, 16 (1): 95–117.

McRobbie, A. (1994), *Postmodernism and Popular Culture*, London: Routledge.

Mellor, P.A. and Shilling, C. (1997), *Re-forming the Body: Religion, Community and Modernity*, London: Sage.

Morgan, D. and Scott, S. (1993), 'Bodies in a Social Landscape', in S. Scott and D. Morgan (eds), *Body Matters: Essays on the Sociology of the Body*, London: Falmer Press.

Muggleton, D. (1997), 'The Post-subculturalist', in S. Redhead, D. Wynne and J. O'Connor (eds), *The Clubcultures Reader: Readings in Popular Cultural Studies.* Oxford: Blackwell.

Polhemus, T. (1995), *Streetstyle: From Sidewalk to Catwalk*, London: Thames & Hudson.

Shields, R. (1991), 'Introduction to "The Ethics of Aesthetics"', *Theory, Culture & Society*, 8: 1–5.

Shields, R. (1996), 'Foreword: Masses or Tribes?', in M. Maffesoli, *The Time of the Tribes: The Decline of Individualism in Mass Society*, London: Sage.

Shilling, C. (1993), *The Body and Social Theory*, London: Sage.

Shilling, C. (1997), 'Emotions, embodiment and the sensation of society', *The Sociological Review*, 45 (2): 195–219.

Simmel, G. (1997 [1905]), 'The Philosophy of Fashion', in D. Frisby and M. Featherstone (eds), *Simmel on Culture: Selected Writings*, London: Sage.

Sweetman, P. (1999), 'Anchoring the (Postmodern) Self? Body Modification, Fashion and Identity', *Body & Society*, 5 (2–3): 51–76.

Sweetman, P. (2001), 'Stop Making Sense? The Problem of the Body in Youth/Sub/Counter-Culture', in S. Cunningham-Burley (ed.), *Exploring the Body*, Basingstoke: Palgrave.

Tseëlon, E. (1995), *The Masque of Femininity: The Representation of Woman in Everyday Life*, London: Sage.

Turner, B. (1992), *Regulating Bodies: Essays in Medical Sociology*, London: Routledge.

Turner, B. (1996), *The Body & Society: Explorations in Social Theory* (2nd Edn), London: Sage.

Veblen, T. (1970 [1899]), *The Theory of the Leisure Class: An Economic Study of Institutions*, London: Unwin Books.

Wagner, P. (1994), *A Sociology of Modernity: Liberty and Discipline*, London: Routledge.

Warde, A. (1994), 'Consumption, Identity-Formation and Uncertainty', *Sociology*, 28 (4): 877–98.

Williams, S. (1998) 'Modernity and the Emotions: Corporeal Reflections on the (Ir)rational', *Sociology*, 32 (4): 747–769.

Wilson, E. (1985), *Adorned in Dreams: Fashion and Modernity*, London: Virago Press.

Wilson, E. (1990), 'These New Components of the Spectacle: Fashion and Postmodernism', in R. Boyne and A. Rattansi (eds), *Postmodernism and Society*, Basingstoke: Macmillan.

Minding Appearances: Style, Truth, and Subjectivity

Susan Kaiser

Style, truth, subjectivity. Linking these three concepts together seems almost heretical. Such a combination points to age-old questions that inevitably frame the interiority of being in opposition to the exteriority of appearing. How can I *know* when I am focused on how I *look*? To what extent does my appearance style represent or create truth(s) about who I am? How do my ways of being, becoming, and appearing interface with those of others?

Questions such as these exceed the scope of this chapter, but I begin here to map out a concept of 'minding appearances' in the spirit of thinking through possible interrelationships among style, truth and subjectivity. The process of 'minding appearances' is both embodied and material. The body itself, of course, is material (biological) and symbolic; indeed, it marks the intersections between the two, and can be described as the 'threshold of subjectivity' (Braidotti 1991: 282). Following Wilson (1985), Entwistle (2000) suggests that dress (which she uses similarly to appearance style) constitutes a marginal space and ambiguously marks the boundary between the body and the social world, including that between self and other. She characterizes dress as a 'situated bodily practice' involving actions directed 'by the body upon the body' and resulting in 'ways of being and ways of looking' in the world.

The mind, of course, is engaged in these situated bodily activities, inasmuch as it is *in* the body and critically frames, organizes, manages and interprets perceptions of the dressed body and its relation to the social world. While it is evident that both the body and its appearance style are independently related to self-awareness, however, the nature of the relationship between the body and how it is dressed or styled remains elusive. Boultwood and Jerrard (2000) offer a helpful review of the clothing literature on ambivalence and argue that ambivalence is at the centre of the intersection *between* the body and style/ fashion.

The process of minding appearances brings together situated bodily practices, streams of consciousness that are themselves embodied, and material dressing. Such a process poses especially compelling aesthetic and ethical challenges in the context of a global economy, where the dominant Western mind/body 'disconnect' becomes situated in a larger disconnect between the efforts of production and the pleasures of consumption. As Boultwood and Jerrard (2000) note, the psychic challenges of linking the body to clothing or fashion are tremendous, and I offer the concept of minding appearances in the spirit of pursuing new ways of thinking about and with the fashioned body.

Here I loosely use 'style' as a process or act of managing appearance in everyday life; this process characterizes the visible identity constructions through which individuals can articulate social psychological yearnings – yearnings that are not only aesthetic but also political in nature (Kaiser 1992). I treat 'truth' as a process of knowledge production that individuals use to negotiate a sense of meaning or purpose with others. As Shapin (1994: 4) notes, truth is 'a matter of collective judgement . . . stabilized by the collective actions which use it as a standard for judging other claims'. That is, no single individual constitutes knowledge; rather, an individual can only offer truth claims that must in turn be socially negotiated. In this sense, truth resembles appearance style; both are individual constructions that must in turn be collectively interpreted and reinterpreted so as to produce knowledge and fashion, respectively. Colleagues and I have suggested that fashion, for example, becomes a process through which groups and cultures can negotiate common ways of expressing complex ambivalences that cannot be easily expressed in words (Kaiser, Nagasawa and Hutton 1991, 1995).

In many ways, 'subjectivity' (a way of being and becoming in the world) is to intersubjectivity (collective understandings of 'how things are') what style is to fashion, and truth is to knowledge. In each case, the former term suggests individual actions and intentions, whereas the latter implies collective negotiations and understandings. However, given the fluidity of all of these processes in everyday life, individual and collective actions become intertwined if not virtually indistinguishable. The idea of minding appearances notes the continual interplay between an individual and his/her various identities and communities, in such a way that combines style, truth and subjectivity. Minding appearances enables the visual, embodied representation of 'who I am and who I am becoming' along with ideas, possibilities, ambivalences and anxieties with which I may find it difficult to grapple, much less resolve, in a verbal, linear, conscious manner. In this sense, appearance style becomes a working model or a tentative truth claim about identity (i.e. who I am, who I am not, who I may be becoming). The process of minding appearance enables the construction of looks, as well as tentative understandings about the self in relation to others and consumer and media cultures, at a specific time and place. Minding appearances becomes a visual vehicle for entering and negotiating intersubjective and discursive spaces that, in cultural studies terms, help to develop a sense of 'what's going on' (see Grossberg 1997: 4).

In particular, nonlinear connections among identities (e.g. among gender, race, and sexuality) can be expressed and interpreted by minding appearances. My involvement with this concept emerges from a larger project on styles and subjectivities representing diverse gender, racial, ethnic, sexual, and socio-economic standpoints (Freitas, Kaiser and Hammidi 1996; Freitas et al. 1997; Kaiser, Freeman and Chandler 1993; Hall 1992; Kaiser and Hall 1999). This larger project attempts to understand varying and shifting power relations, drawing on (a) symbolic interactionism and its 'parent' philosophy of pragmatism (see Blumer 1969a, 1969b; Davis 1992; Diggins 1994; Ferguson 1980; Kaiser, Nagasawa and Hutton 1991, 1995; Kimle and Damhorst 1997; Mead 1934; Rochberg-Halton 1986; Stone 1965), and (b) feminist and cultural studies perspectives on subjectivity and epistemology (especially Braidotti 1991, 1994; Ferguson 1993; Gaines 1990; Harding 1996a, 1998; hooks 1990; Shohat and Stam 1994; Trinh 1991).

Studying style, truth, and subjectivity in tandem inevitably requires a multi-faceted and integrative analysis, building on interdisciplinary studies of the body, clothing, appearance and fashion. In the last twenty years or so, cultural studies has built on earlier work in sociology, textile and apparel studies to foster a better understanding of how individuals and groups actively use and transform popular culture in everyday life, within the context of global capitalism (Wilson 1993). In the process, individuals immersed in the worlds of style and fashion have been alternatively described as (a) mindless fashion slaves duped by consumer capitalism and (b) clever and stylish resistors of consumer capitalism. To the extent that people inevitably style or dress their bodies in some way, using the resources available and affordable to them, and few individuals are immune to fashion in contemporary society, some kind of conceptual, reflexive space is needed between these cultural dope and celebratory models of style and fashion. Somehow people have to construct and interpret appearances; in fact, they have no other means of representing themselves (Wilson 1993: 51). Clothes mark the troubled boundary between the body and the larger social world, ambiguously and uneasily (Wilson 1985). Some of the uneasiness associated with style and fashion probably stems from anxieties and ambivalences about the body, consumer capitalism, garment labour and material inequities. These anxieties and ambivalences, as well as the interface between the body and global capitalism, assume form and become articulated through processes of style and fashion (see Davis 1992; Kaiser, Nagasawa and Hutton 1991, 1995; Wilson 1985). People have to 'mind' their appearances. There is little reason to believe this cannot be accomplished critically *and* creatively.

Part of what needs to be minded in appearance style is an emerging sense of who one is and who one is not. Freitas and other colleagues and I (1997) have shown how it is easier for individuals to express verbally who they do not want to look or dress like than it is to verbalize emerging truth claims about who they are and how they want to look. The world of style, however, affords a visual, nonverbal vocabulary for the creation and presentation of such truth claims. In the process, individuals negotiate and renegotiate identity and community boundaries of various sorts. Warwick and Cavallero (1998: xv) talk about how, because the body is both a boundary and not a boundary, fashion produces an ambiguous space between self and non-self, reminding us daily of how dependent we are on margins and boundaries in our self-constructions.

Silverman (1986: 146–47) suggests that clothing makes the body culturally visible and is 'a necessary condition of subjectivity – that in articulating the body, it simultaneously articulates the psyche'. In cultural studies, the concept of articulation is used to characterize joint processes of expression and connection.[1] In the context of minding appearances, both the processes and the outcomes of articulation are nonlinear and visual, if not ambiguous (see Davis 1992; Enninger 1985; Kaiser 1990, 1997; McCracken 1988).

Perhaps it is, in part, these qualities of style and fashion that have led sociologist Todd Gitlin (1997: 82) to lament cultural studies' 'capitulation' to 'the primacy of visual and nonlinear culture over the literary and linear'. He argues that there has been a trend since the 1980s toward an academic legitimation of 'ecstasies of the moment' – i.e. music, television talk shows, and fashionable clothing. He sees this legitimation as confirming a 'collective withdrawal from democratic hope' (1997: 82). Gitlin (1997) appears to be especially concerned that left-wing scholars engaging these topics are backsliding politically. He argues for maintaining a clear separation between aesthetics and politics. Implicitly, he also contrasts matters of style with intellectual matters.[2]

When I read Gitlin's critique of cultural studies and visual culture in general, I find myself reacting on two levels.[3] First, as one who studies everyday appearance styles and what they mean to people, I question the apparent assumption that how an individual looks cannot possibly be connected with 'real' thinking or, especially, the search for identity and self-truth(s). 'Real' thinking, in Gitlin's analysis, apparently refers to the 'literary and linear' ways of knowing that presumably need to remain the exclusive focus of intellectuals. Such an assumption taps into a larger, tenacious narrative that goes something like this: important, serious issues require 'deep' thinking that goes beneath the obvious or the surface. The 'man of reason' (see Lloyd 1993) who epitomizes this kind of thought employs rational, linear, and logical strategies to arrive at the 'naked truth'. According to this narrative, those who do not follow this way of knowing are unlikely to move beyond the immature and not-yet-fully-evolved 'ecstasies of the moment' (i.e. aesthetics, style, and fashion).

In contrast to this view, I am convinced that, to paraphrase Adrienne Rich (1976: 192), there are ways of thinking that we don't even know about yet. Among these ways are the nonlinear, visual thought processes that express and connect multiple, shifting and embodied subjectivities in everyday life. I recognize that 'minding appearance' sounds somewhat oxymoronic given the legacies of linear reasoning and the mind-body split in modern Western thought. Yet I agree with aesthetic philosopher Ossi Naukkarinen's (1998) suggestion that the problem lies more with traditional academic philosophy than it does with the way people think when they put their looks together in everyday life. He argues that people somehow dress daily and make sense of their appearances in more elastic and integrative ways than traditional philosophy can address. He calls for a new philosophy that can tap that which is visual and nonlinear, moving beyond an exclusive reliance on traditional ways of knowing (i.e. specifying, analysing, critiquing) in modern Western philosophy.

My second concern with Gitlin's analysis emerges from his assertion that intellectual attention to 'ecstasies of the moment' implies a 'collective withdrawal from democratic hope' (1997: 82). To the extent that dominant conceptions of knowledge and 'serious' politics are still coded as white, Western, male, bourgeois and heterosexual, it remains easy to conceptualize appearance style as a trivial, fleeting ecstasy. But based on interviews that tap diverse ways of minding appearances,[4] I am convinced that for many individuals, style is and does much more. It entails and indeed represents the embodied and material limits to dominant fashion images that are often coded as white, Western, female, bourgeois, heterosexual, young and thin. Indeed, for some individuals style becomes a critical and creative strategy for negotiating new truths and subjectivities. That is, it becomes a vehicle not only for being, but also for becoming. As I listen to many people – especially those who do not conform to dominant styles and subjectivities – speak about how and why they mind their appearances as they do, I am struck by the sense of critical hope that I often hear alongside their ambivalences, pleasures and anxieties. Neither the cultural dope nor the celebratory models of fashion subjectivity capture how many if not most people describe their processes of minding appearance.

Listening to people talk about being and becoming in relation to style often reminds me of the tattered copy of Herbert Blumer's (1969b) article on fashion as 'collective selection' that I began to carry around with me in graduate school and which I still (twenty-something years later) find to be helpful in thinking about what fashion can do for individuals and groups in complex, contemporary life. Writing from a symbolic interactionist perspective,

Blumer understands fashion as enabling symbolic adjustment to a rapidly changing world, helping individuals to detach from the past, to resonate with the present, and to anticipate the future. Finkelstein (1996) interprets Blumer as suggesting that fashion helps to reduce social anxiety by embodying change and offering a sense of order. She suggests, however, that Blumer is apolitical in his tacit acceptance of the practices affecting the consumption of fashionable commodities (1996: 101).

Other authors have similarly critiqued symbolic interaction and its parent philosophical tradition of pragmatism for their relatively apolitical nature (cf. Diggins 1994; Ferguson 1980). Denzin (1992) calls for a politically critical interactionism that engages directly with diverse feminist, poststructural, and various cultural studies perspectives. He notes that as interactionism is becoming 'lively' in its engagement with diverse subjectivities, a critical politics of interpretation is emerging.

Perhaps more than ever, there is a conceptual space for theorizing fashion in relation to hope. One modest step towards such a goal necessarily entails recognizing that style and related materials are 'good to think with'.[5] Minding appearances can be a process that brings complex contradictions to the surface. As McCracken (1988) has noted, culture seems to entrust clothes with messages it cannot otherwise express. In at least an incremental way, style can be used individually and collectively to articulate ideas that need to be aired. The ethical challenges posed by globalization – ranging from garment labour to cultural appropriation, hegemonic beauty canons, material inequities, identity politics and environmental impacts – demand more sophisticated, integrative, and contextual ways of knowing than linear and binary traditions of thought can offer. Feminist scholars and scholars of colour have clarified how and why intellectual voices need to become embodied and to call out multiple positionalities, so as to counter all-knowing and disembodied voices 'from nowhere'. Inasmuch as the arena of style offers a rich visual vocabulary to highlight the overlapping and contradictory nature of positionalities (i.e. gender, race/ethnicity, sexuality, class and others), it can also be a useful metaphor for complicating traditional ways of thinking about 'good' thinking in the modern West. Moreover, it can force individuals to confront the many tired, irrelevant, and often gendered, raced, and classed dualisms (for example, mind versus body, politics versus aesthetics, production versus consumption) that pervade Western thinking.

At a minimum, we need to begin to understand minding appearances as embodied, nonlinear, integrative, elastic and shifting ways of knowing that become visible because people inevitably appear (Naukkarinen 1998) and interpret their ways of being and becoming in the world accordingly. In the following sections, I begin to conceptualize the process of minding appearances by focusing on style, truth, and subjectivity in turn, considering each as a frame within which to consider the other two.

Style

> If men and women would only look at each other, really look at each other's appearance, they would be forced to think of transforming social conditions. (Sennett 1976: 170)

For the last 200 years or so, gender and (hetero)sexuality have probably been foregrounded most prominently in dominant constructions of inter-personal difference through Western appearances. Prior to this time and the associated masculine 'renunciation' of style, scholars often regard social class as having been the most potent marker of social differentiation (see Flugel 1930; Silverman 1986; Tseëlon 1995). However, it is problematic to juxtapose class and gender/sexuality in this way, as though the latter became important and the former receded into oblivion. Breward (1999) notes how the new historicism stresses subjectivity and other 'practices of the self' that reveal 'the difficulties inherent in simple and closed explanations of power and its material representation' (1999: 15). His work on masculine fashion subjects in London between 1860 and 1914 challenges the hegemony of 'separate gender spheres' ideology and points to the need for more nuanced under-standings of fashion subjectivity. Such understandings need to be facile in their simultaneous incorporation of multiple positionalities such as race, class, and age, in addition to gender, despite the fact that modern, dominant, white, middle-class culture has highlighted gender as the primary marker of social difference. Depending on one's awareness of or relation to power differences on a number of fronts, some positionalities have been consciously more salient or silent than others. Hence, the complex intersections among positionalities have not been well understood. In the last twenty years, feminist, ethnic, queer, and cultural studies have helped to highlight these formerly muted intersections; their implicit if not direct attention to style and the body has been a key factor in their ability to reveal these intersections.

In particular, interdisciplinary studies of style have revealed how individuals tend to focus in their 'identity talk' (Hunt and Miller 1997) on those positional-ities in which they are conscious of having to struggle for power and recognition. For example, Kimle and Damhorst (1997) describe how white professional women often emphasize the 'danger zones' as well as the pleasures associated with their gender and sexual subjectivities at work. African American males tend to focus on race, rather than gender, as they describe the need to represent their cultural background at the same time they strategically manage to 'beat white men at their own game' of dressing for success (Kaiser and Hall 1999). Both African American men and women use 'style' as a verb, denoting that it is both a process and a way of becoming. It becomes a kind of cultural bond (Hall 1992, Kaiser 1997, O'Neal 1998) as well as a political and aesthetic strategy for expressing and gauging resistance, for 'talking back' (hooks 1989).

The idea that appearance is not merely an image, but also a process, is fundamental to symbolic interaction, which emphasizes the importance of self-reflexivity (Cooley 1902, Stone 1962). Somewhat similarly, Patrizia Calefato (1997) describes how a 'look' functions doubly as an image and as an expression of one's outlook on the world. She argues that a look articulates 'a way of being in the world and of creating a social universe' (1997: 76), and that the 'worldliness' of a clothed body conveys 'relational values, by virtue of a sort of category of otherness' (1997: 76–7).

Those who strive to work through such relational values most consciously are often those who inhabit gendered, raced and sexed bodies that cannot view difference only in terms of 'others.' For these individuals, style becomes a means of entering the discourse of being and becoming in the world. To the extent that fashion helps individuals collectively adapt to a rapidly changing world, everyday appearance style may signify hope as well as resistance. Minding appearances through the discourse of style provides a way of articulating positionalities that otherwise have little space for expression or voice. In this connection, minding appearance entails critical and creative processes of visually melding, mixing, juxtaposing, highlighting, or even muting emerging ways of being in the world. It involves working through the complex ambivalences associated with self-other relations, using the materials at hand. The resulting identity constructions may be ambiguous and require mindful interpretation on the part of perceivers (Kaiser, Nagasawa and Hutton 1991, 1995). Such appearances command attention; they render cultural visibility to individuals and groups. And frustratingly if not tragically, they can be and are easily appropriated in a capitalist context. However, as a gay male architect we interviewed noted, 'It takes me about two seconds to come up with a new look' (Freitas, Kaiser and Hammidi 1996). Working through the politics and aesthetics of style means, in part, knowing when and how to make and do a new look. It means knowing when a new outlook on the world is needed, in Calefato's (1997) terms.

Barnard (1996) reveals the political and aesthetic connections between making and doing looks in his etymology of the word 'fashion'. He describes the political (self-other) connotations implicit in the word's relationship with the Latin words *factio*, associated with factions and power, and *facere* (and the French word *faire*), which connotes making or doing (1996: 37). These associations suggest that appearance style can be regarded as a kind of project

– one that entails attention to power relations as well as subjective and inter-subjective pleasures.

Further, making and doing style implies some faith that it is possible to learn about who one is becoming and in concert with which communities. Such a faith and a sense of becoming tend to pervade the identity talk of European American heterosexual women and other 'others', including people of colour and gay males and lesbians (Freitas, Kaiser and Hammidi 1996; Hall 1992; Kaiser, Chandler and Freeman 1993; Kaiser and Hall 1999). There is often a recognition, in other words, of working through identity issues in relation to others. Style is a way of doing everyday life that anticipates the future and recognizes the need to 'switch it up a bit', in the words of an African American male student (Kaiser and Hall 1999), as necessary to remain freshly committed to the hope of a better tomorrow.

Following Deleuze, Braidotti (1991, 1994) uses the concept of 'minority becoming' to characterize an awareness of emerging subjectivities. Such a sense of emergence can most often be found in the style-related identity talk of those who at least partially or temporarily occupy positionalities outside of dominant masculine discourse. This sense of emergence often leads to an appreciation for those clothes that have 'contextual flexibility', or that can be mixed, matched and worn in a variety of contexts (Kaiser 1997; Kaiser, Chandler and Freeman 1993). These seem to be the clothes that provide a thread of continuity across a range of situations and interactions. These clothes simultaneously afford multiple opportunities for exploring various subject positions. That is, these clothes 'travel' and allow one to 'switch it up a bit', at the same time they reveal self-consistencies across identities and contexts.

In contrast, a different kind of identity talk seems to surface in dialogue with many European American men. There is a greater focus, in their identity talk, on a sense of autonomy and individualism, with favourite clothes serving as mnemonic reminders of special times such as special dates or parties or accomplishments in sports or job interviews (Kaiser, Chandler and Freeman 1993). Rather than revolving around a sense of becoming, this identity talk addresses what one has earned, enjoyed, and experienced in the past. Favourite clothes promise to serve their wearers well in the future, too. They seem to enable fond remembrances and the belief that good times can come again.

Dominant masculine identity talk, like that of other style discourses, reveals processes of thinking with style, although experimentation is often emphasized much less than it is in female, gay and lesbian, and non-white discourses of minding appearances. It can be argued that dominant masculinity has the 'most to lose' in a postmodern play of difference through style. Yet it can also be argued that individuals with less power have the most to gain from borrowing stable symbols of status (for example, a business suit), rather than by expressing contradictions and community values. Neither of these arguments tells the whole story; both need to be complicated and contextualized. And parts of each can be adopted strategically and relationally. It is apparent, for example, that gay men and men of colour often develop strategies that simultaneously allow them to appropriate and to resist dominant masculine discourses of style. A business look can be constructed that is subtly stylish without 'selling out' to white, heterosexual, bourgeois masculinity. So it becomes necessary to find ways of understanding style that move beyond an oversimplifying, binary distinction between power and powerlessness. It becomes important to know not only what a person wears, but also to develop an appreciation for how one wears it within and across looks – adapting it in ways that alternatively challenge and reinforce the status quo. For example, a feminist professor describes how she wears 'pervertized ties' with many of her outfits to undermine dominant masculinity, but she is very aware that she uses a dominant masculine symbol in a professional context in order to do so (Kaiser, Chandler and Hammidi, (2001)).

Articulating contradictions through style may seem like a futile political exercise at times, both because the resulting innovations may in some way reinforce dominant culture and because they can be easily appropriated by designers looking for new inspirations. However, it is evident that those who strive to represent themselves in new ways, or who are committed to subjectivities of renewal are creating syntheses that are beyond the scope of the modern Western 'disconnect' between the mind and the body, or of its reliance on linearity and verbal reasoning. Studying style requires relational and reflexive methodologies that are as contextually flexible as the search for everyday truths that people enact as they mind their appearances.

Truth

> Much of our noble talk about the importance of 'truth for its own sake' is often a tacit way of saying that we want the truth about *others*, at whatever cost it may be to *them*. (Gouldner 1970: 490)

Minding appearance is a visual, embodied epistemology. It is a way of knowing that, despite its visibility, is rarely acknowledged (to say the least) as a form of knowledge production. It does not permit one to pretend to be mindfully disembodied; nor is it linear. Minding appearance is an epistemology of experimentation with the tenuous boundaries among identities. As noted earlier, 'identity-not' truth claims seem to be relatively easy for individuals to articulate in words ('I am not an urban person any more.' 'It's too old for me.' 'I avoid being or dressing like a pretty boy.') (Freitas et al.1997). Apparently it is much more difficult to verbalize affirmative identity truth claims; instead, such claims are more likely to be represented visually as people work through and experiment with various possibilities. In the process, marginalized ways of being can serve as creative resources for reflexively working through ambivalences about self-other relations. Strategic articulations of self-other ambivalences become a vital component of minding appearance.

Minding appearance, then, can be an epistemology of ambiguity. It acknowledges that self-truths are necessarily contingent, as well as embodied. In contrast, as feminist philosophers note in their critiques of positivist epistemologies, voice-from-nowhere truth claims often lack a sense of self-positionality and self-reflexivity. They are presented as though they are disembodied, much less styled. Such truth claims have historically produced women and other 'others' as objects, rather than subjects, of knowledge. The resulting 'S-knows-that-p epistemologies' fail to take the subjectivity of the knower (the capital S, or the voice from nowhere) into account (Code 1996). Hence they can hardly acknowledge alternative epistemologies employed by their objects (persons, with a lower-case 'p') of study. Knowing other people, as knowing oneself, requires constructing a space for constant learning and interrogation. Those who become constructed as 'being seen' (e.g. white middle-class women) or as objects of study, rather than as subjects per se, may use style and fashion as vehicles for subjectivity, for representing themselves in ways that 'interrogate traditional and conventional norms' (Wilson 1993: 51). Such interrogation is nonlinear; it amounts to the visual equivalent of having a voice. Minding appearance enables self-representation that counters the representations of S-knows-that-p epistemologies. Using the materials at hand, individuals who would otherwise only be 'known' can construct everyday truths that represent their best approximation of 'who I am' and 'who I am becoming' at the present cultural moment.

Minding appearance embodies the melding of epistemologies, including those that modern Western philosophy does not adequately address based on its privileging of linear reasoning. Toward an acknowledgment of diverse ways of knowing, feminist philosopher Sandra Harding (1996a, 1998) draws on Gloria Anzaldúa's (1981) concept of 'borderlands' to characterize marginalized epistemologies and the spaces in between epistemologies as sites of discovery. By minding appearance, individuals can explore borderlands epistemologies, recognizing them for what they are: sites under construction – sites that are liminal or hybrid, in between positionalities. Such sites are similar to what Trinh Minh-ha (1991: 30) calls the 'interval' or interim space between truth and meaning – a space without which 'meaning would be fixed and truth congealed'. She notes that what is 'put forth as truth is often nothing more than a meaning' (1991: 30), and that it is the confidence viewers have in what they behold that 'allows truth to take shape' (1991: 35).

There are some interesting parallels between feminist and symbolic inter-actionist perspectives. Although symbolic interaction, and pragmatism before it, has not traditionally highlighted embodiment, it has tried to take subjectivity into account by theorizing how individuals obtain self-understanding through their relations and negotiations with others. Without fully acknowledging issues of race, gender, sexuality, and other embodied positionalities, symbolic interactionists have often failed to take subjectivity into account adequately, but they are increasingly doing so as they engage with cultural studies. Perhaps symbolic interaction's most important contributions to the study of style and fashion lie in its ability to account for *intersubjectivity*. In pragmatism and symbolic interaction, the test of 'truth' is intersubjective understanding in the form of shared community values and meanings (i.e. paradigms). William James identified 'workability' as the criterion by which meaning is evaluated (see Ferguson 1980). This concept refers in part to the initiator's intent and in part to the ability to arouse the intended response by the perceiver. But there is recognition that new understandings emerge from the interaction, some of which can never be anticipated. So truth is an emergent and open-ended process.

Cooley's concept of 'looking glass self' (1902) and Gregory Stone's concepts of appearance programs and appearance reviews (1965) put forth similar ideas about appearance as a process through which self-meanings and, implicitly, self-truths are asserted and assessed. Minding appearance, then, is a process functioning very much like a truth claim whose workability is continually being assessed. Individuals compare ongoing imaginations and evaluations of various communities' responses to their appearance styles. They also come to know themselves as they think *with* appearance. The richest meanings (those approximating a sense of truth?) emerge from thoughtful contemplation of appearances that seem ambiguous and hence arouse mindful interpretations and negotiated understandings (Kaiser 1997; Kaiser, Nagasawa and Hutton 1991, 1995; Stone 1965). In this view, there is no 'essence' or 'true self' waiting to be discovered under the disguise of an appearance. Rather, minding appear-ance facilitates making the best possible approximation of who one is, and is in the process of becoming, in a given cultural moment. This is accomplished through interactive negotiations of looks (i.e. fashion) and meanings with others. So the issue is not one of discovering the 'real there' inside; instead, it is one of engaging in a self-correcting process of understanding oneself and one's various communities by minding appearance.

The pictures of truth, meaning, and appearance described above are quite different from most modern philosophical perspectives on these concepts. Knowing or interpreting appearances within the frameworks of Western philosophy and fashion in the last 200 years has been problematic, especially to the extent that the dominant male subject has been constructed as the one who knows and who sees himself (and thus is seen) as 'the one who looks at women' (Silverman 1986). Perhaps this is changing; one only needs to look at the images of scantily clad young males in recent *Abercrombie and Fitch* catalogues, for example, to realize that the issue of who is looking and being seen is more complicated than traditionally gendered ways of knowing and looking would suggest. Still, the notion that men are the ones doing the looking and women are the ones being seen persists; this notion casts men as natural and true in contrast to women, who mask underlying truths with artifice (see Tseëlon 1995).

At least two S-knows-that-*p* epistemologies can be identified in relation to appearance perceptions, and both need to be unpacked in order to create new spaces for knowing. First, a binary opposition between 'appearance' and 'reality' casts the styles of 'others' into the realm of that which is unlikely to be 'true'. Style becomes conceptualized as that which covers or masks the 'naked truth'. In the nineteenth century, this opposition was resisted through such alternative perspectives as the aestheticism associated with gay male sensibility (see Bergman 1993). Wilson (1993: 62) argues that one of the greatest cultural and ideological (unfinished) battles of the twentieth century has been that 'between those who believe in Nature – the essential, biological core of maleness and femaleness – and those who insist on the constructed and "unnatural" nature of gender'; she notes that lesbians and gay men have been at the forefront in this battle. Gay male culture, for example, has emphasized the ironic use of style to resist, and simultaneously improve upon, dominant masculinist culture for at least a century (see Bergman 1993; Freitas, Kaiser and Hammidi 1996). The concept of 'camp', in particular, relies upon a blending of politics and aesthetics and a strategic play with concepts of temporality. The shared, coded understandings of style within the gay male community meet the criteria of pragmatist and symbolic interactionist concepts of truth.

A second prevailing S-knows-that-*p* view on appearance and reality is based more on their conflation than their opposition. Rather than viewing appearance as something that falsely hides the reality underneath, this view pertains to the idea that personal character can be 'read' (see Finkelstein 1991). Finkelstein (1991: 4) argues, and I would generally agree, that such an effort can be 'better understood as a reading of a cultural moment than it is an analysis of personality'. Yet I differ with what I read as her view of the relationship between appearance and truth. She worries that 'by sustaining an emphasis on image and appearances, we prevent the emergence of a narrative which would give birth to a capacity for reflexivity and subjectivity' (1991: 12).

Following her interpretation of Simmel, she goes on to argue that 'our pursuit of fashion as a source of personal identity is, paradoxically, the primary ingredient in the degradation of identity', because 'if we are relying upon the properties of procured goods for our sense of identity, then we are compelled to procure again and again' (1991: 145). While I share Finkelstein's concerns about consumer capitalism, I find myself coming back to three interrelated points: (a) the inevitability of appearance (see Naukkarinen 1998), (b) the fact that appearance is the only way we can represent ourselves (see Wilson 1993), and (c) the need to confront, and to be self-reflexive about, issues of social responsibility in an inevitably material world. And I question whether minding appearance prevents 'the emergence of a narrative which would give birth to a capacity for reflexivity and subjectivity' (Finkelstein 1991: 12). I would argue instead that minding appearance involves a little-understood kind of knowing that is embodied and, yes, styled. Indeed, minding appearance is a process that can be used to articulate and even to produce reflexivity and subjectivity. Such reflexivity and subjectivity are closer to a visual metaphor than to a linear narrative. The epistemologies needed to create and interpret appearance style are similar to what feminist philosopher Marilyn Frye (1996: 41) describes as pattern perception:

> Our game is pattern perception; our epistemological issues have to do with the strategies of discovering patterns and articulating them effectively . . . Patterns are like metaphors . . . Just as an illuminating metaphor eventually breaks down when persistently pressed, the patterns that make experience intelligible only make so much of it intelligible at a time, and over time that range may change. In the case of pressing a good metaphor, one finds out a great deal by exploring its limits, understanding where and why it breaks down. Similarly with patterns. An important part of pattern perception is exploring the range of the pattern, and a way of going wrong is misjudging scope.

She argues (43) that to advance knowledge, diverse perspectives and metaphors are needed to 're-metaphorize' the world – not to create a unified truth, but rather to make multiple meanings that are united, 'like any yarn, only by successively overlapping threads held together by friction, not riveted by logic'. Frye suggests that truth emerges in and through processes of making and mixing metaphors. In this sense, knowledge becomes more like a collage (see Harding 1996a) than a narrative.

The process of minding appearance is ideally suited to the construction of collages that mix metaphors, individually and collectively. Most likely, the resulting metaphors articulate the complex identity ambivalences that are likely to inspire ongoing experimentation with appearance (cf. Davis 1992; Kaiser, Nagasawa and Hutton 1991, 1995; Kimle and Damhorst 1997; Wilson 1985), for those who have the resources at their disposal to engage in this process. Further, stylized metaphors bring to the surface the 'useful confusion' between ambivalence and ambiguity that Davis (1992) describes so well –

a confusion that probably cannot ultimately be resolved but that can at least be articulated, if not partially clarified, through style.

New knowledge collages – ambivalences intact – may represent individuals' and groups' best and, ideally, most reflexive and critical approximations of who they are becoming at a given cultural moment. But whose styled bodies have been included in the knowledge collages of academic study? The dominant 'knowns' or objects of study are still primarily white, female, heterosexual and middle class, although this is changing. This 'truth centre' of fashion study can no longer hold; diverse and shifting subjectivities need to be taken into account.

Subjectivity

> Mobile subjectivities . . . trouble fixed boundaries, antagonize true believers, create new possibilities for themselves . . . They are relational, produced through shifting yet enduring encounters and connections, never fully captured by them (Ferguson 1993: 154).

The following, traditional ways of thinking about 'good' Western thought have to be complicated before style can be understood in a way that takes diverse subjectivities into account. First, subjectivity has almost exclusively been equated with the realm of dominant masculinity, as captured visually and verbally in Rodin's famous 'thinker' and the parallel idea that 'l'homme pense'. Hence, thinking that matters becomes equated with bodies that matter, to borrow a phrase from Judith Butler (1993). Further, modern evolutionary thought contributes to perceptions of who has 'evolved' intellectually and politically. It follows that the topics and ways of knowing associated with dominant male culture are the most serious and important. This notion, of course, has been challenged by feminist theorizing about new ways of visioning subjectivity (see, for example, Braidotti 1991, 1994; Butler 1993; Ferguson 1993; Haraway 1988; hooks 1990; Trinh 1991).

Second, the Cartesian split between the mind and the body results in a problematic disconnection between subjectivity and style. This split results in a devaluation of the body, nature, woman, and, inevitably, style – all of which become hopelessly conflated in a complex that is contrasted with the model man of reason. The separation of mind and body has been challenged to some extent implicitly, although not adequately, by pragmatist and subsequently symbolic interactionist thought (see Stone 1965). The most direct challenge to this separation has come from strains of feminist, ethnic, and cultural studies that emphasize embodied knowing (e.g. Anzaldúa 1981; Bordo 1993; Goldberger 1996; Harding 1996b; hooks 1990).

Kathy Ferguson (1993) discusses how Hegel conceptualized subjectivity (or, more accurately, dominant masculine subjectivity) as a kind of 'walled city' experience. According to this metaphor, the (dominant masculine) self is complete, autonomous, and self-defining, and shaped, at least in part, by the need to master and utilize nature (1993: 40). Modern Western thought has typically contributed a view of subjectivity – of being a thinking and knowing agent in the world – that is associated with a unitary self capable of rising above the limitations imposed by material (bodily) existence. The American pragmatist philosophical tradition, although rooted in nineteenth-century modernism, never completely brought into the prevailing, modern Western notions of self and subjectivity. In particular, pragmatists (e.g. William James, George Herbert Mead) and, subsequently, symbolic interactionists (e.g. Herbert Blumer, Gregory Stone) offered an alternative to the walled city metaphor by conceptualizing the subject as a dialectical and relational process of negotiating individual agency with social control. Mead (1934) described the 'I' as the individualistic part of the self that can never be totally predicted, due to its agency, creativity, and impulsivity. In a kind of ongoing reality check, however, the 'me' assumes responsibility for social control, reminding the 'I' of collective values and norms within the community. Hence social control becomes self-control through an ongoing, internal conversation that involves both spontaneity and checks and balances. Mead characterizes this ongoing conversation as a process he calls 'mind' – a process that helps to make an individual self-reflective about her/his place in social life.

Similarly, the dialectic, also a contribution of Hegel, is an underlying principle in Simmel's (1904) description of fashion as driven by the incessant interplay between identification and differentiation. Roughly parallel to this interplay is that of individuality and conformity. Both Mead and Simmel, then, used the dialectic to theorize the link between the personal and the social. The following limits to their formulations should be recognized. First, as suggested earlier, neither of their formulations deal well, if at all, with issues of power. Second, they do not directly offer a way of conceptualizing multiple or competing identities and communities. In particular, they do not consider the intersections among gender, race, ethnicity, social class, sexuality and the like. And third, they tend to remain locked into dualities (i.e. 'I' versus 'me', identification versus differentiation, individuality versus conformity), although they at least do so in a way that is relational rather than merely oppositional.

Also using principles of relationality and intersubjectivity, Blumer theorized fashion as a process of collective selection that enables individuals, jointly and symbolically, to mark their detachments from the past, their affinities within the present, and their preparation for the future (Blumer 1969b). Further, Fred Davis's (1992) concept of ambivalence management deals directly with identity issues as driving forces in fashion change through relational and dialectical processes that become aesthetically coded. He describes how ambivalences and tensions between masculinity and femininity, for example, become visually encoded in new clothing styles. Similarly, Kaiser, Nagasawa and Hutton (1991, 1995) describe how processes of ambivalence, ambiguity, and negotiation, in conjunction with the economic forces of capitalism, propel ongoing changes in appearance styles that articulate, but do not necessarily resolve ambivalences.

Still, more theoretical attention needs to be paid to issues of subjectivity in relation to style and fashion. Existing theories help to understand how and why style and fashion change processually, in an ongoing manner. However, the limited 'clothes make the man' metaphor prevails as though it is an ultimate, unspoken truth. There is something highly paradoxical, to say the least, about a 'male-ordered' concept of subjectivity driving our understanding of style and fashion, which are often conflated culturally with femininity.

Feminist conceptualizations of subjectivity offer strategies and metaphors for moving beyond the 'male-ordered' model of subjectivity. For example, Rosi Braidotti's (1991, 1994) concept of 'nomadic subjectivity' and Kathy Ferguson's 'mobile subjectivities' (1993) offer some interesting possibilities for theorizing style in relation to subjectivity in ways that address power relationships and multiple, overlapping standpoints. Neither Braidotti nor Ferguson deal with style or fashion directly, but extrapolating from their conceptualizations seems promising, for several reasons. First, these metaphors deal well with movement, fluidity, and change. They do so in a manner that moves 'beyond binaries' and allows for multiple ways of framing identity negotiations, as appropriate or necessary. Second, both metaphors offer endless possibilities for articulating complex intersections among various standpoints. In this way, gender, race, ethnicity, sexuality and social class, for example, can all be considered simultaneously through the intersections that become especially salient in a given context or community in everyday life. And third, both Ferguson and Braidotti deal to varying extents with power. Ferguson, for example, articulates how mobile subjectivities 'move across and along axes of power (which are themselves in motion) without fully residing in them' (1993: 154). Braidotti (1991, 1994) details a way of conceptualizing 'interconnected nomadism' as a new form of subjectivity that acknowledges diverse and overlapping standpoints.

In her earlier work, Ferguson (1980) addressed Mead's concept of 'mind', or the dialogue between the 'I' and the 'me' in relation to possibilities for theorizing liberatory potential. Although Ferguson does not mention Mead at all in her later work on mobile subjectivities, it seems to me that there are some intriguing possibilities for linking her later work, as well as Braidotti's nomadic subjectivities, to Mead's concept of mind. In a sense, the 'I' can be conceptualized as the individualistic source of movement among the various communities that provide fuel for social construction and control. These communities offer a sense of affinity (Ferguson 1993) arising from the kind of negotiations that take place in the process of mind – be it dialectical or through some other dynamic. In relation to style, the intersections that need to be articulated (and often cannot be verbally) result in a look that feels like a comfortable fit for a given time and set of circumstances. When the fit no longer suffices to capture the necessary affinities and their visual represent-ations, the 'I' is likely to initiate further movement – in some cases, through the subversive power and pleasure of creative thinking (Braidotti 1991, 1994).

An example may be helpful to work through these subjective experiences of affinity and fit through style. In the mid-1990s, a white middle-class lesbian in Northern California described how she shops at GAP, because she appreciates the flexibility and relative androgyny afforded by the casual separates. For that moment, at least, she experienced a personal fit and a political affinity with women in the lesbian community who also shop there. A few years later, however, this subjectivity has shifted. It may be that the store offerings have changed, or maybe it's the style her community is negotiating or mainstream fashion that has changed. Or, perhaps her way of relating to processes of consumption and community are in motion.

Whatever accounts for rest or movement in subjectivities, it is important to recognize that not all individuals are equally creative. Nor do they have equal access to commodities or images that stimulate style change. Many individuals in a global economy are surrounded with images through advertising and other media sources, but lack the economic resources to play out their subjectivities in material form. So there need to be a number of cautionary limits imposed on the use of metaphors that may, when pressed, connote world travel and consumption.

A number of questions emerge from an analysis of mobile or nomadic subjectivities: why are some individuals more interested in mobility, whereas others are content to 'rest' in existing subjective spaces? To what extent are individuals unable to move as freely as they would like 'across and along axes of power' due to limitations in economic, political, or creative resources? How might multiple and mobile subjectivities be reconciled with dialectical ways of conceptualizing change? And should they be? How can we account for identities that individuals barely know they have – as evident, for example, in the case of taking whiteness, heterosexuality or bourgeois experience for granted? How can and do individuals move beyond what Gitlin (1997) calls 'ecstasies of the moment', toward a sense of becoming and hope for a better tomorrow?

Conclusion

I offer the concept of minding appearances as a means to begin to grapple with the interplay among style, truth, and subjectivity. Given the global economic and social forces that shape and reshape what it means to be a person in the world, new epistemologies are needed to theorize material circumstances and socioeconomic opportunity, apparel labour in the factory as well as everyday 'identity work', and hegemonic imagery and modes of negotiations of, or resistance to, that imagery in local circumstances. How do individuals begin to make sense of a staggering array of aesthetic possibilities in relation to what they have and how they can fashion their bodies? Minding appearance involves, in part, sorting through the possibilities and weighing them according to what is attainable and applicable, what begins to tap emerging concepts of current and emerging identities, and what enables the best articulation of ambivalences and ambiguities with which one is currently grappling.

To understand the process of minding appearance is not necessarily to celebrate 'ecstasies of the moment' or 'the primacy of visual and nonlinear culture over the literary and linear' (Gitlin 1997: 82). Nor is it to preclude a search for a more authenticating and reflexive narrative of subjectivity (Finkelstein 1991). Rather, minding appearance is one of the few avenues available to acknowledge and articulate embodied subjectivities that are otherwise stifled or muted. As an epistemology of ambiguity, it enables the expression of complex intersections among and spaces between diverse subject positions and bodily experiences. It helps to blur the boundaries between such binaries as mind and body, inner and outer self, linear and nonlinear, the visual and verbal, concrete and abstract, political and aesthetic, critical and creative, personal and social, local and global.

Minding appearance is not only an academic exercise; it is a vital part of everyday life that enables interactions, the mixing of metaphors, and the renegotiation of tenuous borderlines. It is through the process of minding appearance, at least, that the awareness of even having various identities can be consciously or unconsciously explored and evaluated. Minding appearance enables a sense of moving as well as a sense of resting 'across and along axes of power' (Ferguson 1993). Minding appearance in the context of global travel, the local shopping mall or internet shopping reveals the socio-economic and material limits to the metaphors of nomadism and mobility. Not everyone can afford to be world travellers or active collectors of products and images that add to the repertoire of style. In fact, those with the least power (for example, young women in developing nations) are most likely to spend their days and nights materially producing goods that they cannot even anticipate minding in their own appearances. Still, the process of minding appearance, within the context of what is attainable, touches the lives of individuals world-wide, with a vast array of particular circumstances, yearnings and dreams.

Minding appearance is an embodied process – a situated practice – that moves individuals in and through the agonies as well as the ecstasies of the moment. The mindful and material articulation of complex ambivalences and ambiguities through style may not provide an ultimate sense of resolution or closure. But the process of minding appearance does provide a sense of reflexivity and relationality as individuals construct and contemplate everyday truths. It offers a self-correcting approach that enables adaptability to change within the limits of material circumstances in a world undergoing dramatic social and economic transformations. And it may, at least in an incremental way, contribute to the hope of being taken seriously as an appearing, thinking person in the world.

Notes

1. See Slack (1996) for a helpful review of the theory and method of articulation in cultural studies.

2. See Finkelstein (1991) for a review of some of the literature that has historically made similar claims. She interprets Simmel's work, for example, as characterizing the modern fashionable individual as one with little opportunity to develop reflective or intellectual capacities (1991: 145).

3. It is hard to avoid reading gender and disciplinary issues into Gitlin's analysis, as well. The cultural tendencies that he finds to be most problematic can inevitably be decoded as female and interdisciplinary. See Gouldner (1970) for a rather remarkably foretelling critique of sociology in relation to political activism.

4. See, for example, Kaiser, Freeman and Chandler (1993), Freitas, Kaiser and Hammidi (1996), and Kaiser and Hall (1999).

5. Sandra Harding (1996a) makes a similar point about science – i.e. that it is 'good to think with'.

6. In the US, Abercrombie and Fitch is a very popular retail store that currently makes its catalogue available to customers for $6. The clothes include both male and female casual separates, but one of the catalogue's appeal is clearly the male models. Teenage girls tear out images of shirtless males in seductive stances and plaster them on their bedroom walls.

References

Anzaldúa, G. (1981), *Borderlands/La Frontera*, San Francisco: Spinsters/Aunt Lute.

Barnard, M. (1996), *Fashion as Communication*, London/New York: Routledge.

Bergman, D. (ed.) (1993), *Camp Grounds: Style and Homosexuality*, Amherst, MA: The University of Massachusetts Press.

Blumer, H. (1969a), *Symbolic Interactionism: Perspective and Method*, Englewood Cliffs, NJ: Prentice-Hall.

Blumer, H. (1969b), 'Fashion: From Class Differentiation to Collective Selection', *Sociological Quarterly*, 10: 275–91.

Bordo, S. (1993), *Unbearable Weight: Feminism, Western Culture, and the Body*, Berkeley, CA: University of California Press.

Boultwood, A. and Jerrard, R. (2000), 'Ambivalence, and Its Relation to Fashion and the Body,' *Fashion Theory*, 4(3), 301–22.

Braidotti, R. (1991), *Patterns of Dissonance: A Study of Women in Contemporary Philosophy*, New York: Routledge.

Braidotti, R. (1994), *Nomadic Subjects: Embodiment and Sexual Difference in Contemporary Feminist Theory*, New York: Columbia University Press.

Breward, C. (1999), *The Hidden Consumer: Masculinities, Fashion and City Life, 1860–1914*, Manchester: Manchester University Press.

Butler, J. (1993), *Bodies that Matter: On the Discursive Limits of 'Sex'*, New York/London: Routledge.

Calefato, P. (1997), 'Fashion and Worldliness: Language and Imagery of the Clothed Body'. *Fashion Theory: The Journal of Dress, Body & Culture*, 1(1): 69–90.

Code, L. (1996), 'Taking Subjectivity into Account', in Ann Garry and Marilyn Pearsall (eds), *Women, Knowledge, and Reality: Explorations in Feminist Theory*, 2nd ed., pp. 191–221. New York/London: Routledge.

Cooley, C.H. (1902), *Human Nature and the Social Order*, New York: Charles Scribners Sons.

Davis, F. (1992), *Fashion, Culture, and Identity*, Chicago, IL: The University of Chicago Press.

Denzin, N.K. (1992), *Symbolic Interactionism and Cultural Studies: The Politics of Interpretation*, Oxford: Blackwell.

Diggins, J.P. (1994), *The Promise of Pragmatism: Modernism and the Crisis of Knowledge and Authority*, Chicago, IL: The University of Chicago Press.

Enninger, W. (1985), 'The Design Features of Clothing Codes: The Functions of Clothing Displays in Interaction'. *Kodikas/Code*, 8(1/2): 81–110.

Entwistle, J. (2000). 'Fashion and the Fleshy Body: Dress as Embodied Practice'. *Fashion Theory*, 4(3): 323–48.

Ferguson, K.E. (1980), *Self, Society, and Womankind: The Dialectic of Liberation*, Westport, Connecticut: Greenwood Press.

Ferguson, K.E. (1993), *The Man Question: Visions of Subjectivity in Feminist Theory*, Berkeley, CA: University of California Press.

Finkelstein, J. (1991), *The Fashioned Self*, Oxford: Polity Press.

Finkelstein, J. (1996), *After a Fashion*, Victoria, Australia: Melbourne University Press.

Flugel, J.C. (1930), *The Psychology of Clothes*, London: Hogarth Press.

Freitas, A.J., Kaiser, S.B. and Hammidi, T. (1996), 'Communities, Commodities, Space, and Style', *Journal of Homosexuality*, 31 (1&2): 83–107.

Freitas, A.J., Kaiser, S.B., Chandler, J.L., Hall, Carol, Kim, Jung Won and Hammidi, T. (1997), 'Appearance Management as Border Construction: Least Favorite Clothing, Group Distancing, and Identity . . . Not!' *Sociological Inquiry*, 67(3), 323–35.

Frye, M. (1996), 'The Possibility of Feminist Theory', in Ann Garry and Marilyn Pearsall (eds), *Women, Knowledge, and Reality: Explorations in Feminist Philosophy,* 2nd ed., pp. 34–47. New York/London: Routledge.

Gaines, J. (1990), 'Introduction: Fabricating the Female Body', in Jane Gaines and Charlotte Herzog (eds), *Fabrications: Costume and the Female Body,* pp. 1–27. New York/London: Routledge.

Gitlin, T. (1997), 'The Anti-Political Populism of Cultural Studies'. *Dissent* (Spring): 77–82.

Goldberger, N.R. (1996), 'Looking Backward, Looking Forward', in Nancy Rule Goldberger, Jill Mattuck Tarule, Blythe McVicker Clinchy, and Mary Field Belenky (eds), *Knowledge, Difference, and Power: Essays Inspired by Women's Ways of Knowing,* pp. 1–21. New York: Basic Books.

Gouldner, A.W. (1970), *The Coming Crisis of Western Sociology,* New York: Basic Books, Inc.

Grossberg, L. (1997), *Bringing It All Back Home: Essays on Cultural Studies,* Durham, NC: Duke University Press.

Hall, C. (1992), *Towards a Gender-Relational Understanding of Appearance Style in African-American Culture,* Master's thesis, University of California, Davis.

Haraway, D. (1988), 'Situated Knowledges: The Science Question in Feminism and the Privilege of Partial Perspective', *Feminist Studies,* 14: 575–99.

Harding, S. (1996a), 'Science is "Good to Think With": Thinking Science, Thinking Society', *Social Text 46/47,* 14: 15–26.

Harding, S. (1996b), 'Gendered Ways of Knowing and the "Epistemological Crisis" of the West', in Nancy Rule Goldberger, Jill Mattuck Tarule, Blythe McVicker Clinchy, and Mary Field Belenky (eds.), *Knowledge, Difference, and Power: Essays Inspired by Women's Ways of Knowing,* pp. 431–54. New York: Basic Books.

Harding, S. (1998), *Is Science Multicultural? Postcolonialisms, Feminisms, and Epistemologies,* Bloomington, In: Indiana University Press.

hooks, bell (1989), *Talking Back: Thinking Feminist, Thinking Black,* Boston, MA: South End Press.

hooks, bell (1990), *Yearning: Race, Gender, and Cultural Politics,* Boston, MA: South End Press.

Hunt, S.A., and Miller, K. (1997), 'The Discourse of Dress and Appearance: Identity Talk and a Rhetoric of Review', *Symbolic Interaction,* 20(1): 69–82.

Kaiser, S.B. (1990), 'The Semiotics of Clothing: Linking Structural Analysis with Social Process', in Thomas A. Sebeok and Jean Umiker-Sebeok (eds.), *The Semiotic Web,* pp. 605–624), Berlin: Mouton de Gruyter.

Kaiser, S.B. (1992), 'The Politics and Aesthetics of Appearance Style: Modernist, Postmodernist, and Feminist Perspectives', in Patrizia Calefato (ed.), *Moda, Mondanita, Rivestimento,* Bari, Italy: Edizioni deal Sud.

Kaiser, S.B. (1997), *The Social Psychology of Clothing: Symbolic Appearances in Context,* 2nd edition revised, New York: Fairchild Publications.

Kaiser, S.B. and Hall, C. (1999), 'Reading "Men in Black"'. Paper presented at the International Semiotic Society Institute, June, Imatra, Finland.

Kaiser, S.B., Nagasawa, R.H. and Hutton, S.S. (1991), 'Fashion, Postmodernity, and Personal Appearance: A Symbolic Interactionist Formulation', *Symbolic Interaction,* 14(2): 165–85.

Kaiser, S.B., Chandler, J. and Freeman, C.M. (1993), 'Favorite Clothes and Gendered Subjectivities: Multiple Readings', *Studies in Symbolic Interaction,* 15: 27–50.

Kaiser, S.B., Nagasawa, R.H. and Hutton, S.S. (1995), 'Construction of an SI Theory of Fashion: Part 1. Ambivalence and Change', *Clothing and Textiles Research Journal,* 13(3): 172–83.

Kaiser, S.B., Chandler, J. and Hammidi, T. (2001), *Women and their Wardrobes.* London: Berg.

Kimle, P,A. and Damhorst, M.L. (1997), 'A Grounded Theory Model of the Ideal Business Image for Women', *Symbolic Interaction,* 20(1): 45–68.

Lloyd, G. (1993), *The Man of Reason: 'Male' and 'Female' in Western Philosophy,* 2nd ed., Minneapolis, MN: University of Minnesota Press.

McCracken, G. (1988), *Culture and Consumption,* Bloomington, In: Indiana University Press.

Mead, G.H. (1934), *Mind, Self, and Society,* Chicago, IL: The University of California Press.

Naukkarinen, O. (1998), *Aesthetics of the Unavoidable: Aesthetic Variations in Human Appearance,* Helsinki, Finland: International Institute of Applied Aesthetics.

O'Neal, G. (1998), 'African-American Aesthetic of Dress: Current Manifestations', *Clothing and Textiles Research Journal,* 16(4): 167–75.

Rich, A. (1976), *Of Woman Born,* New York: W.W. Horton.

Rochberg-Halton, E. (1986), *Meaning and Modernity: Social Theory in the Pragmatic Attitude,* Chicago: The University of Chicago Press.

Sennett, R. (1976), *The Fall of Public Man,* New York: W.W. Norton & Company.

Shapin, S. (1994), *A Social History of Truth,* Chicago: The University of Chicago Press.

Shohat, E. and Stam, R. (1994), *Unthinking Eurocentrism: Multiculturalism and the Media,* London and New York: Routledge.

Silverman, K. (1986), Fragments of a Fashionable Discourse, in T. Modleski (ed.), *Studies in Entertainment: Critical Approaches to Mass Culture,* pp. 139–52. Bloomington, IN: Indiana University Press.

Simmel, G. (1904), 'Fashion'. *International Quarterly,* 10: 130–55. (Reprinted in *American Journal of Sociology,* 62 [May 1957]: 541–58).

Slack, J.D. (1996), 'The Theory and Method of Articulation in Cultural Studies', in D. Morley and Kuan-Hsing Chen (eds), *Stuart Hall: Critical Dialogues in Cultural Studies,* pp. 112–27. London and New York: Routledge.

Stone, G.P. (1965), 'Appearance and the Self', in Mary Ellen Roach and Joanne B. Eicher (eds.), *Dress, Adornment, and the Social Order,* pp. 216–45, New York: John Wiley & Sons.

Trinh, M. (1991), *When the Moon Waxes Red: Representation, Gender, and Cultural Politics,* New York/London: Routledge.

Tseëlon, E. (1995), *The Masque of Femininity,* London: Sage.

Warwick, A, and Cavallaro, D. (1998), *Fashioning the Frame: Boundaries, Dress, and the Body,* Oxford: Berg.

Wilson, E. (1985), *Adorned in Dreams: Fashion and Modernity*, London: Virago Press.

Wilson, E. (1993), 'Deviancy, Dress, and Desire', in S. Fisher and K. Davis (eds.), *Negotiating at the Margins: The Gendered Discourses of Power and Resistance*, pp. 48–65. New Brunswick, NJ: Rutgers University Press.

From Fashion to Masquerade: Towards an Ungendered Paradigm

Efrat Tseëlon

This chapter looks for ways of rethinking the relationship between fashion and subjectivity. It starts by reviewing the history of the body as a tool for grounding difference, and an obstacle for ethics and knowledge. It highlights the growing importance of embodied difference as a marker between insider and outsider groups, and as instrumental in identity production. It then moves on to note that the discourse of the body with all its critical theoretical sophistication has consistently avoided dealing with issues of fashion, and by implication, with gender. It suggests that given the tradition of aligning woman and fashion (referentially and representationally) the reason for this avoidance is not necessarily evidence of a dismissive, trivializing attitude towards fashion, and by implication the feminine. It might simply signal a move away from a topic that is heavily marked as gendered in order to avoid unwitting reification and essentializing of a binary closure (which identifies fashion with the feminine, albeit that this kind of essentialism does not appeal to biological truths but to common culture, or history). In short, both history and contemporary culture place fashion within an ideological discourse with a 'symbolic mandate' (to borrow Žižek's term) which repeatedly pins it to the feminine to create an overdetermined effect. It is this identity between fashion and the feminine that I seek to unfix by exploring the paradigm of masquerade as an alternative to the symbolic role of fashion. The conception of masquerade I use does not limit it to notions of truth and falsity, but regards it as a sort of visual performance through artefacts: a vehicle for constructing and decon-structing identities.

In *The Eternal Masquerade* Dennis Bradley (1922) defined masquerade as 'ornamental philosophy'. There he observed that we prefer the beauty of myth and illusion, dress and manners to the troublesome ugliness of reality with its dreary catalogue of wars, pestilences and famines. This observation serves as the starting point for a meditation on the relationship between body, clothes, identity and masking. Since classical and premodern times the body has been used to ground discourses of ethics and knowledge. For the early Church, body (particularly female body) and fashion (as the archetypal artifice) came to signify an obstacle to salvation (Tseëlon 1995). For traditional philosophy body (as opposed to mind) and fashion (as surface and inessential) came to symbolize an obstacle to truth and knowledge (Hansen 1993; Spelman 1982). Modernity saw a number of significant developments that were to change fundamentally the nature of social relationships, and social perceptions.

I want to single out two trends in particular: one trend is the hegemony of science as a guarantor of truth, and as a source of representations. Scientific methods of biological stratification introduced the idea of biological foundation of categories of difference, which was alien to classical, medieval and Renaissance thinking (Bauman 1990, 1991, 1998). The other trend is the rise of the nation-state which, as Foucault tells us, rules not by explicit power, but by the normalising power of surveillance society (1975, 1977, 1980). Unwittingly, science was harnessed in the service of the state to suppress behaviour and groups defined as undesirable. Science has been co-opted to legitimate differences of social power relations along biological lines between men and women (Laqueur 1990), normal and perverse sexuality (Foucault 1980) normality and mental illness (Gilman 1986, 1988, 1991a), as well as white, black and Jewish ethnic groups (Malik 1996). The fear of social change that arose in the wake of the Enlightenment found its expression in the idea of degeneration (genetic predisposition to certain kinds of disease) which helped to create 'difference' out of the materials of bodily reality. It was particularly effective when no identifiable differences actually existed. Myth and fantasy ensured that the dividing line between 'us' and 'them' kept cultural anxieties in check. The idea of degeneration has been applied in turn to the working class in the eighteenth century where the idea of race emerged, to the Jews, and the mentally ill. With regards to those displaying clothing obsessions the discourse of degeneration replaced the discourse of gender (where madness is coded as female, perversion as male) (Matlock 1993).

It is modernity's obsession with order that turned 'difference' into a problem. And it was this obsession which produced such imaginary fabrications as national and personal identity. At the root of identity production (whether social or individual) there are similar dynamics. Illusions of sameness and order are maintained at the cost of excluding the other, the different, or the stranger within oneself. Whether as the polluting object which is excluded from the social order described by Mary Douglas (1966) in *Purity and Danger,* or the unspeakable abject which is repressed into fantasy, according to Kristeva (1982, 1991), the stranger's presence challenges tools of order making. The stranger, maintains Bauman (1990, 1991, 1998), is singled out as a particular problem by the national state – to be excluded, not eliminated – because the stranger, unlike the enemy, poses a greater threat to the social (or psychic) order: it is the enemy within.

Exclusion of the Other is, thus, the basis of identity formation. Paradoxically, the insider and the Other are locked into a kind of symbiotic relationship. Identity formation requires an Other to exclude. It is Foucault's contention (1980) that the contained outsiders (mad, criminal, prostitute, sick, unruly) are what make the insiders insiders. Similarly, Stallybrass and White (1986) observed that 'scientific' categories of difference overlay fantasies of difference. Analyzing the carnivalesque they suggested that in culture as in the body it is the lower strata that are the object of desire and disgust (much like Žižek's reading of Lacan which suggests that the obscene is found at the heart of ideology and is closely bound with it in dialectical relations which conceal the obscene thus rendering power operable (1989). The analysis of Stallybrass and White reminds us that the relationship between the established and the outsider is even more complex. What is expelled as 'Other' returns as the object of nostalgia, longing and fascination, and the bourgeois fantasy life. The result is that what is socially peripheral is symbolically central (Babcock 1978). It was Foucault who rendered embodied 'categories' of difference ideologically suspect. The return to the body in social research has acknowledged, argued and documented the claims first made by Foucault, that there is no purely natural prediscursive body. The body is always already culturally inscribed in a web of linguistic, hegemonic, representational and normative assumptions. Post-Foucaultian criticism has exposed the constructed nature of seemingly transparent, natural, timeless and embodied categories, and has shown them to be culturally and historically contingent (e.g. Bordo 1993; Gilman 1991b; Grosz 1995; Suleiman 1986).

Paradoxically, this critique of Western epistemology for using the body to ground narratives of identity similarly suppresses the body. The body is neither purely natural nor a textual metaphor. The refusal to engage with embodiment other than as a signifier denies the body its materiality. Further, theorizing the body has remarkably managed to avoid the issue of dress and clothing. The body that emerged in social theory (e.g. Featherstone et al., 1991; Shilling 1993) is an anomaly. One cannot talk body without talking clothes. Fashion calls attention to illusions grounded on embodiment, and defines prestige, rank, sexuality and gender. Denial of fashion extends from the philosophical disdain for the body, for fashionable dress, and for the woman – through the account of the civilizing process (Elias 1978, 1982) which charts the production of the refined and contained body by suppressing the physical body – to religious denunciation of the pleasure of the flesh and adornment of the body. Denying fashion a reputable place anywhere other than at the margins of the debate takes various forms. First, the representation of fashion in public culture focuses on objectification of the fashion products or processes, discussing them as aspects of reified reality with immanent meanings, not as dynamic elements in a cultural discourse. Examination, for example, of the over 3,000 references in the Amazon.com bookstore site fashion list, shows that it tends to feature the historical account (generally, or in a specified locale), fashion items, accessories or fabrics, fashion and beauty tips, fashion designers, fashion dolls, as well as some exotic aspects of clothing, those associated with some colourful subculture, or bizarre practices with a touch of sensationalism like tattoo and piercing (the same trend is evident in British television series from *Second skin*, *Adornment* (Desmond Morris's program), *Beyond flesh & blood: body alterations west and world* which featured the anthropological approach in the 1980s, *Painted ladies* (Westwood's program), *Fun with wigs*, *The look* in the 1990s, or the *Dressing for the Oscars* which look behind the scenes of catwalk and designers' world). The second means of marginalizing fashion is through dismissing the topic as not worthy of serious discussion, or by banishing it as trivia. This second point may not be so obvious except when one considers the limited range of venues that exist for publishing on clothing and fashion both among publishers' lists, and within those interdisciplinary social theory and cultural studies journals. Third, it reproduces, however subtly, a cultural outlook which devalues what is typically associated with the woman. Fashion can be hardly theorized without reference to gender. If theorizing fashion is theorizing femininity (Silverman 1986) then the refusal to engage with it signals a desire to avoid a discourse that can be easily mistaken as overdetermined, or to avoid gender issues altogether. Using 'the body' metaphorically also masks issues of embodiment as ungendered. The avoidance of fashion as a topic of research can also indicate a refusal to engage with another binary structure: the distinction between appearance and substance. While fashion habitually occupies the 'appearance' slot (artifice, inauthenticity, duplicity), body – especially when used metaphorically – can be easily slotted into 'substantive' discourse.

My search for critical strategies to theorize body and clothing to transcend a binary closure must involve tools with a reflexive capacity. One such tool is the concept of the performative. Originating from the work of Austin, it draws on the idea that many utterances, or speech acts, are not merely descriptive statements of fact. Rather, they are expressions whose function is to carry out a performance. Austin says that the performative is not concerned with truth and falsity (of a claim) but with felicity and infelicity of a performance. Turner (1969, 1982) introduced the notion of the performative to refer to a feature of ritual, an anti-thesis to 'rules or rubrics' approach. Instead, he emphasized the processual sense of performance over the more mechanistic structuralist implication of 'manifesting form'. The relationship between the performative and subjectivity has been elaborated by Butler (1990a, 1990b) who proposed that identity is constituted in time through what she terms 'corporeal style' consisting of repeated and rehearsed public acts. The notion of performance as a metaphor for social action is not new. It has been introduced by theorists from Jung to Goffman. Jung's persona is a mask or a role with social origins and a misleading individual appearance (1953). For Goffman, the person qua actor plays to an audience and goes to great lengths to display certain aspects of the performance and hide others (1959). For both the act is external to the actor. However, unlike Jung's, Goffman's and Butler's actors do not have an essence 'behind the performance' (cf. my argument in Tseëlon 1995, 2000), they are their performance. The performative thesis has been taken up by queer theory to destabilize gender and sexuality categories. And it has used drag as a vehicle to problematize those very habitual categories (e.g. Case 1990; Garber 1992).

Performance is indeed a liberating and critical tool for interrogating social practices. It does not, however, suggest that by realizing the constructed nature of our categories we can shake them off at will, partly because of the heavy penalties incurred by failing to play the part. Performance, however useful, has limited utility. Some well-rehearsed acts seem remarkably similar to essential attributes. The distinction between them can be more analytical than pragmatic, and is no more illuminating to the cultural observer or the individual performer. To illustrate the limit of the dramatic analogy as a deconstructing device, consider the difference between the improvisational theatre of the commedia dell'arte and the rigid, stylised, 600-year-old Japanese Noh theatre. The commedia emerged in the mid-sixteen century and involved the mix of distinctive stock characters with improvisational texts. The improvisational theatre of Peter Brook went further to eliminate the text, and improvise, without rehearsal, both acts and roles (cf. Heilpern 1979). At the other extreme stands the face of the Noh actor inset in an impersonal, symbolic mask. His every movement is highly controlled and limited, and devoid of any liberty of physical expression. No editing or adaptation is permitted with the hundreds of scripts in the theatre's repertoire (Sekine and Murray 1990). While both the improvisational and the traditional are types of performance, the Noh version appears almost lacking in agency. It has the appearance (if not the spirit) of representing essentialist properties. In contrast, the improvisational theatre seems closer to representing a 'socially constructed act'.

A related but more appropriate paradigmatic concept to interrogate body and fashion beyond an automatic gender linkage is the concept of masquerade. It features in psychoanalytic theories of inessential femininity. This masquerading idea to denote the position of the feminine is a longstanding one in psychoanalysis. It is based on the idea that femininity is a disguise assumed by the woman in order to disarm the male fear of her power (Doane 1982, 1984; Heath 1989; Riviere 1929). Both de Lauretis (1986) and Modleski (1989) examine masquerade as a tool for feminist critical theory. Both dismiss it as insufficient against different alternatives. For Modleski masquerade is limiting as it disavows difference, while de Lauretis sees masquerade as more subversive than mask, which presents imposed constraints. In fact both uses rely on a rather specific sense of mask and masquerade. Mask is limiting only in a discourse where it is viewed as 'the rigid precision characteristic of the "ritualized" behavior of an obsessive neurotic, or a territory-marking animal or bird' instead of a living process which is 'better likened to artwork than neurosis' (Turner 1982: 81). Masquerade as a psychoanalytic (and psychiatric) conception of a feminine strategy of disarmament, is subversive, (although not when appearing (like Madonna and drag queens) to mock hegemonic conventions – only to preserve and consolidate them more effectively). Therefore, it has been employed in a way that disavows difference. Unlike Modleski I don't see the subversive potential of masquerade as exhausted by critique (however difference-blind) of gender performance. Neither do I subscribe to de Lauretis's functional distinctions between mask and masquerade. I use them interchangeably, and I prefer the term of action (masking, masquerading, disguising) to emphasize dynamic similarities over semantic differences. Masquerade is simultaneously an analytic and a critical tool. As such, it can be used both for identity construction, and for critical deconstruction. As an analytic category, it is a 'technology of identity' that deals with literal and metaphorical covering for ends as varied as concealing, revealing, highlighting, protesting, protecting, creating a space from where one can play out desires, fears, conventions and social practices. As a critical subversive strategy it mocks and destabilizes habitual positions and assumptions, transgressing rules of hierarchy and order.

Masquerade is a paradigm particularly suited for 'the clothed body' for a number of reasons. It is rooted both in the material and in the symbolic: a meeting point between the body project and the fashion project. It refers to conscious and unconscious uses of disguise, and to complete covering (costume) as well as token masking (detail). If the concept of masking evokes an epistemology of authentic identity ('behind the mask'), locating it on the epistemological side of the notion of performance moves it away from 'authentic identity' and closer to 'an appearance of authentic identity'. Finally, masking, more emphatically than performance, relies as much on visual artefacts as on metaphorical disguise. And the mask, even when it portrays stereotypes, has the capacity of representing the general without reducing it to the essential. This is best captured in Barthes' reading of 'the face of Garbo' (1989). As a language he sees Garbo's singularity as being of the order of an 'Idea', while the individualized face of Audrey Hepburn as being of the order of an 'Event'. The snowy thickness of Garbo's mask-like make-up, like the white mask of the mime artist, has the effect of transforming her face into an idea of the human creature, and aligns her with the absolute mask: 'the absolute mask (the mask of antiquity, for instance) perhaps implies less the theme of the secret (as is the case with Italian half masks) than that of an archetype of the human face' (1989: 62). Bakhtin also refers to this ability of the mask to capture an abstract quality without implying an essence. In The *Dialogic Imagination* (1981) he compares the epic hero and the hero of popular masks, like the commedia dell'arte. According to him, while the dramatic hero is constrained by his destiny or the plot, the commedia hero is free. Paradoxically, despite the singularity of the dramatic hero as opposed to the stereotypical nature of the commedia character types, he views the commedia characters as: 'heroes of free improvisation and not heroes of tradition, heroes of a life process that is imperishable and forever renewing itself, forever contemporary – these are not heroes of an absolute past'.

Having sketched the theoretical merits of the dialectical masking paradigm for exploring fashion (and body) and its relationship to subjectivity, I now want to illustrate the use of masking for identity construction and critique. This I will do by referring to a number of studies which illustrate how fashion qua mask does not simply reproduce certain codes in a given discursive context, but also acts as a deconstructive presence. Marcia Wynes (1994) examines the creative use of disguise by an outsider Armenian artist Vahan Poladian who exploits his Otherness. Poladian, whose father and brother died during the First World War fled with his mother to Cuba. Unable to enter the US he moved to Paris, got married and had one daughter. Upon returning from the Second World War where he was taken prisoner by the Germans, his wife left him, taking their daughter with her. Forced to start a new life he began trading in antiques, and moved to St Raphael where there was an Armenian community. There he started making his rich and ornate costumes. For the next fifteen years he converted experiences of exile and displacement into defiant, fabulous clothes and splendid hats. His creations were modifications of ready-to-wear garments, decorated with common everyday objects such as bits of bric-a-brac, charm bracelets, feather dusters, Christmas ornaments, bird cages and plastic birds. His unconventional look was a parody of the look of power. Richly ornamented hats displayed luxury, while jackets adorned with stripes, medals and insignias signified military rank. Long robes made of cheap, glittering, brocaded fabrics created a look of simulated wealth. His costumes celebrated Armenian identity by defying traditional Western male attire through an excess of splendour. By majestically parading the streets dressed in his self styled costumes Poladian constructed himself as an Armenian dignitary, but the deceptively rich-looking materials he used, as well as his play with humorous objects such as toys and plastic fruits, simultaneously deconstructed the stately appearance with ironical inversions.

Tali Itzhaki and Avraham Oz (1994) trace the process leading from a naive self-fashioning of the Zionist dream to its inversion at the end of the century as represented by outward appearance. They point out that the ethos and the dress code of the pioneers who settled in Palestine at the turn of the century, as well as their predecessors at the foundation of Israel in 1948, was an ideologically simple one. It consisted of working (preferably short) pants in blue or khaki colour, and cheap fabric, an open shirt, a kafia shawl, Balakawa hat, sandals, or working shoes, and the Sten gun hanging on the shoulder. Both pioneers and fighters, they operated in a milieu which combined military (defence) and civil (setting up agricultural settlements) tasks and blurred the distinction between the two. What distinguished the Israeli rural settlements (like the kibbutz) was the fact that the national civil uniform of working clothes reflected a deliberate motivation to fashion a distinctive new Israeli social and national identity. What this look of simplicity signalled was an ideology of a collective effort of a mobilized society. This society was committed to a social ideal of socialism, and a political ideal of building a home for the Jewish people. In contrast to those idealized, if naive ideals, Itzhaki and Oz discuss the way in which visual features of the pioneer look have been appropriated by right-wing settlers in the occupied West Bank in the 1980s, with some significant modifications like the inclusion of tokens of religion such as dangling talith tassels. They argue that the appropriation of the same attire by fundamentalist right-wing settlers, rather than signalling a continuation of a tradition, in fact managed to signify an inversion, or self-defeating parody of that movement. Their radical nationalism as well as religious radicalism are totally alien to the model of their imitation to which they claim to be a lawful heir. For the Zionist secular movement respect for working the land was a primary value, and socialist values replaced religious ones. In contrast, the right-wing settlers are neither farmers nor poor, and their pioneering conditions, out of keeping with time and place, are more an option than a necessity. The settlers' uniform which builds on the trademark of the fighter and pioneer generation, is a manipulative disguise of a borrowed identity. The settlers' deployment of those pioneer symbols, they argue, was meant to capitalize on the mythological clout that has become attached to the ideological mission of the founding fathers' generation. In this they positioned themselves simultaneously as carrying the can of the ideologies that formed the state of Israel, but also as guardians of the religious roots with which the founding generation has parted company in order to realise their own vision of a new society.

Another form of masquerade is involved in 'clothing and costume perversions' coded, in France at the turn of the century, as signs of homosexuality, masturbation, criminality and degeneracy. The main perversions were inappropriate gender dressing (transvestism), and inappropriate modes of sexual arousal (fetishism). Modes of clothing can only be problematized and pathologized against a symbolic system which allocates rigid space for appropriate (in this case gender) behaviour. When women tried to be men psychiatry debated whether they were lesbians. By deviating from male fantasies, and resisting the masquerade of femininity the woman established her right to own her subjectivity. This inverse masquerade, however, marked her (just like the hysterical who articulates failed interpellation: the subject's inability to fulfil its symbolic designation) not as an author of a new meaning, but as a deviant from a symbolic universe: a pervert. This issue is illustrated by Halla Beloff (2001) through an example of visual rhetoric of the fluency of identity movement between different identity positions. Lesbian identities, she maintains, are negotiated within and without straight gender stereotypes, and bear the mark of 'discreditable spoiled identities' as Goffman put it. During this century, she observes, lesbians seem to have used the complete range of identity possibilities. Choosing the discreet route they have camouflaged their group membership, or used a set of private codes to communicate to insiders while keeping others outside. Camouflage, though, is a strategy used by a marginal, despised, discredited group wishing to remain invisible and unlabelled, and avoid rocking the boat. Another strategy, used by middle- and upper-class women in the first third of the century, is one of open and public lesbian presentations of their chosen selves. It used a kind of elegant austerity (plain silk shirts, tailored suits, cropped hair, elegant tie pin), and an ideal of boyish slenderness to create an ambiguous cultural style. The point of those performances is not to flaunt a crude masquerade of manhood, but to advocate an alternative aesthetic. This is an example of Tajfel's thesis about members of an oppressed group claiming an alternative 'worthy' identity. They do it by choosing their own criteria to turn their ascribed inferior identity to an achieved superior one. The clothes transgressions of male fetishists, however, did not so much pose a threat to a signifying system as underscored its phantasmic foundation. In a psychoanalytic discourse the fetish object, simultaneously denying and embodying a structural lack (the void of our desire, emptiness created by the very act of symbolization), is but a fantasy screen masking that the lack can never be filled: it is a fundamental impossibility. Objects of desire (real people or material artefacts) tempt us with false hope. 'We are all more or less fetishists,' admitted Emile Lauret in 1905. 'Every woman whom a man loves in his heart is forcibly a little bit of a fetish.' Illusion plays a pivotal role in 'normal' as well as 'pathological' fetishism.

Valerie Steele (2001) provides a close-up of the masquerade of fetishist fashion amidst reflection on the constructed nature of the categories of 'normal' and perverse sexuality. Observing that masquerade and sexual identity may be impossible to disentangle, she proceeds to analyze fetish fashion as an example of the relatively modern phenomenon of constructing individualized sexual identities. She traces the trajectory of fetish fashion from a 'closet' deviant sexual interest and practice, to a legitimate enactment of erotic fantasy that has gone mainstream in its fashion-cultural representations. She notes that stock fetish characters such as dominatrix and slave use masks for totally different ends. If the dominatrix is masked like a torturer, the slave's mask or hood implies the victim. Yet their deployment does not imply simple traditional gender-role identifications. In some cases they may actually subvert the 'normal' hierarchy of gender power because they offer multiple identity positions some of which are based on fantasy, not social conditioning.

One could extend the range of examples to include media representation as well as actual behaviour (see Tseëlon 2001a). The Spanish film director Pedro Almodovar uses the motif of disguise in the film *High Heels* (1991) to exploit constant shifts of gender-visual presentation. The film is a murder mystery in which the mother of the protagonist is a singer who looks like a transvestite, but who, in the film is actually impersonated by a drag artist whose look is more feminine, and who is actually an investigating policeman in disguise. The policeman, it turns out, wears an artificial beard even in the home he shares with his mother, who is unaware of the disguise. His previous undercover role, it transpires, has been of a drug dealer. Under this identity he two-timed two girlfriends who were left heartbroken when he disappeared one day at the end of his mission. Alternating between the persona of the drag artist (in love with the daughter) and a police detective (investigating both daughter and singer mother as suspects in the murder) he is cast in a role which embodies and intercepts the investigating gaze. The effect is to destabilize not just notions of gender codes and categories, but the possibility of investigating, or establishing 'the truth'. Gender appearance codes such as beard, earrings, or high heels feature throughout the film in their conventional sense but also as subverting the same conventions that gave them meaning in the first place. They render Almodovar's use of gender bending as ambiguous, not overdetermined; as critique, not a caricature.

In another example of an emblematic filmic disguise Denise York (1994) analyzes the role of the Tallith in Barbra Streisand's Yentl, about a Rabbi's daughter. Seeing that she is such a keen mind, her father chose to introduce her to the world of learning of the Talmud, which in the beginning of the century was still deemed more appropriate for men, and frowned upon in women. When her father dies, Yentl assumes male dress and wins a place at a yeshiva (a Talmudic school) in a different town. The gender masquerade, symbolically marked by the masculine prayer shawl, the Tallith, serves as an entry ticket to a world of learning that belongs exclusively to men. York sees the agenda of this exemplar of the cross-dressing genre as neither a parody of the feminine, nor as its renunciation. Rather, she views the masquerade as concealing androgyny. In assuming the dress and lifestyle of a man, she argues, Yentl (now Anshel) does not seek to project her repressed qualities (released by the masquerade). She simply gives outward appearance to the qualities she knows and values in herself. Thus the film, according to York, is not about a conflict or polarization of gender roles, but about a synthesis that is won through 'lived experience'. The symbolic marker of her transition is the Tallith which is a badge of masculine exclusivity, of her exclusion from 'The law of the Father'. As a woman, even her knowledge of the Talmud does not allow her to don the Tallith. But when she 'comes out' as a woman and embarks on her journey to the new world, to America, she no longer needs to hold on to this symbolism. Confident in her securely won identity she now uses a scarf instead, wearing it, (like a transitional object) in a decorative (non-ritual) way.

Another example comes from an analysis of masquerade practices in carnival. Theo Fransen (1994) takes issue with carnival theories which argue that carnival 'celebrates temporary liberation from the prevailing truth of the established order . . . [and] marks the suspension of all hierarchical rank, privileges, norms and prohibitions' (Bakhtin 1981: 104). Drawing on extensive fieldwork of the Venlo carnival in the Netherlands he suggests, rather like York's point, that participants do not simply liberate a secret identity, but optimize a public one. Masking enhances rather than disguises identities.

From a more historical perspective Ann Ilan-Alter (2001) looks at bourgeois women during the July Monarchy who masqueraded to go to the opera. Masqueraded they managed to satisfy their desire for freedom to enjoy the pleasures of the balls but not quite to escape the threat to their reputation as virtuous women playing their proper part in 'the cult of domesticity'. It was the mask which empowered those women to challenge their traditional roles. Christoph Heyl (this volume) examines a similar period, eighteenth-century England, but focuses on non-masquerade contexts. He notes that wearing the black half-mask became a common device worn by women in public (e.g. the park, or the theatre). Providing a certain degree of anonymity this kind of mask served as a liberating device in a society which had been guarding women's bodies and movements rather closely. Inverting the public gaze, the face mask created a symbolic private space free from surveillance, which enabled the woman to engage in pursuits otherwise denied to her. Finally, from contemporary fashion I note a subversive use of bridal attire which renders it a sort of mask of tradition. While not departing from the connotations of modesty, chastity and purity embedded in the tradition of a 'bride', the symbolism of the white, and the marriage ceremony, those examples nevertheless critique the very convention underlying the custom in a move which constructs both role embracing and role distance, and marks territories of individual identity. They do so by a mixing of provocation and submission. For example, ordinary clothes (slacks, pinafore dress) worn by the bride complete with a bridal veil, or by a tongue-in-cheek combination of a proper bridal gown and a sexy/revealing feature (e.g. sleeveless dress with detachable long sleeves that start in mid-arm and are worn like some form of bracelet, or a gown which is long, including a train from the back, but is ultra short and transparent from the front).

The guiding question I have addressed here is how to theorize fashion and subjectivity without reproducing an essentialist gender discourse which almost habitually identifies fashion with the feminine. Having surveyed the background and various alternatives I have suggested the concept of 'masquerade' which occupies the same symbolic slot allotted to 'fashion' within the symbolic system. The benefits of using the paradigm of the masquerade are that it extends the arena by subsuming fashion (as a particular case) among a range of tools for crafting identities. For rhetorical purposes I have illustrated my thesis with examples that focus on unusual more than on banal examples (but see my analogy between modes of speech and dress to theorize social silence, social acquiescence, and provocation as discursive as well as sartorial strategies, Tseëlon 2001b). Finally, by substituting masquerade for fashion the notion of constructing identities through manipulation of coverings can be easily unhinged from its gender moorings.

References

Babcock, B. (1978), *The Reversible World: Symbolic Inversion in Art and Society*, Ithaca, NY: Cornell University Press.

Bakhtin, M. (1981), *The Dialogic Imagination*, trans. by C. Emerson and M. Holquist. Austin: University of Texas Press.

Barthes R. (1989), *Mythologies*, trans by Annette Lavers. London: Paladin. (Originally published 1957).

Bauman, Z. (1990), 'Modernity and Ambivalence', *Theory, Culture & Society*, 7: 143–69.

Bauman, Z. (1991), 'Postmodernity: Change or Menace?' Centre for the Study of Cultural Values Papers Series, University of Lancaster.

Bauman, Z. (1998), 'Allosemitism: Premodern, Modern, Postmodern', in B. Cheyette and Marcus, L. (eds), *Modernity, culture and 'the Jew'*, Cambridge: Polity.

Beloff, Halla, (2001), Re-telling Lesbian Identities: Beauty and Other Negotiations, in Efrat Tseëlon (ed.) *Masquerade and Identities: Essays on Gender, Sexuality and Marginality*, London: Routledge.

Bordo, S. (1993), *Unbearable Weight: Feminism, Western Culture, and the Body*, Berkeley: University of California Press.

Bradley, D. H. (1922), *The Eternal Masquerade*, London: Werner Laurie.

Butler, J. (1990a), Preformative Acts and Gender Constitution: an Essay in Phenomenology and Feminist Theory, in Case, S. (ed.) *Performing Feminisms*, Baltimore: Juhns Hopkins University Press.

Butler, J. (1990b), *Gender Trouble. Feminism and the Subversion of Identity*, London: Routledge.

Case, S. A. (ed.) (1990), *Performing Feminisms: Feminist Critical Theory and Theatre*, Baltimore: John Hopkins University Press.

de Lauretis, T. (1986), Issues, Terms, and Contexts, in Teresa de Lauretis (ed.) *Feminist Studies, Critical Studies*, Bloomington: Indiana University Press.

Doane, M. (1982), Film and the Masquerade: Theorising the Female Spectator, *Screen*, 23 (3–4), 74–87.

Doane, M.A., Mellencamp, P. and Williams, L. (eds) (1984), *Re-vision: Essays in Feminist Film Criticism*, Los Angeles, American Film Institute.

Douglas, M. (1966), *Purity and Danger*, London: Routledge and Kegan Paul.

Elias, N. (1978), *The Civilizing Process*. Vol. 1. *The History of Manners*, trans. by Edmund Jepchott, Oxford: Blackwell.

Elias, N. ([1939] 1982), *The Civilizing Process*. Vol. 2. *State Formation and Civilization*, trans. by Edmund Jepchott, Oxford: Blackwell.

Featherstone, M., Hepworth, M. and Turner, S. B. (eds) 1991, *The Body: Social Process and Cultural Theory*, London: Sage.

Foucault, M. (1975), *Discipline and Punish: The Birth of the Prison*, trans. Alan Sheridan, NY: Pantheon Books.

Foucault, M. (1977), *Power/Knowledge*, ed. and trans. by C. Gordon, New York: Pantheon.

Foucault, M. (1980), *The History of Sexuality*, Vol. 1: *An Introduction*, New York: Vintage.

Fransen, T. (1994), Carnival as 'Cameleonic Experience' and 'Temporary Change of Social Skin. Paper presented at a conference 'Mask, Masquerade and Carnival', Venice, February, 1–4.

Garber, M. (1992), *Vested Interests: Cross-dressing and Cultural Anxiety*, London: Penguin.

Gilman, S. (1986), *Difference and Pathology: Stereotypes of Sexuality, Race, and Madness*, Ithaca, NY: Cornell University Press.

Gilman, S. (1988), *Disease and Representation: Images of Illness from Madness to AIDS*, Ithaca, NY: Cornell University Press.

Gilman, S. (1991a), *Inscribing the Other*, Lincoln: University of Nebraska Press.

Gilman, S. (1991b), *The Jew's Body*, London: Routledge.

Goffman, E. (1959), *The Presentation of Self in Everyday Life*, New York: Anchor Books.

Grosz, E. (1995), *Space, Time and Perversion: Essays on the Politics of Bodies*, London: Routledge.

Hansen, K. (1993), Aesthetics in Feminist Perpective, in Hilde Hein & Carolyn Korsmeyer (eds) *Aesthetics in Feminist Perspective*, Bloomington: Indiana University Press.

Hart, L. (ed.) (1989), *Making a Spectacle: Feminist Essays on Contemporary Women's Theatre*, Ann Arbor: University of Michigan Press.

Heath, S. (1989), Joan Riviere and the Masquerade, in V. Burgin, J. Donald and C. Kaplan (eds), *Formations of Fantasy*, London: Routledge.

Heilpern, J. (1979), *Conference of the Birds: The Story of Peter Brook in Africa*, Harmondsworth: Penguin.

Heyl, C. (2001), The Metamorphosis of the Mask in Seventeenth- and Eighteenth-Century London. In Efrat Tseëlon (ed.) *Masquerade and Identities: Essays on Gender, Sexuality and Marginality*, London: Routledge.

Ilan-Alter, A. (2001), 'Masked and Unmasked at the Opera Balls: Parisian Women Celebrate Carnival, in Efrat Tseëlon (ed.) *Masquerade and Identities: Essays on Gender, Sexuality and Marginality*, London: Routledge.

Itzhaki, T. and Avraham, O. (1994), Soldiers and Pioneers: The Ideological Deployment of Clothes in Constructing a National Identity in Israeli Society. Paper presented at a conference 'Mask, Masquerade and Carnival', Venice, February, 1–4.

Jung, C. G. (1953). The Persona as a Segment of the Collective Psyche, in *Two essays on analytical psychology* (2nd. edn.), trans. by R.F.C. Hull, London: Routledge & Kegan Paul.

Kristeva, Julia (1982), *Powers of Horror: An Essay on Abjection*, trans. Leon S. Roudiez, New York: Columbia University Press.

Kristeva, Julia (1991), *Strangers to Ourselves*, trans. by Leon S. Roudiez, London: Harvester Wheatsheaf (Originally published 1988).

Laqueur, T. (1990), *Making sex: Body and Gender from the Greeks to Freud*, Cambridge: Harvard University Press.

Lauret, E. (1905), *Féttichistes et érotomanes*, Paris: Vigot.

Malik, K. (1996), *The meaning of race*, London: Macmillan.

Matlock, J. (1993), Masquerading Women, Pathologized Men: Cross-dressing, Fetishism, and the Theory of Perversion, 1882–1935, in Emily Apter and William Pietz (eds) *Fetishism as Cultural Discourse*. Ithaca: Cornell University Press.

Modleski, T. (1989), Some Functions of Feminist Criticism, or the Scandal of the Mute Body, *October*, 49, 3–24.

Riviere, J. (1929), Womanliness as Masquerade, *The International Journal of Psychoanalysis*, 10, 303–13.

Sekine, M. and Murray, C. (1990), *Yeats and the Noh: A Comparative Study*, Colin Smythe: Gerrards Cross.

Shilling, C. (1993), *The Body and Social Theory*, London: Sage.

Silverman, K. (1986), Fragments of a Fashionable Discourse, in Tania Modleski (ed.) *Studies in Entertainment: Critical Approaches to Mass Culture*, Bloomington: Indiana University Press.

Spelman, E. V. (1982), Woman as Body: Ancient and Contemporary Views, *Feminist Studies*, 8, 108–31.

Stallybrass, P. and White, A. (1986), *The Politics and Poetics of Transgression*, London: Methuen.

Steele, V. (2001), Fashion, Fetish, Fantasy, in Efrat Tseëlon (ed.) *Masquerade and Identities: Essays on Gender, Sexuality and Marginality*, London: Routledge.

Stepan, N. (1982).*The idea of race in science: Great Britain 1800–1960*. London: Macmillan.

Suleiman, S. (ed.) (1986), *The Female Body in Western Culture*, Cambridge: Harvard University Press.

Tseëlon, E. (1995), *The Masque of Femininity: The Presentation of Woman in Everyday Life*, London: Sage.

Tseëlon, E. (1998), Fashion, Fantasy and Horror: A Cultural Studies Approach, *Arena Journal*, 12, 107–28.

Tseëlon, E. (2000), Is the Presented Self Sincere? Goffman, Impression Management, and the Postmodern Self, in G. A. Fine and Smith, G.W.H. (eds) *Erving Goffman: Sage Masters of Modern Social Thought*, London: Sage. (Originally published 1992.)

Tseëlon, E. (2001a), Woman and the Gaze, in Dan Fleming (ed.) Formations: 21st Century Media Studies, Manchester: Manchester University Press.

Tseëlon, E. (2001b), On Women and Clothes and Carnival Fools, in Efrat Tseëlon (ed.) *Masquerade and Identities: Essays on Gender, Sexuality and Marginality*, London: Routledge.

Turner, Victor (1969), *The Ritual Process: Structure and Anti-structure*, Chicago: Chicago University Press.

Turner, V. (1982), *From Ritual to Theatre: The Human Seriousness of Play*, New York: PAJ Publications.

Winnicott, D. W. (1953), Transitional Objects and Transitional Phenomena, *International Journal of Psycho-Analysis*, 34, 89–97.

Wynes, M. (1994). Individual Identity and Armenian Tradition: Costumes by an Outsider Artist. Paper presented at a conference 'Mask, Masquerade and Carnival', Venice, February, 1–4.

York, D. (1994), The Cloak of the Tallith: Gender, Disguise and Identity in Barbra Streisand's Yentl. Paper presented at a conference 'Mask, Masquerade and Carnival', Venice, February, 1–4.

Žižek, S. (1989), *The Sublime Object of Ideology*, London: Verso.

Part Two

Historical Case Studies

*When they are veyl'd on purpose to be seene: The Metamorphosis of the Mask in Seventeenth- and Eighteenth-Century London**

Christoph Heyl

This chapter deals mainly with the development and the functional role of masks worn by women in seventeenth- and eighteenth-century London. I shall focus on the practice of wearing masks in a non-masquerade context. Masked women in, for instance, London parks would once have been a fairly common sight. However, this cultural practice is not something to be taken for granted. How did it evolve? What was the status and purpose of these masks? Were they meant to provide a real, efficient form of disguise, or are we dealing with a more complex phenomenon? How did they affect patterns of behaviour, i.e. what were the effects these masks had both on their wearers and on others? These issues will then be related to both the masquerade and other uses of anonymity and disguise in the eighteenth century.

I shall argue that the split between private and public sphere (cf. passim: Habermas 1992; Heyl, forthcoming; Sennett 1977; Stone 1977) which took place among middle-class Londoners from the late seventeenth century (and thus long before similar developments started in most other European countries) gave an altogether new meaning to a range of phenomena associated with masks and disguises. As a new demand for privacy progressively isolated people from each other, the use of, among other things, a mask could offer a way out of this self-imposed isolation and inhibition. By means of deliberately obscuring one's own identity, relatively unrestrained and even new forms of social interaction could become possible.

* This article has been published courtesy of Routledge. © Routledge

A characteristic trait of pre-modern societies is the utter irrelevance of the concept of the individual's right to an inviolable private sphere. Although pockets of privacy always existed, this was very much a phenomenon which mainly affected privileged minorities. Pre-modern societies can be described as face-to-face societies (cf. Stone 1977: 6, 95f) in which groups such as the extended family, the neighbourhood and the guild played a decisive role in guiding and controlling the actions of each of their members. As the concept of privacy was for all practical purposes almost non-existent, every action was conducted in what we today would regard as an atmosphere of publicity. How far this observation went in practice can be concluded from the thousands of detailed denunciations for domestic and moral transgressions received by the ecclesiastical courts between the middle of the fifteenth and the seventeenth century (cf. Emmison 1972).

In this type of pre-modern society, it could always be assumed that each member of a given community knew, and had a right to know a good deal about other members of that community. Under these circumstances, an unknown person was either to be treated as a guest or to be regarded as an outsider and a potential menace.

One of the basic functions of a mask is to conceal or at least to obscure a person's identity, to turn its wearer, at least notionally, into a stranger – and more often than not, it was not a good thing to be a stranger in a pre-modern context. This is why it was possible to use certain forms of masks as a feared shame punishment for women regarded as 'scolds'. In late medieval and Renaissance England as well as on the continent, a contraption known as *scold's bridle* or *brank* was widely in use.

There were two types of scold's bridles. In their simplest form, they consisted of a plain metal cage fitting tightly round a person's head with a metal gag protruding inside. The second type was of a similar construction, but took the shape of a grotesque mask, often fitted with bells and such like to attract even greater attention. Women were exhibited in the pillory or led through the streets wearing these contraptions in a ritual of public humiliation.

Some examples of a particularly unpleasant variety of the 'mask' type are known. These were fitted with a screwing apparatus which, according to a nineteenth-century description, '[. . .] seems calculated to force the iron mask with torturing effect upon the brow of the victim; there are no eye-holes, but concavities in their places, as though to allow for the starting of the eye-balls under violent pressure' (Andrews 1890: 60).

These 'masks' in a sense run counter to modern expectations about what a mask is there for: their purpose is not to protect and conceal, but to torture and expose. Scold's bridles of the 'mask' type were made for being stared at, and this is why it seems to stand to reason that the most cruel of these artefacts

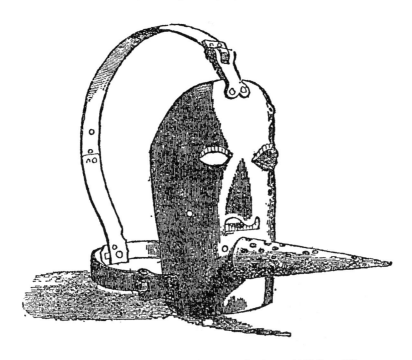

Figure 6.1 *Scold's Bridle*, mask type (Andrews (1890), p 58).

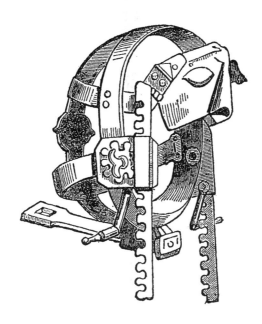

Figure 6.2 *Scold's Bridle* with screwing apparatus (Andrews (1890), p 60).

are masks without eye holes. They are in effect blind masks, not designed in any way to efface the wearer's presence, but to provide a focus for the hostile attention of a crowd of gaping spectators.

While a certain form of mask could assume these functions within the context of a pre-modern society, an altogether different use of masks evolved in the singular social setting of early modern London. A far-reaching process of change was well under way here: as its population increased rapidly, London became the first European metropolis of the day. Urban mortality was so high that this growth was only sustainable by means of a steady influx of people from the rest of the country. Given its sheer size, London was populated by people who were and remained strangers to one another. Here, the days of local communities exercising an exceptionally high degree of social control were numbered, and the kind of urban anonymity we have come to associate with life in big cities came into being. It became 'normal' to live as a stranger among strangers, to accept and to respect the anonymity of others (cf. Sennett 1977: 48, 54f). Under these new conditions, new ideas about acceptable patterns of behaviour spread especially among the urban middle classes. In this unique local and social setting, a demand for privacy first became a mass phenomenon (cf. Heyl forthcoming).

It is under these conditions that new forms of masks began to appear which were soon to undergo a remarkable development. While the phenomenon of the masquerade in eighteenth-century England has been the subject of scholarly studies (Castle 1986; Craft-Fairchild 1993; Ribeiro 1984), the equally interesting use of masks and disguises in a non-masquerade context during the same period and earlier has not yet been studied in depth. There is a body of evidence concerning these phenomena dating from the seventeenth and early eighteenth century, and I shall tentatively chart out what seem to be some relevant aspects of this material.

During the first half of the seventeenth century, a black half-mask (also called *vizard mask*), covering the upper half of the face, was a common winter accessory worn by well-to-do women in London. Numerous prints by Wenceslaus Hollar depict women wearing this type of mask. (Hollar was born in Prague in 1607; he spent a significant part of his life in London where he died in 1677. Prints referred to here will be identified according to the current descriptive catalogue of his work, i.e. Pennington 1982.) Hollar obviously associated the wearing of such masks with England: there are no masked figures in his collection of prints depicting the costume of women from various other European countries (Hollar, 1643). What is more, Hollar associated the wearing of masks as a standard accessory, rather than an element of fancy dress, with London. Women wearing masks appear, for instance, against a panoramic London background as in illustration No. 6.3.

Perhaps surprisingly, the winter costumes and groups of winter accessories shown in Hollar's prints include fans. One does not see these fans in action, but numerous contemporary texts imply that they were used to cover the remaining part of the naked face. Mask and fan go together because they both serve to protect the face, as a couplet from a poem by Samuel Butler (1613–1680) suggests (Butler, ed. Lamar, 1928: 294):

The cold, not cruelty makes her weare
In Winter, furrs and Wild beasts haire
Winter
For a smoother skinn at night
Embraceth her with more delight.

Figure 6.3 *Winter* from Wenceslaus Hollar's full-length *Four Seasons* series, 1643 (cf. Pennington (1982), No. 609, p. 98); original print in author's collection.

There are no Vizard-masks, nor Fans,
To keep Age from a Countenance

Later pictorial evidence confirms that fans were indeed used to *cover* the face and thus to interrupt eye-to-eye contact. (For a striking example cf. William Hogarth's *The Rake's Progress*, No. VII, i.e. the Bedlam scene. Oil on canvas, 1733: Sir John Soane's Museum, London.)

Figure 6.4 Masked lady from Wenceslaus Hollar's *Ornatus Muliebris Anglicanus* series, 1639 (cf. Pennington (1982), No. 1790, p. 293); original print in author's collection.

The main practical reason for wearing these *winter* masks as suggested by their seasonal use and by sub-titles of prints seems to have been the desire to protect the delicate skin of the face from the cold. (Three untitled small prints by Hollar show masks among winter accessories. Cf. Pennington 1982, No. 1948, 1949 and 1951: all p. 310) A poem by Charles Cotton (1630–1687) entitled *Winter* stresses such protective and even cosmetic purposes (Cotton 1689: 62):

> [. . .] out of rev'rend care
> To save her beauty from the Air,
> And guard her pale Complexion,
> Her Hood and Vizard Mask puts on

However, apart from this primary purpose these masks were also a form of disguise. This disguise, however, must necessarily have been rather inefficient: it was still fairly easy to recognize the wearer of such a mask which, after all, just covered the upper half the face. But then even this must have been more than sufficient to introduce the *idea* of anonymity and therefore to modify the behaviour of the wearer. After all, a mask deprives its wearer of certain modes of facial expression and thus affects one's ability to communicate.

These masks offered new possibilities of playing with anonymity, and they probably gave a sense of protection, a sense of almost being invisible. Slowly and steadily, the more utilitarian aspects of wearing a mask became a mere pretext. What had been the mask's side-effect (the price a woman had to pay for 'guarding her complexion' was that it temporarily rendered at least part of her face invisible) now became its main attraction. The mask obscured the wearer's identity, thus temporarily turning her into a stranger of sorts. Although this would have been a most undesirable predicament in a pre-modern community, in the new world of the metropolis it could be regarded as an attractive option. In an urban context where people were more at ease with anonymity than they had ever been before, these masks gradually took on some kind of life of their own which was worlds apart from the scold's bridle and all it stood for.

One should keep in mind that masks both obscure their wearers and attract attention at the same time. The half-masks depicted by Hollar and others could be more of a token disguise than a real one. This point is being made in a poem by John Cleveland (1613–1658) as he mentions the

> [. . .] Cob-web vizard, such as Ladies weare,
> When they are veyl'd on purpose to be seene
> (Cleveland 1647: 33)

Several new developments in the late seventeenth century confirm that the anonymity (be it real or notional) conferred by the mask now became its main attraction and that even the pretence of cosmetic reasons for wearing it was eventually dropped. Under the influence of the new intellectual and moral atmosphere brought about by the Restoration, new informal rules concerning the wearing of masks began to apply. The overall role of the mask underwent a transformation: both its physical appearance and the time and places regarded as appropriate for wearing it changed.

The mask ceased to be a winter accessory and began to be an option available at any time of the year. As its main function came to be its power to confer varying degrees of anonymity, its size increased from the half-mask to a mask covering the entire face. The use of such masks was governed by informal rules: they were only worn in special places such as London parks and theatres.

The new appreciation of anonymity reflected in the development of the mask can be traced in similar, parallel phenomena as it affected patterns of everyday behaviour in numerous ways. A new phenomenon which could well be described as a virtual form of disguise was the incognito ritual. If you made it understood that you were incognito, people could of course still recognize you, but they were nevertheless expected to behave towards you as if you were completely disguised. This apparently bizarre but once common pattern of behaviour demonstrates that the privacy of strangers or of people who wanted to be treated as strangers had become something to be respected. Such a thing would have been unthinkable in a face-to-face society in which every stranger was inevitably incorporated into the existing group as a guest or expelled as an alien and a menace. (The word *incognito* became current in the English language from the mid-seventeenth century. Cf. *OED on CD-ROM* 1992: q.v.)

Eye-to-eye contact among strangers rapidly became a taboo. The anonymous author of a list of 'Rules of Behaviour' (*London Magazine*, February 1734, p. 66 f) advises his readers

> (6) To be cautious of Staring in the Faces of those that pass by us, like an Inquisitor general; for an over-bearing Look has the Air of a Bully, and a prying one that of a Bayley. If we do it by Mistake for a Friend, ask Pardon.
> [. . .]
> (8) Not to fasten your Eyes upon any Person entring into a publick Room, for Fear (by such a broad side) of Shocking his Modesty, and Dismounting his Assurance.

It was a common notion that looking closely at someone's face enabled one to 'read' this face and thus to find out about a person's abilities, inclinations and motivations. The new taboo concerning eye-to-eye contact really meant that it was now regarded as a violation of peoples' private spheres to snatch their secrets from them by 'reading' their faces.

The basic idea that faces can be 'read' was in fact an old one which, however, had developed into something like a science in its own right by the eighteenth century. In 1586, Della Porta drew attention to parallel characteristics of human and animal physiognomy in his illustrated work *De Humana Physiognomia*. The idea was taken up in Le Brun's hugely influential *Traité sur la Physionomie* (1698) and works of a similar nature which were soon translated and became hugely influential in England. Numerous illustrations form an integral part of Le Brun's works. These demonstrate how specific passions affect the human face.

DESIRE.

IF to *Love* be joined *Desire*, that may be represented by the Eyebrows pressed and advanced over the Eyes, which shall be more open than ordinary, with the Eye-ball in the middle and full of Fire; the Nostrils drawn closest next the Eyes; the Mouth also is more open than in the foregoing Action, the Corners drawn back, and the Tongue may appear upon the edge of the Lips, the Colour more inflamed than in *Love*; all these Motions shewing the Agitation of the Soul, caused by the Spirits, which dispose it to desire a Good, represented as convenient for it.

JEALOUSIE,

IT is expressed by the Forehead wrinkled, the Eye-brow drawn down and frowning, the Eye sparkling, and the Eye-ball hid under the lids, turning towards the Object which causes the Passion regarding it cross and sideways, contrary to the Situation of the Face; the Eye-ball should appear unsteady and fiery, as also the White of the Eye and the Eye-lids; the Nostrils pale, open, and more marked than ordinary, and drawn back, which makes Wrinkles in the Cheeks; the Mouth may be shut, and make known that the Teeth are set together; the under Lip is thrust out over the upper, and the Corners of the Mouth drawn back, and very much down; the Muscles of the Jaws will appear hollow.

Figure 6.5 *Desire* and *Jealousie* from Le Brun's *Conference* (Le Brun, 1701), p. 16, p.19; author's collection.

Le Brun in fact provided a key, a kind of an alphabet which could eventually facilitate the 'reading' of faces in everyday life. Later on, this notion was further developed by Johann Kaspar Lavater and others. Thus, belief in the practical value of the science of physiognomy developed from a body of specialist knowledge to a set of commonplace assumptions. Numerous English conduct books propagated these ideas, enabling people to 'read' the faces of others as well as making them aware of the constant danger of 'being read' themselves. A concise version of a popular view of physiognomy is given, for instance, in *The Polite Lady, or, a Course of Education in a Series of Letters from a Mother to her Daughter* (Anon. 1760: 218–19):

Figure 6.6 Ryley/Jeffries, *Inside View of Justice Hall, in the Old Bailey,* 1795 (Jackson, 1795, Vol. I); original print in author's collection.

But, my Dear, not only does the countenance receive a transient tincture from the passion which happens, for the present, to be most prevalent in the mind: what is still more, if we indulge that passion frequently and habitually, it will come at last to give the countenance such a particular cast and air, as it will not be in our power to alter or throw off at pleasure, but will continue fix'd and invariable through our whole lives, and will go a great way to determine our character, at least with the generality of the world, who have no other opportunity to judge of our tempers, but from our looks and appearance; so that we shall pass for proud or humble, peevish or good-natured, impudent or modest, just as our countenance is expressive of any of these dispositions.

Thus, you see, my Dear, there is at least some truth in physiognomy, and that it concerns every young lady to be very careful of her looks, since her character depends as much upon these as upon any other part of her behaviour. The only advice I can give you in this case is, never to entertain any lewd or immodest thought in your breast, and then you will never be in danger of expressing any thing of that nature in your countenance: if you would wish to have a modest look, you must endeavour to have a modest mind; for without the latter, the former can hardly exist.

It was thus a widely received idea that a face could be 'read'. Nothing demonstrates this so clearly as the curious device which was in use in the London criminal courts of the Old Bailey in the eighteenth century and which can be seen in a print from *The Newgate Calendar*. While the defendant was being questioned, his face could be watched in a huge and specially lighted mirror installed for this purpose only (visible close to the right margin of the print). The defendant's facial expression was apparently almost of as much interest to all other parties concerned as his or her words.

It became a part of a middle-class child's education as set out in conduct books to disguise one's feelings by turning one's face into a kind of expressionless mask. The following rules are given in *The School of Manners*, a book written for children and published in London in 1701:

(19) Let thy countenance be moderately chearful, neither laughing nor frowning.
(20) Laugh not aloud, but smile upon occasion.
[. . .]
(18) If any immodest or obscene thing be spoken of in thy hearing, smile not at it, but settle thy countenance as though thou didst not hear it.
[. . .]
(22) Look not boldly or wishfully in the Face of thy Superior.
(Anon. 1701, ed. Whalley, J.I. 1983: 40 f.)

Conduct books for adults continued to make the same point: one may frustrate peoples' attempts to 'read' one's face by deliberately trying to give no clues at all:

[. . .] it is now-a-days considered as a sign of rusticity and ignorance to allow the countenance to be an index of the mind, or to express those particular passions with which it is affected. A certain unmeaning uniformity of face is now studied and practised, or rather to have such an absolute command over our features, as to be able, on occasion, to assume any appearance [. . .]
(Anon. 1760: 219–20)

Given all these alarming assumptions about the countenance being *readable*, it could indeed make good sense to wear a mask of the new type which covered the entire face. In the early eighteenth century, Baron von Pöllnitz, a German visitor, was astonished to see well-to-do women wearing such masks in London parks as a matter of course:

The Ladies here have little to employ them; their Amusement being [. . .] to have the Pleasure of being seen, which really is of all Pleasures that which they seem to take most delight in. This is the Motive that carries them to the public Walks, Concerts, and Theatres; in all which Places, they are mightily reserved [. . .]. [. . .] As for the rest, the Women here enjoy great Liberty. They turn out in a Morning with a black velvet Mask on their Faces, a Coif on in Form of a Hat, with the Brims down, a round Gown, and a white Apron, and in this Trim they go to the Park, or where else they please. (Pöllnitz 1737, II: 461)

Note that on the one hand the author thinks that English women are 'mightily reserved' while on the other hand they delight in the game of seeing and being seen. The mask made it easier for them to do both things at the same time: protected by a mask, an element of privacy could be maintained while frequenting public places.

The very thing described by von Pöllnitz can be seen in a painting attributed to Mario Ricci which shows *A View of the Mall from St. James's Park* (ca.1710). Among the numerous figures promenading in the park (obviously in the summer), there are some women whose faces are entirely covered by black masks.

There are similar examples dating from the late seventeenth century such as two anonymous paintings showing the Horse Guards Parade, one of them including the King and his entourage. (Anon., *Charles II on Horse Guards Parade*. Oil on canvas, 60 × 105 in., painted late in the King's reign. Coll.: Duke of Roxburghe, Floors Castle. Unfortunately, I have not yet been able to obtain permission to reproduce this remarkable painting. Also Anon., *The Old Horse Guards Parade*, dimensions unknown, present whereabouts unknown. There is a photograph of this painting (file 263, British School) in the Witt Library, Somerset House, London.) In both of these paintings, among the numerous figures depicted there is a woman wearing a black mask covering her entire face. The remarkable thing about these paintings is that, as in

Figure 6.7 Marco Ricci, *A View of the Mall from St. James's Park, ca.*1710 (detail). Coll. Castle Howard; reproduction: Courtauld Institute of Art, London.

Ricci's painting, the masked figure or figures are given a most prominent position. In the painting showing Charles II on Horse Guards Parade, for instance, it is not the King with his group of attendants, dogs and a detachment of Foot Guards who provides the unquestionable focus of attention: the figure 'closest' to the viewer is a masked woman, i.e. the anonymous artist chose to diminish the figure of the King and to enlarge that of a nameless masked woman.

Such images strongly emphasize the fact that masked women were present in these places. From the late seventeenth century, women wearing masks seem to have been a feature readily associated with, for instance, St James's Park. Masked women were apparently stock characters connected with certain urban localities, much as foreign merchants in exotic dress were likely to be included in views of the Royal Exchange.

What these paintings strongly suggest is confirmed by a large number of contemporary texts. While early seventeenth-century evidence points to a seasonal use of masks for mainly cosmetic purposes, now the mask's function as a disguise is emphasized time and time again. Numerous references to the practice of wearing masks for the sake of enjoying a certain degree of (at least notional) anonymity can be found in poems, plays and prose texts such as essays, letters and diaries (Heyl, forthcoming).

There are references to masked women walking in parks, references to masked women in theatres and there are, of course, plays featuring park scenes including masked women. Such scenes must have been of considerable immediate appeal as masked actors faced an at least partly masked audience. Given this type of situation, the audience could relate in a very direct sense to what was happening on the stage and issues related to the use of masks could be addressed easily. This may help to explain the fact that allusions to masks abound in some Restoration comedies (for instance: Wycherley 1675, act I, scene 1: 6; act V, scene 1: 91; epilogue): it must have been hard to resist the temptation to point out that what happened on the stage was similar to what went on among the audience. In a situation where part of the audience was masked, the distinction between players and audience almost broke down, turning the theatre into a gathering of professional and amateur performers.

One went to the theatre not only to see a play, but also to enjoy an extra-ordinary atmosphere characterized by the relative absence of restraints which, by the way, never failed to shock foreign visitors. While the players were acting on the stage, members of the audience could don a mask and thus assume an alternative persona, too, escaping from the role they played in everyday life. The semiotic function of these masks was to denote that 'normal' rules of social interaction need not necessarily be observed, that people *might* approach each other more freely than elsewhere. Up to a point, the rules of everyday life (as regards morals and patterns of communication) were relaxed here, albeit only in certain environments such as parks or theatres.

The mask assumed a dialectic function of repellent *and* invitation, its message was both 'I can't be seen, I am – at least notionally – not here at all', and 'look at me, I am wearing a mask, maybe I am about to abandon the role I normally play'. One of the mask's paradoxical attractions was that it could both endanger and protect one's respectability. On the one hand, wearing a mask, one might allow oneself to do things which would otherwise be unthink-able. On the other hand, however, one assumed a different persona (the Latin word *persona* literally means *mask*), i.e. the mask at least notionally protected the identity and thus the integrity of its wearer.

The mask disguises – or more to the point: it pretends to be a disguise; instead of making one inconspicuous, it makes onlookers more inquisitive. This is made abundantly clear in Wycherley's *The Country Wife*. Mrs Pinchwife has just arrived from the country and wants to explore London with all its delightful entertainments:

Mrs. Pin. Well, but pray Bud, let's go to a Play to night.
[. . .]
Mr. Pin. So! the obstinacy already of a Town-wife, and I must, while she's here, humour her like one.   [*Aside*]
Sister, how shall we do, that she may not be seen, or known?
Alith. Let her put on her Mask.
Mr. Pin. Pshaw, a Mask makes People but the more inquisitive, and is as ridiculous a disguise, as a stage-beard; her shape, stature, habit will be known: and if we wou'd meet with *Horner*, he wou'd be sure to take acquaintance with us, must wish her joy, kiss her, leer upon her, and the Devil and all; no I'll not use her to a Mask, 'tis dangerous; for masks have made more Cuckolds, than the best faces that were ever known.
[. . .]
Mr. Pin. [. . .] a Mask! no – a Woman mask'd, like a cover'd Dish, gives a Man curiosity, and appetite, when, it may be, uncover'd, 'twou'd turn his stomack; no, no.
Alith. Indeed your comparison is something a greasie one: but I had a gentle Gallant, us'd to say, a Beauty mask'd, lik'd [sic!] the Sun in Eclipse, gathers together more gazers, than if it shin'd out.
(Wycherley 1675, act III, scene 1: 34–5)

People were apparently very much conscious of the fact that one mainly played with anonymity as opposed to really achieving it. The cultural practice of wearing a mask (i.e. displaying a sign denoting 'I am incognito') while in fact being still very much recognizable can be compared with the convention of the *aside* in the theatre. Once people get used to such rules, they begin to guide their perception and the entire situation very soon ceases to appear contrived and artificial.

However, true anonymity was certainly a possibility when perfect strangers first met and the woman wore a mask. In the correspondence of the second Earl of Chesterfield there is a letter addressed 'To one who walked 4 whole nights with me in St. James's Park, and yet I never knew who she was' in which the Earl requests to see this particular lady's face (Larwood 1877: 107 f).

Parks, like the theatres, were obviously perceived as areas which were set apart in that otherwise unacceptable forms of behaviour were regarded as legitimate there – and *only* there. These were the places, as Wycherley puts it in *The Country Wife*, 'where the men are to be found' (Wycherley 1675, act II, scene 1: 17). In Vanbrugh's *The Relapse* (1696), there is a reference to women wearing masks in 'that *Babylon* of Wickedness, *Whitehall*' (Vanbrugh 1698, act V, scene 2: 59 f.) St. James's Park being one of the prime venues for wearing masks in the open air, it is small wonder that Wycherley's *Love in a Wood, or St. James's Park* (first published 1672) abounds with allusions to masked women and to the relatively free forms of behaviour associated with this practice. Men go to the park to chat up women wearing masks, and Lady Flippant, 'an affected widow', dons a mask to go out in search of a husband (Wycherley 1694, act II, scene 1: 16). Of course one should take care not to take these comedies too easily at face value, but they would seem to confirm the evidence of other sources mentioned.

The fact that these forms of behaviour occurred 'in the open' probably served to control and limit them to a certain degree. All in all, what went on in the parks and theatres appears to be a case of society sanctioning comparatively uninhibited, transgressive types of behaviour in a clearly defined environment. (Another familiar example for transgressive behaviour allowed in a controlled environment and governed by rules and rituals is 'social' and thus legitimate drinking. Ordinary patterns of behaviour may be thrown overboard from time to time if the transgression itself is sanctioned and contained by another set of rules.)

When discussing phenomena associated with masks and disguises, one should keep in mind that, at least according to continental standards, a significant part of the English population habitually disguised themselves in everyday life. In, for instance, the principalities of eighteenth-century Germany, sumptuary laws were still widely being enforced, i.e. there was a clear correlation between the outward appearance of a person and his or her social status (Wieacker 1952: 108). Not so in England: there, the existing sumptuary laws had been allowed to lapse, and hardly anyone even thought of forcibly preventing people of a low social status from imitating the costume and appearance of their betters if they could afford to do so. In many cases they could as it was the custom to give even expensive clothes to servants because these clothes were regarded as being out of fashion after a short period of time.

Travellers from the Continent were invariably confused by this state of affairs which was, from their point of view, completely irrational and reprehensible. They positively resented what they regarded as mere underlings masquerading as fashionable people, especially in places of entertainment. (For one of many such examples cf. Alberti 1752, vol. I: 297.) It is well worth pointing out that, in sharp contrast to most European states of the day, dress and outward appearance were no more expected to be an almost infallible guide to peoples' status in society.

Something which would have been regarded as a masquerade, i.e. a highly exceptional phenomenon in most other countries, was here being taken for granted as a part of everyday life. This points to a comparatively high level of tolerance towards an element of disguise (and the potential confusion that went with it) in English urban society which was indeed remarkable if seen in an international context.

This tolerance extended to what one might call virtual forms of disguise, and a good deal of imaginative use was made of these from the late seventeenth century onwards. A vast number of texts published during this period were anonymous or pseudonymous: their authors chose not to disclose their true identity; instead, they disappeared behind a virtual mask. A continual sort of masquerade was permanently going on in almost all the new periodicals such as John Dunton's *Athenian Mercury* (collected in Anon./ Dunton, 1703) and the vastly successful *Gentleman's Magazine* or the *London Magazine*. Readers frequently engaged in lengthy discussions conducted by means of sending anonymous or pseudonymous letters which were then published. The protection offered by a pseudonym (which is a functional equivalent of a mask) made them feel free to join in an uninhibited public discussion while they themselves remained safely hidden in their own private spheres (cf. Heyl, forthcoming).

Such a discussion would have been impossible without this deliberately created artificial anonymity. It was commonly regarded as a grave breach of decorum to assert and defend one's own ideas against those of someone who occupied a superior position in society. An early eighteenth-century conduct book makes this point quite bluntly:

(11) Strive not with Superiors in Argument or Discourse, but easily submit thine opinion to their assertions.
(12) If thy Superior speak any thing wherein thou knowest he is mistaken, correct not, nor contradict him, nor grin at the hearing of it, but pass over the error without notice or interruption.
(Anon. 1701, ed. Whalley, 1983: 44.)

Rules of this type which governed peoples' everyday behaviour and which gravely inhibited any type of rational discourse could be suspended if face-to-face contact was avoided and if the discussion was transferred to a public and anonymous exchange of letters to the editor of a magazine.

A new use of *actual* masks became current from the 1720s in the shape of masquerades (cf. Castle 1986: passim). Masquerades were events which took place in enclosed spaces such as the pleasure gardens. One gained access by purchasing a ticket at a fixed price. Both women and men attending masquerades were completely disguised; the types of masks and elaborate dress they wore usually ensured that they could not be recognized as long as they chose not to reveal their identities. Although these masquerades were first introduced by a foreigner in 1717 (the Swiss Count Heidegger – cf. Ribeiro 1984:

3), their immediate success can only be understood if one sees it in the context of previous developments and preconditions which could already be found in London.

Bizarre as these masquerades might seem at first glance, people could rapidly get used to them because they represented an attractive amalgam of similar cultural practices which had been familiar to the London public for a considerable time. Londoners were used to the notion of masks being worn *in certain localities only*: the introduction of enclosed spaces with access controlled by the purchase of tickets merely reinforced this element. The old combination of the mask and the park resurfaced in a slightly modified but easily recognizable form in the shape of masquerades held in London's pleasure gardens. The equally established combination of mask and theatre was not lost either as the element of performance by everybody in front of everybody else became much more prominent. Just as in the theatre, the public (and now the *entire* public, both female and male) got a chance of appearing masked. The 'performance' element was now provided not by professional actors but by the public itself for their own benefit.

The main attractions of the older cultural practices associated with wearing masks were presented in an intensified form. Now, one went a step beyond merely playing with anonymity. The masquerades definitely and openly offered a chance to adopt a new persona, an alternative identity expressed in an elaborate costume – and they offered this chance to women and men alike.

The underlying progression informing this development can be traced just by looking at the development of the mask: the early type depicted by Hollar in the first half of the seventeenth century was only a half-mask; by the late seventeenth century the mask covered the entire face, and the early eighteenth-century masquerade introduced elaborate disguises covering the entire body. Thus, the element of anonymity grew steadily.

The masquerade retained elements of what had happened in parks and theatres before. It was less of a new phenomenon than a continuation and culmination of earlier cultural practices associated with previous settings. These earlier practices were replaced by their new incarnation as part of the masquerade scenario: Sources documenting the wearing of masks in London parks (and similarly in theatres) peter out in the 1730s, and it is no coincidence that this was exactly the time when the masquerade had fully established itself in London.

Both the masquerade and its links with the earlier uses of masks discussed above can only be fully understood if one regards this phenomenon as closely linked with the new and extremely powerful concept of privacy which was rapidly gaining ground in late seventeenth- and eighteenth-century London. Age-old networks of intimate social contact and communication had been eroded by the mass retreat into innumerable isolated private spheres. The masquerade gave a new chance of satisfying the still existing desire for social contact and communication while at the same time it satisfied the new desire for privacy. By means of a strategy of complete disguise, one could break the new taboos imposed on modern urban society. One could approach strangers and communicate with them without any fear whatsoever of exposing oneself.

As the element of anonymity was increased to a maximum, unprecedented liberties (especially between the sexes) could be taken – a circumstance much commented upon in the eighteenth century. Without a doubt, part of the masquerade's appeal lay in the fact that rules of propriety which had otherwise to be obeyed were relaxed or dropped altogether. Hence there are numerous contemporary warnings against the dangers associated with masquerades:

A Masquerade is almost the only Place where a Man has an Opportunity of entertaining a Woman alone. 'Tis the only Place in which a man, who is an absolute Stranger, can speak to you. The Custom of the World allows a Liberty in the Discourse there, that cou'd not be permitted any where else in the World: There is an Air of great Pleasantry, and great security, in saying the most tender and the boldest Things between Jest and Earnest; and he will stop at nothing whose Insolence you encourage, while you suffer it, and whose Presumption is nothing, while in a moment he can turn it all to Raillery; and as soon as he finds he cannot succeed, pretend that he never design'd it.

The Woman who is mask'd, under the Pretence of being between known and unknown, will bear a thousand Things, which if she was under a Necessity of confessing who she was, she cou'd not: And the Assistance of this to the Liberty which he takes, who pretends to be between Jest and Earnest, gives Opportunities to Things the most intolerable [sic!]. (Seymour 1753: 217 f)

On the one hand, the masquerade setting offered a higher potential of transgression than the park/theatre setting where wearing a mask had just been an option. On the other hand however, this new practice was much more circumscribed and limited both spatially and temporarily than what had been going on in parks and theatres. Masquerades were commercially organized events which were planned for a certain day and which took place in architecturally enclosed spaces. One had to hire a masquerade dress and purchase a ticket in order to participate.

The boundaries between the masquerade and 'normal' everyday life were thus made very obvious. Blatant transgression 'inside' a sphere designated for masquerades in a sense affirmed the status quo reigning 'outside'. Parks and theatres where one *could* but *did not have to* wear masks, in which one could just pretend to be an invisible observer or choose to become more active had been spaces characterized by a certain ambiguity. It was there that the world of the mask with its potential for anonymity and transgression over-lapped with the everyday world of what was taken to be 'normal' behaviour. This ambiguity was lost, and the practice of wearing masks was transferred to spaces of its own. All in all, the practice of wearing masks was being contained; its transgressive potential was both increased and at the same time crucially limited by the introduction of masquerades. Wearing a mask ceased to be an option which was freely available on an ad-hoc basis and became part of a commercialized, escapist form of entertainment.

It is a long way from the pre-modern face-to-face society, in which masks could be used as a punishment, to the manifold uses masks and disguises were put to in the early modern, urban social context of London. The mask lost all its possible sinister connotations of a pre-modern shame punishment and underwent a remarkable and significant metamorphosis from a cosmetic accessory to a notional and eventually an actual disguise.

Only a society which at least began to appreciate and to cherish privacy, and in which a stranger was respected as an unknown rather than feared as an alien and an outsider could be more or less at ease with the manifold use of both real and virtual masks and disguises. This is why, in the unique social context of London, forms of artificially created anonymity could proliferate from the late seventeenth century onwards.

Acknowledgements

The author would like to thank Penelope Corfield (Royal Holloway, London), H.R. Forsyth and Mireille Galinou (Museum of London), Ralph Houlbrooke (University of Reading), Paul Langford (formerly of Lincoln College, Oxford), Lynne MacNab (Guildhall Library, London), Diana Patterson (Mount Royal College, Calgary), Roy Porter (Wellcome Institute, London), Aileen Ribeiro (Courtauld Institute, London), Sarah Winbush and Jane Cunningham (Witt Library, London) for their manifold advice and assistance.

References

Alberti, M.G.W. (1752), *Briefe betreffende den allerneuesten Zustand der Religion und Wißenschaften in Groß-Brittanien* [sic!], 3 Vols, Hannover: Johann Christoph Richter.
Andrews, W. (1890), *Old-Time Punishments*, London, Hull.
Anon. (1760), *The Polite Lady: or, a Course of Female Education in a Series of Letters from a Mother to her Daughter*, London: J. Newbery.

Anon. (Dunton, J.) (1703), *The Athenian Oracle: being an entire Collection of all the Valuable Questions and Answers in the Old Athenian Mercuries*, London: Andrew Bell.

Anon. (probably Garretson), J., ed. Whalley, J.I. (1701, reprint 1983), *The School of Manners*, London: V & A Publications.

Brewer, G. (1812), *The Juvenile Lavater; or, a Familiar Explanation of the Passions of Le Brun, calculated for the Instruction and Entertainment of Young Persons*, London: Minerva Press.

Butler, S. (ed. Lamar, E.) (1928), *Satires and Miscellaneous Poetry and Prose*, Cambridge: Cambridge University Press.

Castle, T. (1986), *Masquerade and Civilization. The Carnivalesque in Eighteenth-century English Culture and Fiction*, Stanford.

Cleveland, J. (1647), 'The King's [sic!] Disguise' in *The Character of a London-Diurnall: With several select Poems: By the same Author*, London.

Cotton, C. (1689), *Poems on Several Occasions*, London.

Craft-Fairchild, C. (1993), *Masquerade and Gender. Disguise and Female Identity in Eighteenth-Century Fictions by Women*, University Park: Pennsylvania State University Press.

Crew, A. (1933), *The Old Bailey. History, Constitution, Functions, Notable Trials*, London: Bell.

Emmison, F.G. (1972), *Elizabethan Life: Morals and the Church Courts*, Chelmsford: Hutton.

Gordon, C. (1902), *The Old Bailey and Newgate*, London.

Habermas, J. (1992), *Strukturwandel der Öffentlichkeit*, Frankfurt/M.: Suhrkamp, (English translation – Habermas, J. (1991), The Structural Transformation of the Public Sphere: An Inquiry into a Category of Bourgeois Society, Cambridge, MA: MIT Press.

Heyl, C., A Passion for Privacy. Untersuchungen zur Genese der bürgerlichen Privatsphäre in London, ca. 1660–1800 (forthcoming).

Hollar, W. (1640), *Ornatus Muliebris Anglicanus*, London.

Hollar, W. (1643), *Theatrum Mulierum sive Varietas atq. Differentia Habituum Foeminei Sexus, diuersorum Europae Nationum hodierno tempore vulgo in vsu a Wenceslao Hollar, etc. Bohemo, delineatae et acua forti aeri sculptae*, London: V.A.M. [sic!].

Jackson, W. (1795), *The New and Complete Newgate Calendar, or, Villany displayed in all its Branches*, London: Alexander Hogg.

Larwood, J. (1877), *The Story of the London Parks*, London: Francis Harvey.

Le Brun, C. (1701), *The Conference of Monsieur Lebrun, Cheif [sic!] Painter to the French King, Chancellor and Director of the Academy of Painting and Sculpture; upon Expression, General and Particular. Translated from the French, and Adorned with 43 Copper-Plates*, London. *London Magazine* (February 1734), London.

Le Brun, C. (1713), *Conférence de Monsieur Le Brun [. . .] sur l'Expression Générale et Particulière des Passions*, Amsterdam: Picart.

Oxford English Dictionary (OED2) on CD-ROM, Version 1.01 (1992), Oxford: Oxford University Press.

Pennington, R. (1982), *A Descriptive Catalogue of the Etched Work of Wenceslaus Hollar, 1607–1677*, Cambridge: Cambridge University Press.

Pöllnitz, C.L.v. (1737), *The Memoirs of Charles-Lewis Baron de Pollnitz* [sic!], *being his observations he made in his late Travels from Prussia thro´ Germany, Italy, France, Flanders, Holland, England &c,* 2 Vols. London: Daniel Browne.

Ribeiro, A. (1984), *The Dress Worn at Masquerades in England, 1730 to 1790, and Its relation to Fancy Dress in Portraiture*, New York, London.

Sennett, R. (1977), *The Fall of Public Man*, Cambridge: Cambridge University Press.

Seymour, J. S. (= Hill, J.) (1753), *The Conduct of a married Life*, London.

Stone, L. (1977), *The Family, Sex and Marriage in England 1500–1800*, London: Faber.

Vanbrugh, J. (1698), *The Relapse; or, Virtue in Danger*, London: R. Wellington.

Wieacker, F. (1952), *Privatrechtsgeschichte der Neuzeit*, Göttingen.

Wycherley, W. (1675), *The Country Wife*, London: Thomas Dering.

Wycherley, W. (1694), *Love in a Wood, or St. James's Park*, London: H. Herringman.

Performing Selfhood: The Costumed Body as a Site of Mediation Between Life, Art and the Theatre in the English Renaissance

Ronnie Mirkin

The body in modern scholarship serves as a focal point for numerous avenues of research. Michel Foucault and Norbert Elias have even introduced a distinct area of historical research – the 'history of the body'. As Bryan Turner has stated, 'any comprehensive sociology must be grounded in a recognition of the embodiment of social actors' (Turner 1984/1989: 1). This has become an accepted fundamental notion and a major component in contemporary sociological, cultural, philosophical and historical scholarship. The body, in Turner's formulation, is paradoxically, a material, physical, organism but is also a metaphor (Turner 1984/1989: 7). It acts and is acted upon in the real world, but it has also an elusive quality, which makes it function as a sign and a symbol, as, for example, in the medieval and early modern notion of the 'body politic', or in the concept of the body as a microcosm, analogous to the macrocosmic universal structure. In contemporary studies bodies are considered as sites, environments and locations for a multitude of practices and discourses concerning the ordering and regulation of society (Turner 1989: 7–8). According to Outram, bodies can act as 'prisms', concentrating rays of understanding from different sources, which otherwise could never intersect (Outram 1989: 36). This chapter will follow Outram's image of the body as a prism, which brings together in the same space different rays from the surrounding world and re-emits a recharged light of comprehension to certain aspects of culture in a given period (Outram 1989: 5). I shall look at the costumed body in the English Renaissance as a prism where the ideologies, practices and the aesthetics of contemporary culture could converge. The costumed body in that period was, as I shall show, a site of mediation between real life, the visual arts and the art of the theatre. All these areas of human activity participated in the discourse of performance, which was paradigmatic to the age.

The major artistic genre in Elizabethan and Jacobean England was the art of portraiture. This is the medium through which the costumed body in Renaissance England can be examined. Portraiture actively participated in the social and political life of the day. It was used as a public means of self-advertisement for the powerful members of English society and has since remained the main source for the study of the costume of the period. The Renaissance was also the golden age of the English theatre, the age of Shakespeare and his contemporaries. It seems that the proximity between these two arts of self-presentation and representation is not accidental. The English Renaissance has been characterized as a period with a strong dramatic sense of life, where an intensified consciousness of the theatrical element in human interaction was felt (Greenblatt 1973). Real life, the art of portraiture and the art of the theatre are, therefore, joined by the performative element their 'actors' shared. As Stephen Greenblatt notes: 'the boundaries between life and art completely break down, and . . . the conventional distinction between reality and the imagination must give way to a sense of their interplay' (Greenblatt 1973: ix).

Most studies which take account of socio-historical embodiment or focus on the study of the body in society tend to overlook the obvious fact that human interaction takes place between costumed people, between selves who are constantly emitting and transmitting messages through their appearance – their visual, bodily self-presentation. Costume historians and semioticians of fashion tend to do the opposite – they analyze fashion and clothes while the body beneath takes a secondary position. I propose that an awareness of the 'costumed body' as a unified, functioning entity, embedded in social life, can open new ways for studying cultural phenomena. A site can be created in which various discourses may converge, allowing for the investigation of areas which otherwise lack sufficient documentation. I shall suggest that seen thus, a way might be found to explore the visual and behavioural aspects of performance on the English Renaissance stage, for which no real visual evidence has remained.

According to Victor Turner, the existential need to explain and give meaning to human experience entails what he terms 'cultural performance'. This is a ritualistic process of drawing forth through forms of bodily expression in space and time, prior to verbal formulation, a purposeful enactment which organizes the interaction between people and their world in every 'unit of experience' (de Coppet 1992: 16–17; Turner, V. 1982/1992: 12–19). This process is seen as a 'journey', a 'rite of passage', from one phase of existence to another. In the light of this idea, dressing and self-presentation through costume can be considered a ritualistic cultural performance, taking place at a liminal phase (Turner 1991: 94–5; 1992: 41) in the passage between private and public selfhood and between private-intimate and public-formal spaces (Turner, B. 1984/1989: 37).

The nature of social interaction as performance has been formulated by Goffman (1959) in our times, and illustrated by Shakespeare some 400 years earlier (*As You Like It*, 2.7, 138–65). When 'all the world's a stage', the passage from the private intimate realm into the arena of public selfhood, through the ritual of dressing for the role to be played in real life, is analogous to the process of the actor putting on his costume behind the scenes, preparing for the passage from his individual selfhood to the character he is about to perform on the stage. The procedure of portrait painting can be regarded in a similar way: the relationship between sitter and artist is described as a consensual ritual to fabricate the public identity of the painted subject (Brilliant 1991: 89–90). Thus real life, the art of portraiture and the art of the costumed actor on the stage, from various points of view, manifest the performative element in human interaction and in the process of the fashioning of selfhood. This theatrical strain is especially evident in Renaissance England.

Members of the elite of Elizabethan and Jacobean society are meticulously documented in the numerous portraits that have survived from that period. Portraits were one of their most important means for self-display. The costumes that encase their bodies, exhibiting the highest fashion of the time, are the main and most emphasized component of the composition. The flat and detailed style of the painting and the body language through which the images communicate to the viewer are a clear testament as to contemporary aesthetic and rhetorical norms, if we learn how to read them. Tudor portraiture in the tradition of Holbein, which developed in England during the sixteenth-century, and for which Waterhouse coined the term 'costume pieces' (Waterhouse 1978: 31), established a formula of a three-quarter length figure. This formula lasted through the first three decades of Elizabeth I's long reign (Fig. 7.1). From the 1590s onwards a full-length image became a favoured format (Hearn 1995: 171), giving the fullest information about the sitter and his or her costume (Fig. 7.2). Although they are painted in a non-realistic style, these portraits should be regarded as representations of real people, wearing real clothes artfully constructed, people who were embedded in a culture with strict rules of behaviour and demeanour (Bryson 1990). The works of art appear to become momentarily transparent. In Brilliant's words: 'It is as if the art works do not exist in their own material substance but, in their place, real persons face me from the other side' (Brilliant 1991: 7).

Figure 7.1 *Elizabeth I*, attributed to Federigo Zuccaro, *c*.1575, the 'Darnley' Portrait. (© By courtesy of the National Portrait Gallery, London.)

Figure 7.2 *Henry Wriothesley, 3rd Earl of Southampton*, Unknown artist, *c*.1595.
(© By courtesy of the National Portrait Gallery, London.)

The detailed information about the bodily costumed reality of the members of Elizabethan and Jacobean society in portraiture can serve as a means for a reconstruction of the theatrical presentations of the same period and the actors' performance on the stage for which visual documentation in this period hardly exists. This is an avenue of research that has not been dealt with before, although the visual aspect of the structure and space of the Elizabethan theatre has been fully studied, depending on a small number of questionable sketches, verbal descriptions, speculations and attempts at reconstruction. The rebuilding of the Globe is a result of such efforts (Mulryne and Shewring 1997). However, although scholars agree that costumes, not scenic devices, created the predominant visual effect on the open and sceneless Elizabethan stage (MacIntyre 1992: 2), and research has also shown that one of the major expenses of any acting company at the time was on costumes (Stallybrass 1996: 29; Gurr 1995: 194), hardly any iconographic evidence has survived of the costumed actors in the English Renaissance theatre. The growing body of performance studies concerning acting and audience response in the English Renaissance theatre practically ignores the importance of costume in the overall performance and the rhetoric power of the costumed actor on the stage. When dealing with the interrelationship between actors and audience in the Elizabethan and Jacobean theatre, and the messages and meanings that might have emanated from the stage at the time, this aspect of research is not considered. As Jean MacIntyre says, there is a 'blind spot' concerning the study of theatrical costume as part of the overall production (MacIntyre 1992: 2).

It is well known that the basis for the wardrobe of theatrical costumes was everyday apparel, which was purchased by the companies or loaned or donated to them (Stallybrass 1996: 298–302; Carson 1988: 51–2). But it is not enough, in my view, to 'translate' directly from the visual arts onto the stage the information about the nature of the costume, as it is usually done in designing period plays. The visual data has to be incorporated into the cultural context of the period, with its ethical and aesthetic norms and customs of behaviour. Only in this way does the possibility open for recapturing the nonverbal language and the rhetorical and communicative power of the costumed actor, in a period, which has left no visual traces of the relation between costume and acting on the stage (Fischer-Lichte 1992: 146). At the same time the theatrical event has to be understood as a communal experience that united audience and performers in one discursive world (Gurr 1989: 12, 50–4, 68–70; Mullaney 1995: 52–4). We can assume that among the members of the audience in the various theatres there were people who had donated their costumes to the acting companies (Stallybrass 1996: 301–4). Peter Stallybrass has demonstrated the lively circulation of clothes between real life and the theatre in

Renaissance England and the role of the theatres as engines of fashion (Stallybrass, 1996: 289–320). We could further presume that nobles and gentlemen who visited the theatres also trusted themselves to the hands of artists to have their portraits painted, dressed in their most elaborate attire. This proximity between costumes worn in daily life and by actors on the stage might serve as a clue as to a behavioural relationship between 'acting' in real life and in the theatre. An acquaintance with the normative, civilized, social codes of the period and with the structure of Elizabethan and Jacobean costume, and an understanding the range of gestures and movements which the current fashion allowed, will enable the scholar to decipher the messages transmitted through the body language and the costumes in the motionless portraits. I suggest that it is a similar visual rhetoric and body language that was also used by the actors on the stage.

One should not forget, however, when looking at the portraits of English women and men in the last decades of the sixteenth century and the first decades of the seventeenth as a source for reconstructing the costumed actors on the English stage, that the Elizabethan and Jacobean theatre had an all-male cast of actors. Women did not participate in this art of performance as they did in the contemporary Italian theatre of the Commedia Dell' Arte. This is to say that young men were impersonating the female parts in the plays, wearing women's clothes. Thus an added layer of performativity emerges, which engages questions about gender identities and anxieties that existed in the period (Orgel 1996: 31 passim). These problems have been extensively dealt with in recent Renaissance scholarship, but are beyond the scope of this chapter.

The use of the costumed images in the portraits as a source for the study of theatre costume offers two paths of investigation, which have close connections between them – the 'behavioural' and the 'structural'. By the 'behavioural' method I mean regarding of the overall event of portrait painting as a theatrical situation. The sitter, male or female, had to prepare, rehearse, his or her role in order that the result, which is the painted portrait, would suit the aim of the staging of the painting so as to create the desired effect. The elaborate, extravagant and complicated fashion of the period under consideration is a testament to the length of time and the assistance needed in the ritual of dressing for the part to be played in the portraits, in which the costume was the dominant feature and the carrier of meaning.

Queen Elizabeth I is the foremost example of this theatrical apparatus. She, who declared before her Parliament, 'We Princes are set on stages, in sight and view of all the world duly observed' (Greenblatt, 1984: 167), was considered the greatest actress of her realm. She is known to have used her wardrobe as a vehicle in the theatre of power (Arnold 1988: xv; Strong 1963: 20–1, Strong 1987: 20–1). Her costumed body, the way it functioned in her public appearances and in her numerous portraits, attests to the theatrical sense of life that prevailed in her age. Nicholas Hilliard, her favourite portraitist, recalls in his treatise the *Arte of Limning,* how she advised him about the best way to seat her in order to get the required results for her painted image, 'seeing that the best to showe onesselfe neadeth no shadow of place but rather the open light' (Pope-Hennessy 1943: 97) (Fig. 7.3).

Figure 7.3 *Elizabeth I,* by Nicholas Hilliard, *c.*1572–6, the 'Phoenix' Portrait. (© By courtesy of the National Portrait Gallery, London.)

Most of the Elizabethan and Jacobean portraits, especially the full-length ones, situate the sitter on a kind of private stage, often with a curtain draped to one or two sides of the figure (Figs. 7.4 and 7.5). The space in which the image is placed is not an illusionistic-perspectival Renaissance space but rather a symbolic one in the Mannerist style (King 1994: 33). A prop, such as a chair or a corner of a table covered with a heavy fabric, adds to the setting. One or two attributes, a book, a hat, a piece of armour (see Fig. 7.2) and heraldic and emblematic devices, add contextual data about the painted person. The body of the sitter, face and costume alike, is frontally well lit, with no shadow, in order to expose its every detail. The posture is upright and erect. The preferred gesture, especially but not uniquely for men, is that of one arm set 'akimbo'. Thomas A. King terms it 'that proud mannerist gesture' (Fig. 7.6). It connotes performativity, theatricality, aristocratic self-display. It registers the inherent, legitimate, courtly *sprezzatura* as described in Castiglione's *The Book of the Courtier* (King 1994: 24–5, 33, 37). The influence of Castiglione's *Cortegiano* in England is well known. Starting from its translation into English by Thomas Hoby in 1561, and all through the English Renaissance, it became the foremost guide to ideal conduct (Della Casa – Pine-Coffin 1958: 108; Kelso 1964: 13; Mason 1971: 34–5). As Wayne R. Rebhorn notes, 'the ideal courtier is essentially a performer, who produces beautiful spectacles continually before an appreciative audience' (Rebhorn 1978: 23). He is constantly and self-consciously playing a role and creating himself as a work of art. Bearing this in mind we should listen once more to Hamlet's instructions to the players:

> Nor do not saw the air too much with your hand, thus, but use all gently;
> for in the very torrent, tempest, and as I may say the whirlwind of your passion,
> you must acquire and beget a temperance that may give it smoothness.
> (3.2. 4–7)
> Be not too tame, neither; but let your own discretion be your tutor. Suit the
> action to the word, the word to the action, with this special observance: that
> you o'erstep not the modesty of nature. (3.2. 15–18)

These words sound as if Hamlet is quoting Castiglione:

> I have discovered a universal rule which seems to apply more than any other in all
> human actions or words: namely, to steer away from affectation at all costs . . . and
> to practice in all things a certain nonchalance which conceals all artistry and makes
> whatever one says or does seem uncontrived and effortless. (Castiglione 1967: 67)

It is probable that Shakespeare had read Castiglione in the English translation. But even if he did not, these were the ideals in the light of which the aristocracy

Figure 7.4 *Elizabeth of Bohemia,* by Robert Peake the Elder, *c.*1610.
(© By courtesy of the National Portrait Gallery, London.)

Figure 7.5 *Richard Sackville, 3rd Earl of Dorset,* attributed to William Larkin, 1613. (By kind permission of English Heritage, Ranger House, the Suffolk Collection.)

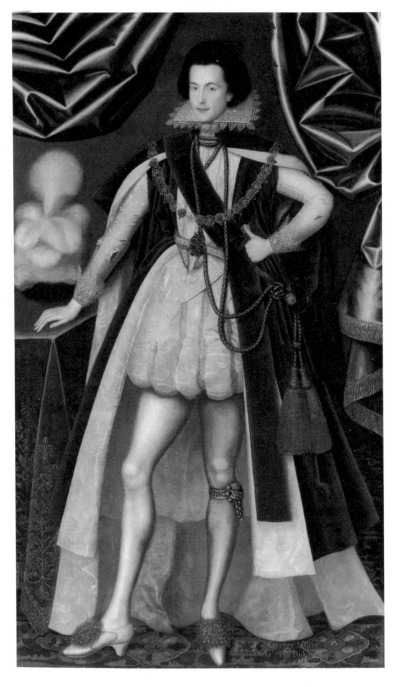

Figure 7.6 *George Villiers, 1st Duke of Buckingham,* attributed to William Larkin, *c.*1616. (© By courtesy of the National Portrait Gallery, London.)

of the time cast itself. As Bryson says: 'Through his manners the gentleman was supposed to proclaim his "natural" virtue and title to authority, but such manners were self-evidently the product of education, effort and artifice' (Bryson 1990: 153). Shakespeare must have been well aware of that when he created his fictive characters, which he arranged according to the social scale. Castiglione's rules for courtly behaviour must also be understood as underlying the visual and bodily messages and ideology, which the portraits of the period were meant to transmit when immortalizing the members of high society. Therefore it is most probable that Castiglione's behavioural instructions also provided the model of conduct actors who played noblemen and kings were supposed to adopt. As Greenblatt notes, 'The Manuals of court behavior which became popular in the sixteenth century are essentially hand-books for actors, practical guides for a society whose members were nearly always on stage'. (Greenblatt 1984: 162). The question is not whether Hamlet is instructing the players to act realistically when he asks them 'to hold as 'twere the mirror up to nature' (3.2. 20). For the ideal courtier, 'nature' was artificiality and his 'art' was to conceal all artistry. In Castiglione's words:

> The courtier has to imbue with grace his movements, his gestures, his way of doing things and in short, his every action . . . this is very often a natural, God-given gift, and that even if it is not quite perfect it can be greatly enhanced by application and effort. (1967: 65)

Effortless effort, the virtuosity of artificiality, or, in the words of Castiglione: 'we can truthfully say that true art is what does not seem to be art' (1967: 67), was the essence of the style and spirit of Mannerist art which reigned in Europe from the mid sixteenth to the early decades of the seventeenth century. It is this ethos, which is also an aesthetic, which brings together the art of portrait painting and the art of the theatre as participating in one cultural context.

The 'structural' method for exploring the rhetorical power of costume in art and in the theatre demands the study of the structure of the costumes of high fashion worn in the period. It is evident that Elizabethan and Jacobean costume was built so as to enforce the body to act according to correct rules of conduct. Right behaviour would strike the spectator with awe; wrong deportment would have a comical or grotesque effect. The most important items of clothing to determine the correct position of the body were the rigid whaleboned doublet and the stayed corset – stiff instruments for encasing the torso of both men and women and setting it upright. Georges Vigarello has shown how, as from the sixteenth century, conduct books and the emerging form of costume were teaching a similar doctrine. Careful attention was given to rectitude, which was becoming a moral as well as a civilatory-aesthetic symbol.

Beauty, proportion and decorum were considered outward signs of inner nobility (Vigarello 1989: 149–99, esp. 154 passim). Garments, instead of following the outline of what they covered, imposed their own shape to adhere to contemporary conventions (Vigarello 1989: 155).

To the upward enforcement of the torso by the doublet – the same term was used for this part of the costume for men and women alike (Arnold 1988: 142–3) – was added the starched, delicate, lace ruff encircling the neck, disjoining the head from the body and restricting its movement. Tight or stiffened blown-up sleeves separated the arms from the torso by means of 'rolls' or 'epaulettes', hindering any spontaneous movement. To restrict untamed movement there were further devices built into the structure of fashionable costume: the padded, inflated melon-hose for men and the wide, circular hoop farthingale for women (Fig. 7.7).

Going back to Hamlet's direction to the player not to saw the air too much with the hand, we realize that it is in accordance with the cut of fashionable costume: it did not allow for abrupt gestures, and thus abided by the rules for graceful aristocratic movement of the body. In Hamlet's words:

> Now this overdone, or come tardy off, though it make the unskilful laugh, cannot but make the judicious grieve; the censure of which one must in your allowance o'erweigh a whole theatre of others. (3.2. 22–5)

Whether it is Shakespeare or only the fictive character of Hamlet speaking through these words, they reflect the cultural norms of the day. High art was primarily designed to affect a select, educated, refined and appreciative audience and was guarded against being brought down to the level of 'a whole theatre of others'. This exclusivity of high art applies to both painting, and especially to the enigmatic art of portrait painting, which, through a series of codes, displayed and disguised the painted person, and to the new professional theatre emerging in Renaissance England, with its skilled actors bringing to life the sophisticated drama that was being created at that time.

By examining the structure of costume, a similar observation emerges as to the overall effect the costumed body created as was seen by looking at the codes of behaviour of the time: costume was designed to impose difficulties on the body, that had to be overcome with effortless effort. Wearing such a tyrannical costume demanded of the wearer to exercise *sprezzatura* in order not to look ridiculous. It demanded skill, agility and self-control, usually expected of actors, so as not to display the strain it caused the body, but rather to imbue it with grace 'the seasoning without which all other attributes and good qualities would be almost worthless' (Castiglione 1967: 65).

Figure 7.7 *Henry Frederick, Prince of Wales,* by Robert Peake the Elder, *c.*1610.
(© By courtesy of the National Portrait Gallery, London.)

Norbert Elias has explained the imposing of strictures on the body in early modern Europe as part of the 'civilizing process' and the emergence of the individual, the 'self', in this period. 'The transformation of interpersonal external compulsion into individual internal compulsion . . . leads to a situation in which many affective impulses cannot be lived out as spontaneously as before' (Elias 1978: 257). Thus the notion of self-control gives new meaning to the idea of 'Renaissance self-fashioning' as formulated by Greenblatt (Greenblatt 1984), when seen as an internal exercise of power relations. In this light, the art of portraiture and the performing art of the theatre can be interpreted as participating in the creation of modern subjectivity. They display through the costumed bodies of their actors, in the small theatre of the picture frame as in the open-air auditorium of the public theatre, 'that within which passeth show' (*Hamlet*, 1.2. 85). The two major theatrical arts of performance of the period become the arenas of an invisible psychological process, where selfhood is created.

The politically conscious English recognized the near-magical power of portraits and their ceremonial presence in the space they occupied, in which they could replace the persons they represented (Marin, 1988: 10–11). For Elizabeth I and her courtiers portraits played an important part in the strategies of government all through her reign. They were manipulated, through the representation of her Body Politic (Axton 1977; Kantorowicz 1957/1997) and the active participation of her enormous wardrobe, for the transmission of the messages of her rule in a symbolic and emblematic language (Fig. 7.8).

Elizabeth had a powerful presence in real life, but not so her successor to the throne of England, James I. He was, it seems, a physically repulsive and coarse person (Akrigg 1963: 5). There was therefore an urgent need, immediately upon his becoming the new King, to create for him a suitable official image, although he did not like sitting to painters (Hearn 1995: 184). Using the well-tested formulas of body language and costume, the court painters managed to overcome the obstacles of nature, and immortalized him and his Queen, Anne of Denmark, who was not a great beauty herself, in a series of impressive official portraits (Figs. 7.9 and 7.10). The structure of fashionable costume, with its ethical and aesthetic codes, helped the new rulers to perform the *sprezzatura* they naturally lacked.

Through the idea of theatricality and performance as fundamental constituents in the formation of selfhood in early modern England, the costumed male and female body, dressed in the extravagant fashions of the day, was seen as a site in which life, the art of portraiture and the art of the theatre could interact. Through the prism of the 'costumed body' of the period, the intersecting discourses of codes of behaviour, artistic style and theatrical performance open for modern researchers a methodology for exploring areas

Figure 7.8 *Elizabeth I,* by Marcus Gheeraerts the Younger, *c*.1592. The 'Ditchley' Portrait. (© By courtesy of the National Portrait Gallery, London.)

Figure 7.9 *James I,* by John de Critz, *c.*1606. (© By kind permission of the Dulwich Picture Gallery.)

Figure 7.10 *Anne of Denmark,* by Marcus Gheeraerts the Younger, *c.*1611–14.
(© By kind permission of the Marquess of Tavistock and the Trustees
of the Bedford Estate.)

otherwise obscured from sight for lack of visual evidence. The still portraits which continue to gaze at us today in galleries and museums are a silent testimony to a vital and vigorous culture, in which the body acted in the social arena, always aware of the eyes of an audience attentively watching (Freedman, 1991: 20).

References

Akrigg, G.P.V. (1963), *Jacobean Pageant or The Court of King James I*, Cambridge Massachusetts: Harvard University Press.

Arnold, J. (ed.) (1988), *Queen Elizabeth's Wardrobe Unlock'd*, Leeds: Maney.

Axton, M. (1977), *The Queen's Two Bodies. Drama and the Elizabethan Succession*, London: Royal Historical Society.

Brilliant, R. (1991), *Portraiture*, London: Reaktion Books.

Bryson, A. (1990), 'The Rhetoric of Status: Gesture, Demeanour and the Image of the Gentleman in Sixteenth- and Seventeenth-Century England', in Gent, L. and Llewellyn, N. (eds), *Renaissance Bodies. The Human Figure in English Culture c.1540–1660*, London: Reaktion Books; 136–53.

Carson, N. (1988), *A Companion to Henslowe's Diary*, Cambridge: Cambridge University Press.

Castiglione, B. (1967), *The Book of the Courtier* (1527), translated and with an introduction by Bull, G. Harmondsworth: Penguin Books.

de Coppet, D. (ed.) (1992), *Understanding Rituals*, London and New York: Routledge.

Della C. (1958), *Galateo or the Book of Manners* (1551–5), a new translation by R.S. Pine-Coffin, Harmondsworth: Penguin Books.

Elias, N. (1978), *The History of Manners. The Civilizing Process: Volume I*, translated by Edmund Jephcott, New York: Pantheon Books.

Fischer-Lichte, E. (1992), *The Semiotics of Theatre*, tr. by Gaines, J. and Jones, D.L. Bloomington and Indianapolis: Indiana University Press.

Freedman, B. (1991), *Staging the Gaze. Postmodernism, Psychoanalysis, and Shakespearean Comedy*, Ithaca and London: Cornell University Press.

Goffman, E. (1975), *The Presentation of Self in Everyday Life*, Harmondsworth: Penguin Books.

Greenblatt, S. (1984), *Renaissance Self-Fashioning from More to Shakespeare*, Chicago & London: Chicago University Press.

Greenblatt, S. (1973), *Sir Walter Ralegh. The Renaissance Man and His Roles*, New Haven and London: Yale University Press.

Gurr, A. (1989), *Playgoing in Shakespeare's London*, Cambridge: Cambridge University Press.

Gurr, A. (1995), *The Shakespearean Stage 1574–1642*, Cambridge: Cambridge University Press.

Hearn, K. (ed.) (1995), *Dynasties. Painting in Tudor and Jacobean England 1530–1630*, London: Tate Publishers.

Kantorowicz, E. H. (1957/1997), *The King's Two Bodies. A Study in Mediaeval Political Theology,* Princeton, New Jersey: Princeton University Press.

Kelso, R. (1964), *The Doctrine of the English Gentleman in the Sixteenth Century,* Gloucester, Mass.: Peter Smith.

King, T.A. (1994), 'Performing "Akimbo". Queer pride and epistemological prejudice', in Moe Meyer (ed.), *The Politics and Poetics of Camp,* London and New York: Routledge; 23–50.

MacIntyre, J. (1992), *Costumes and Scripts in the Elizabethan Theatres,* Edmonton, Alberta: The University of Alberta Press.

Marin, L. (1988), *Portrait of the King,* translation by Martha M. Houle, Minneapolis: University of Minnesota Press.

Mason, J.E. (1971), *Gentlefolk in the Making. Studies in the History of English Courtesy Literature and Related Topics from 1531 to 1774,* New York: Octagon Books.

Mullaney, S. (1988), *The Place of the Stage. Licence, Play and Power in Renaissance England,* Ann Arbar: University of Michigan Press.

Mulryne, J.R. and Shewring, M. (eds) (1997), *Shakespeare's Globe Rebuilt,* Cambridge: Cambridge University Press in association with Mulryne & Shewring.

Orgel, S. (1996), *Impersonations. The Performance of Gender in Shakespeare's England,* Cambridge: Cambridge University Press.

Outram, D. (1989), *The Body and the French Revolution. Sex, Class and Political Culture,* New Haven and London: Yale University Press.

Pope-Hennessy, J. (1943), 'Nicholas Hilliard and Mannerist Art Theory', *Journal of the Warburg and Courtauld Institutes,* 6: 89–100.

Rebhorn, W.A. (1978), *Courtly Performances. Masking and Festivity in Castiglione's 'Book of the Courtier',* Detroit, Wayne State University Press.

Shearman, J. (1977), *Mannerism,* Harmondsworth: Penguin Books.

Stallybrass, P. (1996), 'Worn worlds: clothes and identity on the Renaissance stage', in M. de Grazia, M. Quilligan and P. Stallybrass (eds), *Subject and Object in Renaissance Culture,* Cambridge: Cambridge University Press; 289–320.

Strong, R.C. (1963), *Portraits of Queen Elizabeth I,* Oxford: Clarendon Press.

Strong, R. (1987), *Gloriana. The Portraits of Queen Elizabeth I,* London: Thames and Hudson.

Turner, B.S. (1989), *The Body & Society. Explorations in Social Theory,* Oxford: Basil Blackwell.

Turner, V. (1991), *The Ritual Process. Structure and Anti-Structure,* Ithaca, New York: Cornell University Press.

Turner, V. (1992), *From Ritual to Theatre. The Human Seriousness of Play,* New York: PAJ Publications.

Vigarello, G. (1989), 'The Upward Training of the Body from the Age of Chivalry to Courtly Civility', in *Fragments for a History of the Human Body,* Part Two, M.F. with Ramona Naddaff and Nadia Tazi (eds), New York: Zone, (4); 149–199.

Waterhouse, E. (1978), *Painting in Britain 1530 to 1790,* Harmondsworth: Penguin Books.

Manliness, Modernity and the Shaping of Male Clothing

Christopher Breward

At the turn of the nineteenth century writers in the trade press for the men's garment industries found themselves caught between the older rhetoric of restraint which characterized traditional discourses of masculine fashion and the need to promote an increasingly expansive range of new clothing items marketed on the promise of health, vitality and the palpable display of the youthful and attractive manly body. *The Hosier and Glovers' Gazette* offered a critique of the modern man which set the arising poetics of male narcissism in high relief:

> We wrong women when we hold them up to ridicule for wearing three different costumes in a single day. There are men, and plenty of them, who change their clothes twice as often. Early in the morning the man of this class appears for a moment in a suit and hat of daintiest dove-colour. Then he mounts a horse, not so much because he wants to ride as for the sake of his white breeches and his yellow riding boots. Later on you see him, swathed in flannel, walk out with the ladies. But his brow is clouded. You imagine him saying sweet things? Far from it. The man has graver things to consider. He calculates in secret whether he will have time, before luncheon, to put on the proper attire for afternoon calls. And no sooner has he paid these visits and delivered himself of some gossip, than he hurries home and puts himself inside his lawn-tennis costume. Later on he wears evening dress, or his smoking jacket, which abroad goes by the name of shmoking. (Anon 1894: 28)

As this commentary reveals, modish clothing for men, far from conforming to the constraining dictates of renunciation, traced the demands of the social calendar as closely as the female wardrobe. In a sense, this tracing was far more clearly embodied than the decorative and largely immobilizing aesthetic that according to contemporary critics of the fashion-system still defined women's fashionable dress into the 1890s. (Wrigley 1995; Montague 1994).

A code of masculinity which stressed athletic vigour alongside moral fibre gave rise to a fashionable manly 'look' that was overtly physical in its appeal whether the wearer was dressed for riding, walking, tennis, dancing or even business. This chapter draws on recent studies of the social and sexual reconstruction of 'manliness' in this period to illustrate how a concurrent sartorial shift both reflected dominant debates in the field and offered a site on which arising visual and erotic models of masculine selfhood, could quite literally be pinned. I will argue that it is in the very seams and tucks of the modern man's wardrobe that rising concerns over the effeminizing effects of commodity culture and the declining state of the British physique can be most profitably read.

Dress historian Anne Hollander (1995) has shown how the transition from bespoke to ready-made forms of production in male clothing during the second half of the nineteenth century retained intact the design principles and antique ideals that had underpinned the emergence of the suit as an idealized repository of modern values in the late eighteenth century. The introduction of the tape measure and an interest in standardized measuring and cutting techniques from the 1820s which eased the move into mass-production, simply offered the promise of democratization to a tailoring industry already enamoured with the potential of platonic notions of the 'model' body. Where previously clients' physical details were recorded as notches on individualized lengths of paper whose marks came together to construct a unique cloth carapace, now the provision of published rules which presented systems of proportion as universal law lent tailors the ability to fit a generalized pattern to anyone who desired it. The transformative effects of padding, lining and darting ensured a fit as seemingly perfect as that achieved by more traditional methods. Furthermore, as standardized templates replaced archives of personal measurements, the potential for controlling and speeding up fashion change on a national and international scale multiplied significantly. Bodies could now be imposed on a massive scale, rather than simply disguised on an ad hoc basis and support for this developing trend is clearly communicated in the tailoring press. In a sense, new tailoring systems provided maps for the navigation of the ideal fashionable body: the guides for a terrain that in the context of a commodity culture was becoming subtly eroticized.

Edward Giles, editor of *The West End Gazette*, a journal for high-class London tailors, reported in 1887 that 'between 1796 and 1872 we have published, to my knowledge, fifty three coat systems' (1887: 190) and went on to illustrate the impact made on the tailoring trade by the circulation of these abstract systems which were engineered to produce idealized templates for the efficient cutting and construction of men's clothing, building on the technical advances noted above. From the 1820s in particular, and the introduction of standardized external measures, tailor publishers promoted a series of methods for reducing the mystery of cutting to the figure to a series of geometrical equations. *Mr Golding's Tailor's Assistant* of 1818 was one of the first. It proposed that all measures should be taken from the notion of a perfectly proportioned male figure 'whose breast measure exceeds the waist about an inch, and whose waist length exceeds the breast width an inch' (Giles 1887: 118). Giles noted that in retrospect such early templates could not avoid association with the fashionable line of clothing in the early part of the century, that strivings for 'grace and elegance' based on abstract proportions merely produced temporal approximations of corporeal beauty based on sartorial taste. In Golding's case this meant that 'the hollow curved lapels, the skimpiness of the waist, the amplitude of the skirts, the extreme fullness at the tops of the sleeves . . . combine to make a man appear to us as a figure of fun' (1887: 124).

Later pattern cutting systems abandoned a striving for the ideal in prefer-ence for the closer study of anatomy and geometry. In this way systems could be applied to remedy the imperfections of real bodies through the skilful manipulation of scale. Rather than attempt to make idealized models fit all physical variations, systems published after the middle of the century acknow-ledged the need for flexibility. In *The Complete Guide to Practical Cutting* published by Edward Minister and Son in 1847, the rigidity of a method relying on the precision of geometrical instruments for drafting purposes was softened by a realization that some men's bodies could not be reduced to the angle of a set square and the relationship between notional measures. The authors 'found by experience that a corpulent man's coat, when cut by proportions of his breast measure, produced a coat too large behind and consequently too small in front' (Giles 1887: 133). Similarly C. Compaing and Louis Devere in *The Tailor's Guide*, published in ten parts during the 1850s, offered a comprehensive survey of various body shapes and postures for consideration by cutters which gave priority to the careful observation of corporeal idiosyncrasies:

Inventors have neglected the fact that no machine can give a correct measure, of a flexible substance like the human body, because a piece of wood, leather or metal cannot feel as the hand does, whether the pressure or stretching is hard enough, which is an essential thing in measuring . . . It would be ridiculous to call on a customer and wrap him in a machine. Any man, whatever his build, can always be measured with the greatest accuracy by means of the common inch-tape . . . Many customers seem not to have patience enough . . . They do not like to be measured, and looked at in every way, as they well know that the aim of measurement is to ascertain where there is any imperfection in their body, and they are vexed that their tailor sees they are not the very type of the Apollo Belvedere. (c.1855: 18–19)

Herein lay a profound contradiction between the reality of the tailor's proximity to, and understanding of his customer's individualized, indeed sensile body, and a growing pressure to assimilate physical differences into a celebration of scientific progress. George Atkinson, who claimed to have pioneered the use of the tape measure as early as 1799, asserted in a self-promotional pamphlet of the 1840s that 'I reduced the trade of a tailor to a system.' Yet in the same article he also insisted that new methods and tools, improved rather than undermined more traditional, tactile and intuitive creative skills: 'I found that by constantly using [the measure] I could judge the size of a gentleman by my eye' (Giles 1887: 144).

The issue of judgement, skill and taste were raised most forcefully in the writings of Dr Henry Wampen, a German mathematician whose books on tailoring perhaps made the biggest impact on the practice of cutting and bespoke tailoring methods in the late nineteenth century. Wampen first published *The Mathematical Art of Cutting Garments according to the Different Formations of Men's Bodies* in 1834. In the 1850s he produced his *Anatomy* and *Anthropometry,* and in 1863 his most influential work *Mathematic Instruction in Constructing Models for Draping the Human Figure,* synthesized the findings of these earlier works. All of his texts were swiftly translated into English and Giles paraphrases his method thus:

> He states that as every body in nature possesses the two proportions of height and breadth, they must be both taken with consideration in draping the human figure. Every human figure can be placed under one of these categories, ie 1. The height proportion will be equal to the width, 2. Greater than the width, or 3. Less than the width. He urges that as tailors have to clothe the body some knowledge of this structure is requisite. By applying geometrical measurement to the various parts . . . he was enabled to deduct positive principles. (1887: 152)

The manner in which these principles were communicated was highly technical and Wampen's self-consciously academic discourse was engineered as an improving aid in raising the professional standing of the tailoring trades and as an encouragement for the setting up of tailoring academies. As he himself claimed: 'culture of the mind is the first element wherefrom arises all that civilises and improves us and by which means all men become equalised' (Giles 1887: 150).

Beyond raising the level of debate to an abstract discussion of the relationship between mathematics and sartorial aesthetics that fitted more comfortably within the rhetoric of the university than the trade manual, Wampen also inferred that the consideration of platonic ideals of beauty and the appreciation of the naked male form in its most perfect state might have some role to play in the design and manufacture of contemporary men's clothing. Recalling his early career Wampen noted that:

> I went as a student to Berlin, to complete my studies. I took a great interest in art and philosophy, and a question was then much discussed whether the Grecian ideal of beauty was simply ideal or founded upon scientific basis . . . I was induced to measure certain statues, and I came to the conclusion that the Grecian sculptors worked on scientific bases . . . One day a tailor who worked for me, a Mr Freitag, saw my sketches on a table when he said 'You are just the man we want; you must write something for us tailors.' (Giles 1887: 150)

The claims made on classicism, on an understanding that the exemplary physique of the ancient Greek athlete provided a fitting template for the production of a rationalized modern wardrobe, were visible not only in the propaganda of rival pattern cutters. Whilst the expansion of fashion publishing from the 1860s onwards clearly set the context in which competing tailoring systems could reach a wider audience, their material impact on the output of tailors is more difficult to ascertain. It is most unlikely that their complex equations meant much to the daily practice of jobbing tailors, and in the growing field of mass-produced men's clothing such theorizing must have been largely irrelevant. But in a broader sense the circulation of such ideas mirrored prevalent concerns, both in attitudes towards the display of the contemporary male body and to its fitting out in fashionable clothing. These concerns were especially visible in descriptions of the moment at which abstract pattern became second skin. The practical role of the tailor in translating chalk dust, tacking thread and pins to a bespoke suit of clothing fitted to the frame of the customer has generally been overlooked, overshadowed by those adjacent moments in the workshop or out in the street that have been prioritized by economic and labour historians or by literary and cultural historians, concerned as they have been with tracing histories of the sweated industries or with the footsteps of the dandy and the flaneur.

The key ritual of fitting-up may also have slipped from view due to its intensely personal, almost erotic characterization. Undoubtedly it was at this point that the tailor came into the closest contact with the body of his client. Here was a problematic proximity whose social implications did not escape the attentions of trade journalists, music hall lyricists and popular novelists. The transactions of the tailor moved towards the transgression of a fragile cultural terrain in which the potential breaching of corporeal, sexual and class taboos became dangerously real. Yet the awkward negotiations around limbs and torso also marked a process that was rapidly being superseded through the 1880s and 1890s by the more impersonal provision of the hosier's

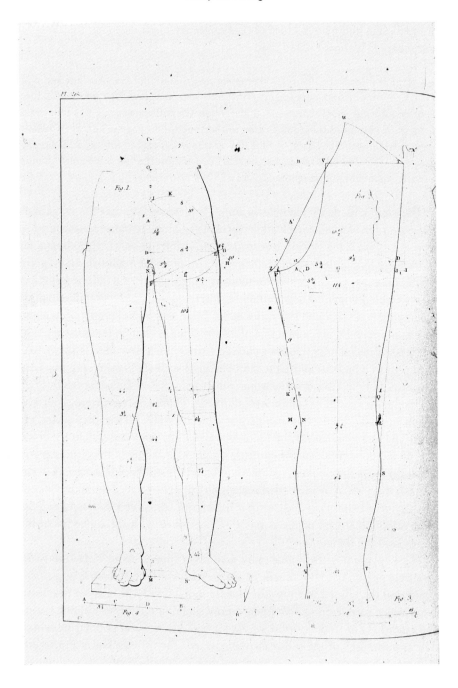

Figure 8.1 H. Wampen: Anatomy *c*.1850. By Kind Permission of London College of Fashion Learning Resources: Tailoring Archive.

and the outfitter's shop, where the pre-packaged nature of ready-to-wear products dictated a retail transaction in which the body was described in a less directly physical manner, at one remove from the cold hands and insistent tape measure of the tailor.

The columns of *The Tailor and Cutter*, a leading trade journal founded in 1866, reveal the strict protocol that surrounded the direct application of measuring systems to living bodies during the 1880s. The aptly named correspondent T.H. Holding, himself the publisher of several pattern-drafting tracts, urged readers who were making the transition from theory to practice to 'remember always that your hands are going about a sensitive intelligent man, and not a horseblock. First rule – never stand whilst taking any measures in front of your man, but on his right side. To do so is to commit a gross piece of familiarity, rather offensive in all cases.' Having established the appropriate position, the delicate manoeuvres required for the taking of leg measurements received particular mention as

> the leg measure is one of the very chief measures in a pair of trousers, and is often taken very faultily. With great quickness place the end of your measure close up into the crutch, then pass down your left behind his thigh . . . take thigh measure close if you use them . . . If a man's dress is right, well two measures thus 24, 22, will at once indicate which side that has to be cut out. (1880).

By this date, the revolutionary advice of system publications written at mid-century, such as that of Compaing and Devere or Wampen, had become codified into a series of gestures whose role in sculpting the body had become obscured by habit and glossed by etiquette. Clearly though, in adjacent cultural spheres the sexual primacy of the male physique played a central, if necessarily veiled role in formulating attitudes towards a modern masculine fashionability.

As previously noted, a shift from the use of traditional tailors to a much wider acceptance of the ready-made clothing offered by outfitters and hosiers characterized the consumption of men's clothing across social sectors in the United States and Great Britain from the 1880s onwards and to some degree this must in some part account for the self-consciously modernizing rhetoric of sizing systems and pattern-cutting techniques which formed the tailors' riposte to the competition of mass-production. This transition in taste was marked particularly in terms of style, broadening the remit of the ideal wardrobe to include standardized garments associated with sport and leisure whose adoption could increasingly be tolerated for more formal situations. The lounge suit for example, whose soft, simplified and comfortable cut had previously been reserved for relaxation in a domestic setting, had been accepted by 1910 as a regular component of business dress on both sides of the Atlantic

(Barraclough Paoletti 1985). Associated with this appropriation of sporting styles and fabrics for regular wear was an expanding range of goods designed specifically for new physical activities: cycling, tennis and rowing, promoted especially by new progressive retail companies including Austin Reed, Thomas Burberry and Gustav Jaeger. The knitted sweater for example emerged in the 1890s as an article suitable for strenuous activities, eminently muscular and hygienic in concept, though its design took some time to stabilize as this comment from the popular journal of masculine pursuits *The Modern Man* suggests:

> Sweaters are most excellent things, but they are nearly always too tight under the armpits. A garment which is essentially made for the athlete would, one would imagine, allow for a fairly robust physique, but this the average sweater does not do . . . In the matter of colour, I shall never be persuaded to wear a sweater that is not white. Those of grey and brown may be very nice and clean, but they don't look it. (12 December 1908: 24)

Similarly in bespoke tailoring trends at the turn of the century, methods of design strove to produce a finished article which both revealed the glowing physique beneath and promoted an image of hygienic rationality. Interestingly the process by which this effect could be achieved gave rise to internal debate in the industry focusing on the rift between systems that relied on padding and stiffening for a dramatic muscular effect, and those that saw the role of the cutter as one of more subtle means, where an understanding of anatomy and proportion revealed underlying forms rather than created them. The editor of *The London Tailor* clearly saw the latter method as the more tasteful, though both practices laid claim to associations with modernity:

> The new style is what we have termed the 'cast iron pattern of tailoring' . . . We made for a . . . customer a very soft Vicuna coat without stiffening or padding, nothing more, in fact, than French canvas and a bit of the thinnest horsehair in the shoulder. The coat was nice to the touch . . . and . . . fitted him like a glove. He goes 200 miles away for a sojourn in a health resort and gets a [new] coat . . . packs it up together with his ideal coat and sends it to us to re-make up . . . The coat he objected to had darts and slashes let into the canvas in every direction on the shoulder . . . from the front part of the skye back to the shoulder seam, the shoulder skye had been strained out until the pattern in the check Tweed was enlarged almost double the width . . . The shoulders were like epaulettes . . . The one was neat and natural and the other unnatural and absurd. But then from Portsmouth to Aberdeen it is the style . . . Nothing we can say is ever going to bring us back to that natural free-like tailoring that is to us so artistic . . . It is much easier to put a piece of cloth on a man's breast, and stiffen it out as though . . . with thin tin than to get a coat right that shall sit in its place. (1898)

At the centre of both trends – in forward-looking outfitting and scientific tailoring – sat a continuing preoccupation with the healthy and beautiful male body. The double bind was amusingly expressed in a series of Du Maurier cartoons published in *Punch* in the autumn of 1882. Titled 'Lost Illusions' they depicted the contrasting effects on the male figure and psyche of sporting and formal wear, reflected through the desirous glances of a potential female suitor. In the white flannel and knickerbockers of the tennis court the young

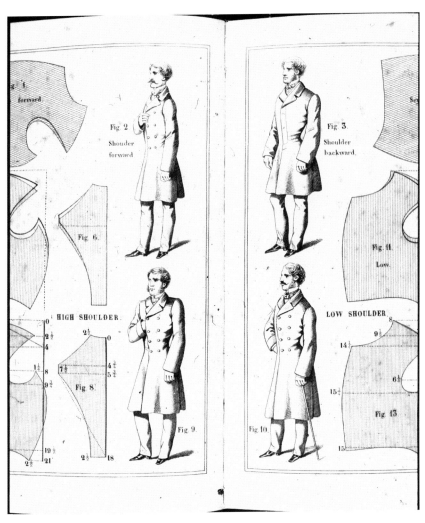

Figure 8.2 C. Compaing and L. Devere: The Tailor's Guide *c*.1850. By Kind Permission of London College of Fashion Learning Resources: Tailoring Archive.

athlete of the first plate 'looked like a young Greek god, fresh from Olympus'. In its contrasting pair, attired in the dapper morning suit of a London street 'he looked for all the world like a commonplace young clerk in some City bank – which oddly enough, he just happens to be' (1882). In a reversal of the sequence, published as 'More Lost Illusions' in the following issue, the new paramour, now a stately art pundit in the imposing great-coat of the intellectual, looks according to his admirer 'like a Greek god even in his every-day clothes! What must he be when he's playing lawn tennis!' Predictably expectations suffer a blow when his puny frame emerges from its well-cut covering to assume the requisite sporting garb: 'Poor Agatha! The spell is broken for ever' (1882). Whilst the widened choice of appropriate dress provided men with the opportunity to mythologize their physical attractions through recourse to the powerful effects of self-fashioning, their real bodies were at this stage more resistant to disguise. Yet as Captain L.H. Saunders, an advice columnist, affirmed twenty years later, even flesh could be co-opted for the purposes of fashion:

> Some men look better in a thirty shilling suit than others do in outfits costing ten guineas. The former have the gift of setting off clothes . . . something depends on the man's face, but most on his carriage and physique. He who is too short or too tall is never the possessor of this valuable asset. It seems to be the peculiar property of the man of medium height and athletic build. I am convinced that physical culture can do quite as much for a man's appearance as can the tailor, and I would urge my readers to develop their physique as well as to study fashion . . . But don't overdo it . . . the ideal from a clothes point of view being he who is possessed of rather more than the average amount of muscle but whose carriage is not rendered stiff by being musclebound. I believe the more active type of sports rather than such things as weight-lifting would give the desired result. (1908)

During the 1890s and 1910s the physical results of weightlifting provided a site for the spectacular celebration of the male form in London and other Western capitals. Pivoting around the near-naked figure of the body-builder this cult of muscularity found outlets on the music hall stage, in the circus and in the pages of physical culture magazines. Its broader political and social ramifications have received much attention in recent years from historians of popular culture, art historians and historians of masculinity (Anderson 1992; Boscagli 1996; Garb 1998) but, the relationship between these pre-occupations and the development of men's clothing has yet to be fully explored. This is surprising, as the fearful discourse of a degeneration of the national physique, from which the movement drew much of its strength, constantly used descriptions of clothed men's bodies to illustrate the woeful condition of the modern urban male. Anderson shows how the publications of J.P. Muller, a Danish gymnast and pedagogue, bracketed the promotion of military exercise regimes with a wide-reaching critique of the indolence of contemporary society. Published in England in 1905 and running into several reprints, his book *My System* equated the feminizing attractions of fashion with the muscle-weakening enforced immobility of office work, so that the feebleness of the clerk's body and the rise of blatant consumerism in city life were yoked together as the cause of a wide-ranging fin de siècle malaise:

> The typical office worker in big cities is often a sad sight. Hunched over in early years, his shoulders and hips made crooked by the awkward position at his desk, his face pale pimply and powdered, his thin neck sticking out of a collar that a normal man could use as a cuff, his foppish, fashionable suit rotating around pipe cleaners that are supposed to be arms and legs. (1992: 80)

Further attacks on the state of men's bodies made similar connections between stunted form and inappropriate attire, though to differing ends. Popular journalist Edwin Pugh displayed a visceral distaste for the inhabitants and fashions of London's East End in 1908, using a similar tone to Muller, but directing his polemic towards an attempt to arrest the erosion of the social order threatened by the increasing availability of ready-made clothing. For Pugh ugliness and degeneracy were symbolized by the inappropriate meeting of coarsened working-class bodies with the newly accessible trappings of modish living:

> This is 'Arry... He is small. Bad and insufficient air, bad and insufficient food, too much hard work at too early an age, and not enough healthy play at any stage of his development, have retarded his growth, have warped and stunted him. But he is tough and wiry. He is brimming over with super abundant vitality... His feet are big and clumsy: cheap, ill-fitting boots account for that ... one suspects from a certain slackness and abrupt bulginess about his sleeves and the legs of his trousers that his joints are disproportionately large ... He works hard, in factory, workshop, warehouse or office. He is not well-dressed, but he is at least decently clad in ready-made clothes, or clothes made to measure by some cheap cash tailor. Indeed he reeks of cheapness. Cheapness is his undoing. He has suitable clothes for every occasion ... but they are all of a like shoddy quality, and seem all to have been made for somebody else. And the effect of his big hands and big feet, his stringy sinewy neck and loosely hung limbs, is to accentuate this distressing element ... Fortunately, however, he is vain enough not to be self critical. He has enough self esteem to blind him to those fine shades and delicate nuances of costume and speech and deportment that he mimics so ... unconvincingly ... He insists on himself in public places ... he is the young man who gives each new catch phrase its vogue ... You cannot escape him. He pervades every phase of London life (1908: 41–3).

Thus the under-privileged East End body, suggested Pugh, could be appropriated for the nefarious ends of fashion, undermining any residual survival of the noble body of the manual worker. 'Arry's attempts to mimic the clothing and deportment of the aristocratic man about town as a means to project his self-image, to 'insist on himself', calls directly on historian Peter Bailey's conception of 'glamour' as an important motor for fashionable innovation and the control of sexual impulses in the chaotic context of the modern city.

THE IDEAL MODEL FOR THE NEW SUPREME SYSTEM

Figure 8.3 The Red Book of Men's Tailoring *c*.1918. By Kind Permission of London College of Fashion Learning Resources: Tailoring Archive.

Though 'Arry's posturing is a source of ridicule for commentators like Pugh, its description evokes a very corporeal projection of the self in city culture. Here a well-proportioned physical frame, with dress cut tightly to suggest muscular form and brightly to accentuate the possession of fashionable knowledge, could stand as a symbol of modernity; and to the wearer at least these attributes could come together to constitute a form of sexual attractiveness. Through a parallel study of the Victorian barmaid, Bailey has positioned this 'sexualisation of everyday life' at the centre of debates regarding the gendered experience of metropolitan material culture. The phenomenon of glamour, defined as a visual property utilized in the management of arousal, positioned its subjects in an illusory realm, physically or emotionally distanced from the material world of poverty, work or ill-health. Its forms were engineered to encourage an engagement with the practices of fashionable consumption and organized leisure: 'a dramatically enhanced yet distanced style of representation, display or address, primarily visual in appeal' (Bailey 1990: 168). The most familiar application of the device can be seen half a century later with the elevation of screen actresses to the role of Hollywood love goddesses. But its effects can also be seen in the alluring organization of shop windows, the sensual displays of the public bar, and the paraphernalia of popular theatre that marked London's West End in the nineteenth century.

The notion of glamour can also be read as the visual code of a broader sexual ideology which Bailey identifies as the 'parasexual'. This he defines as 'an inoculation in which a little sexuality is encouraged as an antidote to its subversive properties' (1990: 148). In other words parasexuality was a strategy for managing the everyday circulation of sexualized codes and practices in a culture that otherwise viewed the open display of the erotic as a destructive force. Here was a practice that could be utilized by the 'expanding apparatus of the service industries and a commercialised popular culture' in which the garment trades played a full role. As Bailey continues:

> It is on this distinctive terrain that the less august branches of capitalism converted sexuality from anathema to resource, from resource to commodity, in the development of a modern sexualised consumerism. Parasexuality, with its safely sensational pattern of stimulation and containment, was a significant mode of cultural management in the construction of this new regime . . . It is plain from its operation . . . that it worked primarily to valorise male pleasures . . . in a self conscious and mutual working out of new modes of relationship between men and women (1990: 167).

Taking into account the powerful 'sexual' element implied in the fitting and cutting of men's clothes to an idealized notion of the male figure, the sensual attractions of dress itself and the highly theatrical performance of its shapes and textures in public life, I would argue strongly for the application of a parasexual reading to the development of masculine sartorial taste and production in this period. The refinement of the proportions of the suit, the rise of sportswear and the popular communication of fashionable formulae amongst young male consumers from all social classes, allowed young men to assess themselves visually against other men in an increasingly competitive sexual marketplace. This led to a heightened awareness of their own sense of glamorous fashionability, as well as placing them under the critical gaze of potential female suitors. (In the homosocial realm of the club and the amateur sports team or the developing subcultures of homosexual prostitution and pornography this emphasis on viewing the bodies of other men was even more important to the negotiation of social formations and hierarchies, but work remains to be done on the role of fashion in these spheres.)

One muscular public figure in particular fully incorporated the characteristics of glamour with the celebration of an embodied masculine fashionability at this pivotal moment, smoothing the tensions inherent in hegemonic readings of manliness between the possession of moral fibre, the promotion of a healthy, athletic body and the duty to display status and distinction through dress. The music hall strongman Eugene Sandow was a Prussian subject, born in 1867, whose career as a performer developed in the context of an emergent north European health culture characterised by the work of both Wampen and Muller. Having studied sport and human anatomy at the universities of Göttingen and Brussels, he enlisted the growing influence of the advertising, entertainment and publicity industries to promote tours of Britain and the United States in which he set his own body on display. His act combined the aesthetic and erotic pleasures of the poses plastiques troupes who froze into three dimensional tableaux of famous paintings and sculptures, and the spectacular physical accomplishments of the acrobat or weightlifter. Sandow's particular contribution to the genre, however, lay in his use of his body as an agent in the moralizing crusade for an improvement of national health and as a site for a more commercialized celebration of male beauty. His emergence into the public consciousness was marked by *the Daily Telegraph* in November 1889 when their correspondent noted that:

> Personally he is a short but perfectly built young man . . . with a face of somewhat Ancient Greek type, but with the clear blue eyes and curling fair hair of the Teuton. When in evening dress there is nothing specially remarkable about this quiet mannered, good natured youth; but when he takes off his coat and prepares for action, the extraordinary development of the arms, shoulders and back muscles is marvellously striking . . . the muscles stand out under a clear white skin in high relief, and suggest the gnarled roots of old trees. (Mercer Adams 1894: 44)

Following acclaimed runs at the London Aquarium and the Royal Music Hall in Holborn, Sandow's reputation as 'Strongest Man on Earth' was assured and his fame was celebrated in popular song, as the subject of an early film by Edison, and in plaster cast at the British Museum. In the first two decades of the twentieth century his expertise was called upon by institutions as varied as the British Army where he advised on exercise regimes, and by the concert pianist Paderewski who credited Sandow as his personal finger trainer. Amongst the wider public his cultural currency was crystallized in the phrase 'as jolly as a Sandow', an expression indicating the innocent vitality and optimism of health, and publicized through several reprints of his 1905 book *Strength and How to Obtain It* (Boscagli 1996: 106).

However, what is especially significant about the Sandow phenomenon, other than its pervasiveness in the contemporary culture, is the way in which his image worked in juxtaposition alongside other public ciphers for a modern masculinity to promote a very avant-garde take on the male body as a site for fashionable discourse. So, whilst the puffing of such products as a pair of Sandow dumb-bells in journals like *The Modern Man* was entirely to be expected, bringing the promotion of physical education and pride in selfhood to its 'natural' subaltern constituency, the fixing of the strongman's image by society photographer Napoleon Sarony was far more piquant. A decade earlier Sarony had been responsible for capturing the self-promotional essence of Oscar Wilde in high-aesthetic mode, and in a sense both subjects engaged directly with the same issue of how to represent masculine sartorial desire on the body, though from opposing positions. As Boscagli notes whilst 'the polished exaggeration that popularised the aesthete's image had been achieved by dressing the subject up, in Sandow's photographs the bodybuilder is shown practically naked' (1996: 106). In another strikingly apt coupling, Sandow's theatrical friend, the male impersonator Vesta Tilley remembered him as

> a handsome, beautifully proportioned man, and a born showman. The ladies were particularly attracted by his performance, and he once showed me a good sized box containing all sorts of jewellery . . . which had been thrown on stage to him . . . He married the daughter of a well known Manchester photographer, and when, shortly after his marriage, he retired from the stage, ran a big physical culture business in London. (in De Freece 1934: 54)

Tilley's admiration for Sandow is telling. Both performers cast the paradoxes of contemporary fashionable masculinity in high relief. Tilley aped the gestures, phrases and appearance of a newly commodified and highly popular mode of public presentation for men, appropriating the very physical trappings of that mode, its tightly cut modern suits and sporty accessories, in a manner that served both to accentuate its validity in the minds of the audience and to reveal the oppositional power of the performer's biological gender. Like Sandow's, hers was a performance that could only have succeeded at a moment of profound transition in the practice and representation of the gendered body and in the organization of the clothing industries, for both acts revealed the manner in which masculinity was a case of directed consumption and public masquerade as much as it was an accident of nature. Their acts could well be used as examples of the bizarre, the artificial and the infamous, subjects that have been isolated as markers of a fin de siècle sensibility, undermining stable readings of gender and contributing towards the defining features of decadence (West 1993). And this despite Sandow's careful promotion of himself as a reforming force, purging all elements of physical and moral degeneration from the social body. Yet as the literary historian John Stokes has claimed, seemingly irreconcilable cultural forms were often viewed as coherent in the logic of late-nineteenth-century moral and aesthetic debates. The environment of the theatre formed a fitting arena for arising discussion:

> The study of acrobats left a trail of aesthetic paradoxes. There was the realisation that the spasmodic sense of danger felt by the spectator depended upon the fine equilibrium of the performer . . . It followed that the appreciation of acrobats benefited from a scientific approach, especially when their feats involved some distortion of the body that shifted the line between grace and deformity . . . requiring [the spectator] to demonstrate his sensitivity to the natural along with his openness to the abnormal, his wide eyed amazement with his cool headed analysis. (Stokes 1989: 86)

The endeavours of the men's garment industry, from the reforming of sizing and cutting systems to the wider provision of sports-derived garments offers a clear parallel to the display of the acrobat, the strongman or the male impersonator on the music hall stage. Men's bodies as a site of desire were being reappraised and redrawn. Responding to fears of degeneration and contamination the figure of the athlete presented the ideal formula for twentieth-century notions of masculine fashionability and attractiveness, though the maintenance of a fine distinction between vain excess and sartorial perfection ensured that the logical destination of fashion, a kind of sexual self-love, remained safely in check. As *The Modern Man* confirmed, by the first decade of the new century the male wardrobe was capable of concealing all manner of corporeal sins:

> At some time or another you must have seen a photograph of one of our leading 'strong men' in ordinary attire, and you must have been struck by the fact that he did not look any better than an ordinary individual, although you knew that his muscular development was exceptionally fine. (1908)

References

Anderson, M. (1992), *Kafka's Clothes: Ornament and Aestheticism in the Hapsburg Fin de Siècle*, Oxford: Clarendon Press.

Anon (1894), 'Fashions for Men' *The Hosier and Glovers' Gazette* (15 January).

Anon (1898), 'The New Style of Tailoring', *The London Tailor* (13 August): 1.

Bailey, P. (1990), 'Parasexuality and Glamour; The Victorian Barmaid as Cultural Prototype', *Gender & History* 2: 2.

Barraclough P., Jo (1985), 'Ridicule and Role Models as Factors in American Men's Fashion Change, 1880–1910', *Costume* XXXIX: 121–34.

Boscagli, M. (1996), *Eye on the Flesh: Fashions of Masculinity in the Early Twentieth Century*, Oxford: Westview Press.

Compaign, C. and Devere, L. (c.1855), *The Tailors' Guide*, London: Simpkin, Marshall & Co.

De Freece, V (1934), *Recollections of Vesta Tilley*, London: Hutchinson & Co.

Du Maurier, G. (1882), 'Lost Illusions', *Punch* (October 21): 186, 'More Lost Illusions', *Punch* (November 11): 222.

Garb, T. (1998), *Bodies of Modernity: Figure and Flesh in Fin de Siecle France*, London: Thames & Hudson.

Giles, E. (1887), *History of the Art of Cutting in England*, London: T.H. Holding.

Holding, T. H (1880), *The Tailor and Cutter* (15 July): 245.

Hollander, A. (1995). *Sex and Suits: The Evolution of Modern Dress*, New York: Kodansha.

Mercer A.G. (1894), *Sandow's System of Physical Training*, London: Gale & Polden.

Montague, K. (1994), 'The Aesthetics of Hygiene: Aesthetic Dress, Modernity, and the Body as Sign', *Journal of Design History* 7: 2: 91–112.

Pugh, Edwin (1908), *The City of the World: A Book about London and the Londoner*, London: Thomas Nelson.

Saunders, Capt. L.H. (1908), 'The Outer Man', *The Modern Man* (7 November): 24 (December 12): 24.

Stokes, J. (1989), *In the Nineties*, London: Harvester Wheatsheaf.

West, Shearer (1993), *Fin de Siecle*, London: Bloomsbury.

Wrigley, M. (1995), *White Walls, Designer Dresses: The Fashioning of Modern Architecture*, Cambridge, MA: MIT Press. 90–1.

Embodying the Single Girl in the 1960s

Hilary Radner

The dominant position in feminist studies exemplified by scholars such as Susan Bordo (1997) claims that consumer culture oppresses women by holding them to impossible standards. Scholars such as Elizabeth Wilson (1985) and Angela McRobbie (1991) emphasize how consumer culture in general and fashion in particular offer women the means of gratifying desires and pursuing pleasure. Here I will argue that photography in the 1960s illustrates the difficulty of assigning a fixed value to the relationship between women and the fashionable. Fashion photography in the 1960s offered a new ideal for women, one in which she is represented as autonomous and as democratic. Models were no longer anonymous and as household names were able to assume control of their careers. Nonetheless, the body that these photographs privileged was that of an adolescent. The adolescent body was freed from the constraints of previous fashions that controlled the feminine body through external means; however, these external constraints were replaced by strict regimes of diet and exercise. The 1960s ideal of the Single Girl, which would continue to dominate feminine culture, depends upon creating a seemingly impossible and delicate balance between self-gratification and social control. The woman is encouraged to adopt a mode of self-policing that she initially exercises on her own body. The complexity of this relationship to a self that owes its existence (its identity) to the very system by which it is controlled or policed should make us wary of either condemning culture as social control or praising it as self-gratification. This paradox should lead us to question our notions of 'freedom' and its possibilities. The development of fashion photography in the 1960s as a means of embodying a new mode of femininity illustrates the problems posed by the representations of freedom and action in consumer culture.

The Paradox of the 'New' Girl

In the 1960s, fashion photography and women's fashion were 'on the move' as a result of the confluence of a number of factors, which eventually would produce the very vocal feminisms of the 1970s. In the 1960s Second Wave feminism was only beginning to understand itself as such; however, it was preceded by the consolidation of a new feminine ideal. Young, single, economically self-sufficient, the ideal incarnated the notion of movement, of a culture in transition. The degree of control that women had over this 'movement' that they embodied was ambiguous. Fashion photography of this period expresses the paradoxes of the position of this new feminine, the Single Girl, as she would come to be called. Since she represented 'movement' her capacity to move was limited by the fact that her primary function was to signify the ideal of a period. This ideal is formulated through the publication of such popular works as Helen Gurley Brown's *Sex and the Single Girl* in 1962. Both in appearance, waif-like and adolescent, and in goals, to be glamorous and adored by men (in the plural) while economically independent, the Single Girl defines femininity outside a traditional patriarchal construction. At the same time, the Single Girl establishes consumerism as the mechanism that replaces maternity in the construction of the feminine.

Typical of the contradiction inherent in this new ideal is the evolution of fashion photography during the 1960s. Fashion photography in this period shifted stylistically, giving expression to the Single Girl ethos. The model is shot outside, often walking, or running; she is 'active'. This activity is not, however, without its contradictions. The body as an object constructed through consumerism also becomes an important element in feminine culture that is transformed and sold. As often remarked by contemporary feminists, this body emphasizes youth as the crucial characteristic of the new feminine ideal. Though fashion photography undergoes significant changes during this period, the meaning of these changes remains ambiguous.

Fashion and Art

Tom Wolfe recalls:

> Once it was power that created high style, but now high style comes from low places, from people who are marginal . . . who carved out worlds for themselves, out of the other world of modern teenage life, out of what was for years the outcast corner of the world of art, photography, populated by poor boys. (in Castelbajc 1995: 130)

Whether indeed, 'style' originated in the 'margins' of society is debatable; certainly, 'low' became 'high'. As art historian Martin Harrison observes, fashion photography undergoes a transformation during the 1960s in terms of both its subject and its style. Like many phenomena associated with the 1960s, these changes do not suddenly erupt transforming social discourse; they are symptomatic of larger and gradual mutations in culture during the post-Second World War era. 'New wave' photography freed the women from a domestic mise-en-sène and from the studio. It emphasized fluidity and movement, a certain style rather than a set of commodities. Harrison refers to this photographic mode as 'outside fashion', a mode that he sees as a representation of a new feminine ideal grounded in activity. These aesthetic and social issues were associated with economic changes in major consumer industries, clothing in particular, as well as such diverse events such as the shifts in Hollywood that resulted in a fragmentation of the film industry and the rise of the independent film. This new cinema, characterized by young European film-makers, for example, had a marked influence on fashion photography and its reception. According to Harrison: '*Blow-Up* (1966) defined the public's image of the 1960s fashion photographer. Ironically, Antonioni's earlier films had strongly influenced many fashion photographers' (Harrison 1991: 187). Indeed, David Bailey, (a primary exponent of New Wave photography and the 'model' for Antonioni's protagonist) claimed that his work had been influenced by 'films like *Jules et Jim* and Fellini's *8 ½*' (Harrison 1991: 211).

Fashion and the Working Girl

If the film industry was reformulating itself in response to the Paramount decision in 1948, the rise of television and the move to suburbia, the fashion industry was also in the process of transformation, as was the woman's magazine. The 'working girl', for whom Helen Gurley Brown revamped *Cosmopolitan Magazine* in 1965, was the new preferred customer, rather than the socialite of the pre-war years. 1960s designer Mary Quant asserts in her autobiography:

> There was a time when clothes were a sure sign of a woman's social position and income group. Not now. Snobbery has gone out of fashion, and in our shops you will find duchesses jostling with typists to buy the same dress. (Jackson 1998: 43)

Haute couture catered to the wealthy woman of leisure, who had the time and money to afford a wardrobe. Ready-to-wear assumes a woman of limited time and funds for whom fashion was practical as well as pleasurable. *Funny Face* (1957) designer Givenchy's ode to his muse Audrey Hepburn marks a transitional moment in the move from haute couture to prêt-à-porter, seemingly anticipating the new ideal promoted by Helen Gurley Brown. *Funny Face* is the working girl's (although paradoxically an intellectual one who despises fashion) fantasy: a story in which a shop girl becomes an haute couture princess. Yet it is not Audrey Hepburn in designer Givenchy's gown at the film's conclusion that will inspire future fashion. She is remembered for the black turtleneck and capri pants that she wears to frolic as yet unreformed in the cafés of Paris. Similarly Jean Seberg's blue and white striped cotton sailor's jersey seen in *Breathless* (Godard, 1959) has become an anti-fashion staple, from the boutiques of Agnès B. in the 1970s to the catalogues of J. Peterman in the 1990s. This image of a young woman, unattached and uninhibited, represents an ideal that continues to dominate public imagination, from Françoise Sagan's *Bonjour Tristesse* in the 1950s to US television's *Ally McBeal* in the 1990s.

The new ideal was young and single, but not necessarily economically or socially privileged, seemingly as accessible to the typist as to the duchess. The 1960s notion of 'the look' tended to undermine a concrete definition of style as ownership, something achieved through assembling a set of objects. 'The look' (a termed coined by Mary Quant, one of its primary proselytisers) also emphasized the element of surprise, of the unanticipated, of the continually new, as an attribute of the 'stylish'. 'Image, attitude and association – in other words, "the look" – were as important as the actual content of the product itself, whether this be a painting, a record, a dress, or a chair,' claims Lesley Jackson in *The Sixties: Decade of the Design Revolution* (1998: 38, 40). As Terence Conran, one of the designers responsible for Habitat, stated in 1965 'Expendability is no longer a dirty word,' or more picturesquely, 'Taste is constantly on the move' (Jackson 1998: 36). 'Activity' was a style, a mode of representation but it also implied an 'active' subject. Magazines stressed the importance of exercising and dieting. 'Underwear' and 'home appliances' highlighted in the 1950s (Castelbajac 1995: 130) were supplanted by products that promoted a body that was the result of self-control and that was ultimately concerned with its 'self' rather than others.

Fashion and Spectacle

Harrison (1994) argues:

> Women's fashion magazines were the first medium to present images of women for the consumption of women, rather then men, and the women depicted in these photographs – who after all represented their readers – began to be cast in active as opposed to the passive roles traditionally assigned to them in art.

Within Harrison's argument, the displacement of the fashion model from the studio to the outdoor mise-en-scène signified the construction of an 'active' as opposed to 'passive' feminine. This 'active' genre emphasizes the contradictions inherent in fashion photography, which hinge upon the coincidence of seemingly inconsistent terms such as 'street' photography and high fashion; spectacle and activity; provocation and commercialism. Unlike art, fashion photography obviously functions primarily within a marketplace that serves to sell clothes. Only belatedly does fashion photography sell itself as art, almost as an after-thought. The boundaries between art photography and fashion photography have always been blurred – photographers themselves crossing easily between genres. Institutions such as Condé Nast, a major publishing house that specializes in magazines, and women's fashion magazines in particular, were among the first to promote art photography as such in the twentieth century.

Ultimately, as a commercial genre that itself follows 'fashion' and the dictates of magazine editors, fashion photography resists the requirement of con-temporary high art, which arguably sees the work's fundamental goal as the expression of individual genius. Harrison attempts to define certain photo-graphers such as William Klein as having such a personal vision. Yet, if the photographer William Klein pioneered the 'street' look in fashion photography, it was the lesser known Frances McLaughlin or Karen Radkai who were equally responsible for furnishing *Vogue*[1] with these images of a new urban femininity. In his book *Appearances: Fashion Photography Since 1945*, Harrison himself underlines the significance of McLaughlin's work: 'Liberman saw in Frances McLaughlin, then only twenty-four years old, the ideal inter-preter of junior fashions' (1991: 42). In fact, the 1933 image that Harrison claims provides the seeds for this genre, which would flourish in the post-Second World War years, was commandeered by editor Carmel Snow. Harrison (1994) comments:

> (A) burgeoning new commodity she had to propagate was sports wear. Of all aspects of clothing, sports wear most clearly exemplified the modernist fascination with speed – streamlining, motor-racing, air travel, movies – all testified to the faster pace of urban life.

Martin Munkacsi, a sports photographer, who 'creates' the historic image at Snow's request 'not only instructed his model to move, but to run' (Harrison 1994). The genre develops in response to a 'client' that required a new aesthetic to promote a new type of clothing. The effect of spontaneity is a construction, designed to articulate this new aesthetic of urban life, produced through a hierarchy of 'instructions', of stage directions, geared towards creating a certain market. Stylistically, the genre exploits the techniques of immediacy (and disposability) that characterize the mass media in general. The Munkacsi photograph of Lucile Brokaw (according to Carmel Snow) is 'the first action photograph made for fashion' (Harrison 1994)[1]. This action is staged, made rather than taken, affirming the duplicity of the moment. The model is 'to be looked at'. She sells the new 'sports-wear' look as well as a set of specific items. She is not an athlete or soldier performing a designated task with an external goal. She represents something other than her 'self', even as she offers a model of this 'self' for the woman reader.

Yet, the contrast between this image and others of the period is undeniable. Brokaw seemingly moves outside the frame – her hand blurred, her leg extending beyond the formally inscribed field of the image. Her body is draped with a cloak – some sort of after-bathing apparel. Both the details of what one must assume is a bathing suit and the cloak are obscured by the lines of movement. The body itself as an entity defined by specific physical attributes overwhelms the structural attributes and details of her outfit: the musculature of a thigh is sharply delineated, one white shoe visible at the bottom of the page, the neckline of the suit itself hidden, her crisp hair softened by air rushing past.

In clear counterpoint (as Harrison demonstrates) a series of fashion photographs shot by Edward Steichen that appeared in the 1 May 1927 issue of *Vogue* emphasizes the image as a process of containment: the model is triply framed by the page and then within the page itself. The photographs portray a woman carefully posed for the camera, immobile, her body fully and conspicuously displayed, captured in its entirety. This body takes its identity from the clothes that cover it. Rather than asserting its independence, the body is subsumed, rendered abstract, by the clothes that cover it. Every detail is visible, including the details of jewellery and hose. Here, the image functions as a means of enumerating a set of items, which assembled constitute the fashionable look. Stylistically the image draws explicitly on fashion illustrations that offered similar portraits of an anonymous model, or even actual details of hats, shoes, jewellery, accessories, etc.

Transformations

This transformation of the feminine begins in the 1930s but does not take on its full importance until after the Second World War. In post-Second World War culture, mass-produced 'ready-to-wear' dominated the market. Style is reinterpreted in terms of the new economy of non-durable consumer goods. The new rather than the 'well-made' innovation, rather than quality, became increasingly the signifiers of 'style'. Ellen Leopold remarks:

The mechanisation of tailoring skills did replace this attribute of clothing with an alternative idea of apparel as a consumer durable designed to be worn until literally worn out. Instead, it preserved the possibility for a high turnover of an unlimited elaboration of styles. Constant renewal of designs substituted for high levels of output (1993: 115).

In the 1960s the new ready-to-wear lines replaced the individualized fashions of couture, in which a dress was made for a given client, as the expression of 'high style'. These ready-to-wear lines were important not only in terms of how they were manufactured but also in terms of what they 'sold'. They represented a shift away from formal evening gowns and a European look. Fashion increasingly concerned itself with day-wear and in particular 'working' clothes. This shift implied another setting for the fashionable woman. By the 1960s, it was the so-called 'working girl' (as Mary Quant observes above) who set fashion standards. For practical and aesthetic reasons the formal attire of the socialite (though still important to the scene of fantasy that fashion magazines offer their readers) no longer was constructed as the locus of 'correctness' and 'authority'.

Not coincidentally, the proper and the improper – the career girl and the working girl – the woman in the streets and the streetwalker – become less and less distinguishable. If the body that emerges is a minimized attenuated body, a childlike body, it is nonetheless a body that inhabits clothes as body. 'Nipples reappeared as a normal part of the anatomy' (Castelbajac 1995: 130). The body refused effacement, asserting its identity much as does the model that can no longer be contained within the image. During this period models develop an independent identity, a signature. The model emerges, the supermodel, as a significant author in fashion discourse, as a recognisable and recognized agent in the production of the fashion spectacle. Harrison signals this transition by including the names of the models alongside those of the photographer in his attribution. Steichen's models remain anonymous, though the collection – the couture line – is noted.

Individual and Identity

Fashion photography illustrates that it was not the politics of the 1960s activism that wrought changes in contemporary social fabric, changes now associated with the 1960s. Rather it was popular culture itself, far from resisting change, that posited the personal rather than the political as the new primary arena of experience and citizenship. The formula 'the personal is political' comes to characterize the new feminist values of the 1970s and the 1980s. This position, however, far from challenging consumer culture, affirmed its continued attempts to collapse the public and the private, to eliminate the public sphere as the forum of a specifically political engagement. This is not to negate the feminist's legitimate contention that private space had a political dimension, but rather to question the direction that this assertion has taken in contemporary everyday life. Fuelled by consumer industries' increasing need for new markets, popular culture encouraged the emergence of discourses that formulated an individual whose major preoccupation was the fulfilment of his or her needs and desires as the significant expression of citizenship. Helen Gurley Brown, and Betty Friedan, if divided in their sense of how best to achieve this objective, had in common their conviction that each woman had the right to fulfilment defined in her own terms. The sexual revolution in this context is a logical extension of social transformations in the twentieth century that posit the individual as the location of identity and fulfilment.

The anxiety generated by the construction of a social hierarchy in which identity is assumed in the workplace rather than the home – in which the salaried individual rather than the family became the fundamental economic unit – has been well documented. Media scholar, Lynn Spigel (1989), among others, has mapped out the cultural anxiety surrounding the domestic status of the feminine in her studies on advertising in the late 1940s and early 1950s. She claims that from 1948 to 1955 'women's home magazines . . . held to an out dated model of femininity, ignoring the fact that both working class and middle class women were dividing their time between the family work space and the public work space'. In fact, 'the fifties witnessed a dramatic rise in the female labour force – and, in particular, the number of married women taking jobs outside the home rose significantly' (Spigel 1989: 34). The Single Girl represents a strand in popular culture that embraces rather than denies work and 'singleness' as the emblem of a new sexual order. Helen Gurley Brown's enormously successfully transformation of the ailing *Cosmopolitan Magazine* in 1965, a magazine that clung to the outmoded domestic ideal described by Spigel, into a publication that spoke to and legitimated the working woman, or 'girl' as she was more popularly known, testified to the importance of these changes.

Symptomatic of the solution was a conflation of the categories of woman/girl into the category of working girl. In *Sex and the Single Girl*, Brown thus proposes, whether married or not 'a single woman is known by what she does rather than by whom she belongs to' (Brown 1962: 89). For the Single Girl, then, her identity is determined in the workplace rather than the home. The term girl maintained or at least represented the woman's status as nubile–marriageable–long past her youth or even childbearing years. Significantly, Helen Gurley Brown never had children and, as Nora Ephron points out, she is, forty-three when she takes over *Cosmopolitan Magazine* in 1965 and revamps its format from women's service magazine to handbook for the working girl. In so doing, she increases circulation from under 800,000 to over one million copies a month in five years, from 259 advertising pages a year to 784 (Ephron 1970: 22, 23, 29).

If the transformation of *Cosmopolitan Magazine* into 'Cosmo' illustrates the social diffusion of a new ideal, the figures within the fashion world that best represent this shift, the culmination of which is largely a 1960s phenomenon, are David Bailey, the photographer and Jean Shrimpton, the model. A brief analysis of a few crucial images of this period illustrate how these multiple discourses operated in terms of a 'thick' representation of the new femininity and its relations to fashion. Here we can see the formalization of the movement that we have traced from Munkasci in the 1960s itself.

Jean Shrimpton and David Bailey

In the 1960s, fashion editors looked for a 'face' that was somehow 'new', or different, while focusing on a certain almost perverse image of girlishness. The elfin Twiggy who was five feet and six inches tall, and weighed 91 pounds, measuring '31–22–32' at the time of her fame was one of the first models to be identified with the 'youthquake' (Gross 1995: 179). Yet Twiggy, one might say, was also the victim of the same phenomenon which saw the new ideal as one which depended on 'the dichotomy of youth and very high fashion' in the words of fashion photography Steven Meisel (Meisel 2000: 98). Twiggy epitomized the prefabricated face, the 'paper face', a face, reputed to be constructed and managed by Nigel John Davies. Twiggy lacked flexibility. She can only sell her 'self', and thus she retires at the age of nineteen (Gross 1995: 183). Shrimpton represents the new model. She is not anonymous. She must be both recognizable as star and capable of transforming her looks in order to conform to the demand for the continually new. Shrimpton continues to model into her thirties; she too, however, officially retires at the age of twenty-six (Liaut 1996: 108). Shrimpton as an icon functions as the synthesis between an older ideal of style as 'breeding' and the new ideal of style as 'disposable consumer object'. At five feet and eight-and-a-half inches, weighing 118 pounds, her measurements were '34–24–35' (Liaut 1996: 103). In spite of her height, Shrimpton projected an image of youth, wearing her hair in braids, carrying toys, often appearing dishevelled, un-made. Like Cindy Crawford in the 1980s and 1990s, Shrimpton had a certain wholesome quality that could be transformed but that never strayed too far from its origins. She always projected a defined and reproducible image.

In contrast, Wilhelmina, later a successful agent, who was perhaps the most financially successful model of the period, was too anonymous in her presentation. Not coincidentally she was known as 'last star of the couture era' (Gross 1995: 193). Her stature and dimensions also recalled an outmoded ideal. When she began her career as a model, she was five feet nine, and her measurements were recorded as '36–24–37'. She claimed 132 pounds but in fact weighed 159, 56 pounds more than the emaciated Twiggy. Though by 1967 she was in such demand that designers were willing to rip open seams in order to accommodate her size, her image remained of less importance than the clothes she wore. Wilhelmina was an expert in the art of self-transformation. One of her admirers reported: 'I was fascinated by how fast she could change hairpieces' (Gross 1995: 193–8). Though she had a defined image, unlike Wilhelmina, Shrimpton was also a 'working girl' who contrived a 'self' suited to a given occasion. She adapted to a given photographer while conveying a sense of identity, and continuity to the public. From the upper-middle classes, she moved easily between the demands of haute-couture and the new ready-to-wear market. Yet with her wide-set eyes, her winged eyebrows, generous mouth, thick hair, and almost coltish limbs, she appeared in a state of perpetual adolescence, a girl forever on the verge of womanhood. Though eventually she worked with most of the noted photographers of the period her relationship with David Bailey marked her as a model. To a degree she as his first star legitimated him, assigning the photographer a new role, as star-maker. The figure of the photographer as star-maker in this period comes not only to have an economic significance but also a highly charged erotic connotation. David Bailey is himself of working-class origins and is presented as a photographer who saw fashion as primarily a means of achieving a certain economic status in the world:

(F)or me, the sixties were really more about a class-structure thing anyway. It was about the emergence of a class that never had a voice before, the working class and kind of vaguely lower middle class. Until the sixties, the class structure here was almost like a cast system in India. If things had gone on as they were, I would have ended up an untouchable. But that all broke down in the sixties. (Gandee 1999: 540).

He also frequently remarks on the erotic aspect of his work, his relations with his models. He is infamous for remarks such as 'the only reason I ever did fashion was because of the girls', or 'a model doesn't have to sleep with a photographer, but it helps' (Gross 1995: 165–167).

Bailey, though at the beginning of his career himself, helps Shrimpton to create her 'look'. Yet in another sense he discovers her as 'the beauty of the century in a kind of democratic way'. He claimed that she 'was the first supermodel ... At one point in the mid-sixties, she was on the cover of *Newsweek*' (Gandee 1999: 540). Twiggy's look underlined her status as a 'paper face'; however, Shrimpton's look was as a set of gestures, a vocabulary of the body as it was a specific hairstyle and make-up. This new vocabulary of the body emphasized the body as such, the fact that it could not be contained by the image. This code of movement and gesture would be something that Bailey would teach generations of models, each transforming the vocabulary to suit the specificity of a new body and face displayed for the camera gaze. Harrison (1997: 27) elaborates in his study on Bailey:

> motion had been a touchstone of modernism (rapidly appropriated in fashion photography throughout the twentieth century), and the emphasis on exaggeratedly angular and anxious permutations of the fluid body was a central component of the imagery that Swinging London presented to an intrigued world audience in the Sixties (Harrison 1999: 27).

In order to represent this 'fluid body', to develop what Harrison calls Bailey's 'vocabulary of gesture', Bailey needed Shrimpton who was able to embody his particular vision, one that coincided with the historical moment (Harrison 1999: 28).

Bailey's genius, his acute sense of the moment is caught in that same moment. To be caught in the moment is also his great failing as an 'art' photographer. William Klein, who more successfully makes the transition to artist than does Bailey, self-consciously plays with the codes of the fashion photograph. Bailey fixes and formalises these codes. Shrimpton, in his photographs, has escaped the confines of the family manor. She has other possibilities than marriage to 'a Mr. Collins', the set of constrained choices presented to the heroines of a Jane Austen novel in which wife or spinster delineated the range of occupations open to a well-bred young woman; however, she does not have the purposeful stride of Klein's models who seem fiercely intent on breaking through the frame. Shrimpton as a model and as a professional, as the agent of her own interests, remained caught in her status as image. She never, for example, achieves the economic stability and flexibility of a Cindy Crawford who is able to control her distribution as image. Similarly, Shrimpton seems captured by the photograph, its prey and never its mistress. The model in Klein's photographs appears to have a very different relationship to the camera.

In Klein's photograph of Simone D'Aillencourt taken in 1960, the model walks directly towards the camera (Gross 1995: 184). She does not even flinch as a man on a scooter crosses behind repeating the horizontal movement of the white stripes painted across the street that she is crossing. Her inexorable passage is precisely perpendicular to the horizontal lines of movement literally inscribed upon the earth. The man on the scooter too seems unaware of her.

Another woman, another model, turns back to look as she moves, we sense almost regretfully, across the street towards a point somewhere in the distance, at which the white stripes will form a tiny triangle, the point to which all representation in 'perspective' must refer – *le point de fuite*. In the right-hand top corner of the frame, two figures move along the white horizontal lines, cropped such that only their legs are visible. The world is 'in movement', in an ordered pattern, articulated if not explained by the formal composition of the photograph. At the bottom of the frame, we see the backs of the heads of men turned towards the woman who advances upon them, oblivious to the manner in which they seem to block her path. The heads are fixed, a moment of stasis which the movement of the image must eventually confront. Indeed, it is the position that we, as the readers, of this image must inevitably take – arrested in front of it, blocking the very movement of the image in our attempts to decipher it. The figure of the woman advances upon us, intent on her own goals.

A famous photograph of Shrimpton, which appeared in British *Vogue*, April 1962, presents her similarly caught in the nexus of urban life (Harrison 1999: 46). Instead, however, of a series of trajectories that lead the eye out of the frame, Bailey reinscribes the frame through the telephone booth in which Shrimpton is literally encapsulated. The strong horizontal line of her black-gloved hand, even the black and white plaid of her suit, repeat the formal motif of the frame. If in some sense Shrimpton seems too small for her little box, her sinuous limbs not quite mastered by the geometry of the phone booth, she is at least momentarily captured. Her immobility serves a certain purpose: that of displaying the details of her outfit, the hemline, the cut of the skirt, the shape of the collar. And as if to recall the little girl that she really is, her teddy bear is perched atop the 'phone looking down upon her. A man in a fedora (a big teddy bear perhaps himself) stops and looks at the camera. He seems to lack the sense of purpose and integrity that we note in Klein's figures.

In another photograph published in the same issue, from the same series 'New York: Young Idea Goes West', still holding her teddy bear, Shrimpton stops at a corner and stares almost aggressively into the camera, though the crossing light clearly says: 'Walk' (Harrison 1999: 47). Should we fail to under-stand, another sign barely attached to the post instructs us to 'cross at the Start of the Green'. Shrimpton does not cross – rather she displays her outfit for us, for the camera, the clean lines of her coat, the rakish tilt of her hat, and the height and shape of her heel. We could say that there is a brutal honesty in her stare. It recognizes her function, which is to sell clothes, and then more clothes – clothes that will go with a woman/girl wherever she chooses, but clothes that nonetheless must be constantly renovated 'on the move' themselves.

Yet, something has happened. The comparison to the Streichen is remarkable. Shrimpton's stance aggressively calls our attention to her role as 'model'. Steichen's anonymous model is almost apologetic. Her eyes are modestly averted, looking off-screen, away from the camera, her legs are positioned in a lady-like manner, crossed one in front of the other, classical ballet's third position. Even in a studio shot such as that of Shrimpton and Terrence Donavan that appeared in *Vogue*, 15 September 1961 we notice a marked change in demeanour (Harrison 1999: 59). Shrimpton wears a neat little suit, her white gloves draped over her handbag (no teddy bears) placed on the ground. However, her stance, her legs akimbo, her torso off kilter, her arms and hands extending awkwardly along the lines of the body: these suggest a body in all its viscerality, and a body in movement at that. In contrast, Terence Donovan seems constrained, his body muffled by the frumpy and rumpled lines of his sports jacket and slacks. Yet, we note again that, if Shrimpton does not seem quite the proper lady, she is careful to display the details of the clothing and accessories she wears down to the chunky bracelet that adorns her wrist. She may be independent but she knows her job.

Klein and Bailey

Two details from American *Vogue* illustrate this contradiction at the heart of fashion photography represented by the careers and work of Klein and Bailey. In an unattributed series of photographs on 'rainwear', an unidentified model with Shrimpton's 'look' stops in mid-step as she crosses a street, adeptly displaying her coat, boots, gloves and hat (*Vogue*, 1 April 1962: 148). The motion of her foot serves to draw attention to the line of the boot, emphasized by the curb. In spite of the poor quality paper and printing, the fashion 'commodity' is clearly recognizable as a silhouette, the length and shape of the heel, and the column of leather sheathing the calf, are highlighted against the asphalt. The model may be free to wander but it is in a direction that serves the purposes of that which she sells. In the 1 August 1962 issue (62) the photographs are attributed to Klein and again they feature women 'outside', on the 'street'. Even in a detail, we note how Klein plays with the conventions of fashion photography, using them against the grain.[2] Here the image of the woman is that of her reflection in a series of glass planes rather than that of her 'self', a process of reflection that is doubled (a reflection of a reflection) such that woman and garments seem almost about to disappear. This effect of the disappearing woman is intensified by the poor quality of the paper and printing: she is strangely doubled. Ghostly and transparent, she is too many but not entirely present. The human is not recuperated in the work of Klein. Rather the aesthetic formal qualities of the model's face transformed through the camera render her beautiful as an art object, an 'objet d'art' but an object nonetheless that works hard in the service of consumerism. Thus even the work of Klein finally says: with the proper cultivation of the face and body through the use of consumer products all women can improve themselves. Only the camera, however, that renders them not 'themselves' – only reflections, shadows, traces – can capture beauty, a beauty that is ultimately inhuman, a technological invention.

Conclusion

This analysis should encourage us to greet the ethos of 'consumer empowerment' propagated by the fashion world with a certain scepticism. The active woman more often than not seeks girlishness as the goal of this activity. Her activity, then, entails the purchase of an array of products designed to promulgate and preserve this girlishness. This activity then impedes her movement along other uncharted lines into new and unknown territory. Where is the whole woman, 'woman' in her entirety?

The intimate connection between the feminine body and consumerism has been reiterated by a range of scholars. These arguments divide more or less between those who see consumerism as an invitation to own the feminine body as one's self and those that see it as a new form of domination. The articulation of fashion within the broader context of feminine consumption is symptomatic of these larger issues. In post-Second World War culture, high fashion clearly draws upon the subcultures of street life and of the avant-garde – subcultures generally thought to represent the extremes of social subversion by the dominant class in the United States. The new woman who roams freely represents the ideal individual as a free agent, who is most free in her control over the body. Fashion photography in the 1960s reflects a new vision of the consumer who consumes, but consumes freely. These expendable images point to the underlying contradictions inherent in a culture of consumption that posits individual fulfilment as its goal.

Notes

1. For example, see *Vogue*, 15 April 1947: 141 and *Vogue*, 1 November 1954: 86.
2. Klein's film *Qui êtes-vous Polly Magoo?* (1963) is a vicious parody of the fashion world that nonetheless depends on the same aesthetic that it critiques for its effect.

References

Bordo, S. (1997), *Twilight Zones: The Hidden Life of Cultural Images from Plato to OJ*, Berkeley: University of California Press.

Brown, H.G. (1962), *Sex and the Single Girl*, New York: Random House.

Castelbajc, Kate de (1995), *The Face of the Century: 100 Years of Makeup and Style*, New York: Rizzolli.

Ephron, N. (1970), *Wallflower at the Orgy*, (New York: Bantam.

Gandee, C. (November 1999) '1960s: photographer David Bailey revisits Swinging London', *Vogue*: 540.

Gross, M. (1995), *Model: The Ugly Business of Beautiful Women*, New York: William Morrow, 1995.

Harrison, M. (1991), *Appearances: Fashion Photography Since 1945*, New York: Rizzolli.

Harrison, M. (1994), *Outside Fashion: Style and Subversion*, New York: Howard Greenberg Gallery.

Harrison, M. (1999), *David Bailey: The Birth of Cool: 1957–1969*, New York: Viking Studio.

Jackson, L. (1998), *The Sixties: Decade of Design Revolution*, London: Phaidon.

Leopold, E. (1993), 'The Manufacture of the Fashion System', in J. Ash, E. Wilson (eds), *Chic Thrills: A Fashion Reader*, Berkeley, CA: University of California Press; 101–17.

Liaut, J.-N. (1996), *Cover Girls and Supermodels: 1945–1965*, trans. Robin Buss, London: Marion Boyars.

McRobbie, A. (1991), *Feminism and Youth Culture: From 'Jackie' to 'Just Seventeen'*, Boston: Unwin Hyman.

Meisel, S. (April 2000), 'The Moving Image', *Vogue*: 98.

Spigel, L. (1989), 'The Domestic Economy of Television Viewing in Postwar America', *Critical Studies in Mass Communication*, 6: 17–55.

Wilson, E. (1985), *Adorned in Dreams: Fashion and Modernity*, Berkeley: University of California Press.

Part Three

Contemporary Case Studies

Desire and Dread: Alexander McQueen and the Contemporary Femme Fatale

Caroline Evans

Alexander McQueen graduated from the MA Fashion Design course at Central Saint Martins in London in February 1992. His first collections were Victorian in inspiration, drawing on the dark side of the nineteenth century, rather than its picturesque representations. His graduation collection was based on Jack the Ripper and Victorian prostitutes who sold their hair to be made into locks which were bought by people to give to their lovers: he stitched locks of human hair under blood-red linings. Here, as in so much of McQueen's subsequent work, the themes of sex, death and commerce intertwined. For the show he encased locks of his own hair in perspex, creating an object which was both souvenir and memento mori; he had the idea of giving himself to the collection.

The *Independent* fashion report of his second collection was entitled 'McQueen's Theatre of Cruelty'. It read:

> Alexander McQueen's debut was a horror show . . . McQueen, who is 24 and from London's East End, has a view that speaks of battered women, of violent lives, of grinding daily existences offset by wild, drug-enhanced nocturnal dives into clubs where the dress-code is semi-naked. (Hume 1993: 29).[1]

The review spoke of violence and abuse, but not of the historical eclecticism which also permeated the show. This collection set the tone for those to follow over the next few years. Their mood was doomy and lost, savage and melancholic, yet also darkly romantic. In them McQueen developed an aesthetic of cruelty culled from disparate sources: the work of sixteenth- and seventeenth-century anatomists, in particular that of Andreas Vesalius; the photography of Joel-Peter Witkin from the 1980s and 1990s; and the films of Pasolini, Kubrick, Bunuel and Hitchcock. Through the mid-1990s McQueen explored and developed this aesthetic in a series of spectacular fashion shows. This chapter looks primarily at his first four years, from 1993 to 1997, surveying his early work by way of introduction before moving on to focus on two collections, *Dante*, shown in March 1996 for McQueen's own label, and *Eclect Dissect*, shown over a year later for Givenchy, where McQueen was, by then, principal designer.

His first show after his graduate collection took place in March 1993 and was inspired by the film *Taxi Driver*. The models were inadequately wrapped in cling-film and were styled to look bruised and battered. His second show, *Nihilism*, was staged in October 1993. It featured Edwardian jackets in corroded gilt, over tops apparently splattered with blood or dirt to create the impression of bloody, post-operative breasts under the sheer muslin. The collection attracted shocked, if not universally hostile, press coverage (Hume 1993) which McQueen continued to garner in subsequent collections. The aesthetic shock-tactic continued in the fourth, *The Birds*, featuring very hard tailoring which was based around the idea of road kill (Heath 1995: 102). The models at the show were bound in sellotape and streaked with oily tyre marks; these tyre marks were also printed on some of the jackets to look as if the model had been driven over. However it was the styling and presentation of McQueen's fifth collection, *Highland Rape,* shown in March 1995 and his first show to be staged under the aegis of the British Fashion Council in its official tent during London Fashion Week, which attracted the greatest criticism. The collection mixed military jackets with McQueen tartan and moss wool, contrasting tailored jackets with torn and brutally ravaged lace dresses and ripped skirts. On a runway strewn with heather bracken McQueen's staggering and blood-spattered models appeared wild and distraught, their breasts and bottoms exposed by tattered laces and torn suedes, jackets with missing sleeves, and skin-tight rubber trousers and skirts cut so low at the hip they seemed to defy gravity.

The show was described as 'aggressive and disturbing' (*Women's Wear Daily* 1995: 10). Much of the press coverage centred around accusations of misogyny because of the imagery of semi-naked, staggering and brutalized women, in conjunction with the use of the word 'rape' in the title. But McQueen claimed that the rape was of Scotland, not the individual models, as the theme of the show was the Jacobite rebellion. 'I'd studied the history of the Scottish upheavals and the Clearances . . . *Highland Rape* was about England's rape of Scotland' (cited in Lorna V 1997: 26). The harsh styling was intended to counter romantic images of Scottish history: 'I wanted to show that the war between the Scottish and the English was basically genocide' (*Women's Wear Daily*, 1995: 10). This was also the period of considerable coverage of atrocities in Bosnia and Rwanda in the Western press, a period in which the historical meaning of the word 'genocide' acquired a contemporary resonance.

However, the criticisms of his work as misogynist during this period tended to obscure its defining characteristic, the theatrical staging of cruelty. Although most apparent in the styling of his collections, his aesthetic of cruelty also extended to his designs where it was not only thematic but also intrinsic to his cutting techniques and his methods of construction. In the early collections cloth was usually slashed, stabbed and torn, and each garment was a variation on the theme of abuse. When he arrived at Givenchy in Paris in 1997 as principal designer the staff described their terror as they saw him approach a garment with the scissors, knowing he was about to cut up the couture model they had just produced, like a malevolent Edward Scissorhands. 'I'm intent on chopping things up' he said in an interview early in 1997 (cited in *Cutting Up Rough* 1997). Apart from the slashed garments, McQueen also developed a distinctive style of tailoring for which he became famous: razor sharp, its seams traced the body's contours like surgical incisions, skimming it to produce pointed lapels and sharp shoulders.

The *Vogue* stylist Isabella Blow who became his patron commented on the way his cutting techniques and his practice of historical collage came together:

> What attracted me to Alexander was the way he takes ideas from the past and sabotages them with his cut to make them thoroughly new and in the context of today. It is the complexity and severity of his approach to cut that makes him so modern. He is like a Peeping Tom in the way he slits and stabs at fabric to explore all the erogenous zones of the body. (in Hoare 1996: 30)

Blow, who said McQueen combined 'sabotage and tradition, beauty and violence' (in *Cutting Up Rough*, 1997), referred here to Michael Powell's film *Peeping Tom* in which the protagonist is a photographer who murders women in the act of photographing them by means of a bayonet attached to his tripod – thus the camera becomes the instrument of the death it records.

In McQueen's 1996 catwalk show for his collection *La Poupée* the black model Debra Shaw walked contorted in a metal frame fixed to her wrists and ankles by manacles. Disavowing the obvious connotation of slavery, just as he disavowed the accusations of misogyny in *Highland Rape*, McQueen claimed he wanted the restricting body jewellery to produce the jerky and mechanical movements of a doll or puppet (Lorna 1997: 26). The collection was based on Hans Bellmer's dolls of the 1930s which the artist compulsively took apart and reconstructed for a series of photographs, a process described by Rosalind Krauss as 'construction through dismemberment' (Krauss 1986: 86). Although McQueen's collection was not a literal reinterpretation of Bellmer's *poupée* in all his work of this period he shared with the artist a compulsion to dissect and probe. Bellmer's 1933 doll had six miniature panoramas fitted inside her stomach; illuminated by a torch bulb, operated by a button on her left nipple, and viewed through a peep-hole in her navel, the tiny panoramas displayed a collection of bric-à-brac which represented 'the thoughts and dreams of a young girl' (Webb 1985:29–30). Going beneath the skin of conventional fashion, McQueen's first collections explored the taboo area of interiority, breaching the boundaries between inside and out. The fantasy of exploring and probing the interior of the body, although commonplace in contemporary art, is habitually disavowed in fashion by its emphasis on surface, perfection and polish. McQueen, by contrast, actively explored the tropes of abjection in relation to the female body. In a television interview while he was working on the collection for *It's a Jungle Out There* he held up to the camera a piece of cloth with blond hair trailing from it like a pelt and said, 'The idea is that this wild beast has eaten this really lovely blond girl and she's trying to get out' (*Cutting Up Rough* 1997).

The cruelty inherent in McQueen's representations of women was part of the designer's wider vision of the cruelty of the world, and although his view was undoubtedly a bleak one it was not, I would argue, a misogynist one. And this was not because the designer often talked of the 'strong', uncompromising women for whom he designed[2] but did have something to do with his fascination with an uncompromising and aggressive sexuality, a sexuality which, in his *Dante* collection, shown in March 1996, came to resemble that of the fin-de-siècle femme fatale, the woman whose sexuality was dangerous, even deathly, and for whom, therefore, male desire would always be tinged with dread. And, in this context, McQueen's fascination with lesbian 'decadence' was significant in his production of the femme fatale:

> Critics who labelled me misogynist got it all wrong, they didn't even realise most of the models were lesbian. (in Lorna 1997: 26).[3]

> I'm not going to say my clothes are for lesbians, but a lot of my best friends are strong lesbians and I design with them in mind. If anyone's going to say my shows are out of order or anti-women it's going to be them, not some dainty housewife sitting in the front row. You can't please everyone when you design. (in Heath 1995: 102)

For the *Dante* collection McQueen used notoriously 'blue-blooded' models (Honor Frazer, Elizabetta Formaggia and Annabel Rothschild) whose make-up emphasized their chiselled features with pale skin and dark lips. The collection featured fine boning and military embroidery, braid-trimmed hussars' jackets and an eighteenth-century style gold brocade admiral's coat worn with a shredded lace dress and a black jet-encrusted headpiece made by the jeweller and art director Simon Costin. Costin's previous jewellery, which McQueen had used in his graduate show at Central Saint Martins in 1992, used the techniques of taxidermy and dissection. The deathly references were explicit in this collection in which fashion became the locus of darker meanings. Costin's jet headpiece made the memento mori imagery explicit, as did a McQueen lace top which extended over the head to cover the face like a hangman's hood. Costin was also responsible for the figure of a plastic skeleton seated in the front row of the audience. Further references to death included models wearing masks set with crucifixes, imagery which McQueen 'appropriated' from the grand guignol photography of Joel Peter Witkin; Simon Costin's earrings of dangling bird claws; arms caught in silver crowns of thorns; and Victorian jet beading. Stella Tennant modelled a mauve and black lace corset which drew on the collection's mourning colour palette of black, bone beige, mauves and greys (Menkes 1996: 10).[4] The model's berry-coloured lips, against her pale flesh, were vampiric and deathly. The high, constraining lapels of the corset, like an exaggerated wing collar, forced her chin up in a pose which also suggested an orthopaedic brace or truss. But in its dark sexuality, her image also recalled the Salomés, Judiths and Delilahs of the fin-de-siècle whose terrifying sexuality was so fatal to men.

The nineteenth-century femme fatale was, arguably, a fearful representation which configured female sexuality as perverse, even deathly, and which echoed fears about the social, economic and sexual emancipation of women at the turn of the century (Dijkstra 1986; Showalter 1991). Turn-of-the-century fears about syphilis were also articulated specifically in images of women whose sexuality was toxic, tracing a link between contagion and sexuality by suggesting that such women were the carriers of disease (Bronfen 1992; Buci-Glucksmann 1994; Dijkstra 1986; Doane 1991.) McQueen's designs, a hundred years later, although similar stylistically, conjured up a very different concept of the femme fatale. Like her nineteenth-century counterpart, the late twentieth-century femme fatale could be thought of in relation to fears about illness, death and sexuality, fears which were raised in relation to HIV and AIDS from the mid-1980s onwards. The ubiquitous rise of 'the body' as a subject for artists and cultural theorists in this period was linked, partially, I believe, to this. Specifically, the imagery of both art and fashion was permeated by Kristeva's concept of the abject, Freud's uncanny, and Bataille's *informe*, each of which was the subject of major exhibitions in the USA and Europe in the 1990s.[5]

What differentiated McQueen's late twentieth-century representation of the femme fatale from her turn-of-the-century counterparts, however, was that she was no longer depicted as an object of fear: rather, she became a frightening *subject*. Her highly sexualized appearance was a defence, but one which shaded into a form of attack. In the *Dante* show a model wearing Philip Treacy's headpiece of stag's horns created an image of a feral woman, only half human, recalling Baudrillard's phrase in *Fatal Strategies*: 'imagine a thing of beauty that has absorbed all the energy of the ugly: that's fashion' (Baudrillard 1990: 9). Her spiky, hybridized beauty and deathly pallor echoed Virginia M. Allen's description of the femme fatale as the antithesis of the maternal: 'sterile or barren, she produces nothing in a society which fetishizes production' (Allen 1983: 4, quoted in Doane 1991).

This, and other images from the collection, recalled the etymology of the words 'glamour' and 'vamp'. 'Glamour' is a Scottish variant of 'grammar' which, because of the association of learning with the occult, means a charm or spell. It was first used in its modern sense by Walter Scott in the nineteenth century. 'Vamp' (used in the early twentieth century as a verb 'to vamp') is an abbreviation of vampire. Allying glamour with fear rather than allure, McQueen's avowed intent was to create a woman 'who looks so fabulous you wouldn't dare lay a hand on her', a statement which was illuminated by the knowledge that one of his sisters had been the victim of domestic violence (Hume 1996: 82).

> I design clothes because I don't want women to look all innocent and naïve, because I know what can happen to them. I want women to look stronger. (Cited in Hume 1996: 82)

> I don't like women to be taken advantage of. I disagree with that most of all. I don't like men whistling at women in the street, I think they deserve more respect. (Cited in Marcus 1998: 148)

> I like men to keep their distance from women, I like men to be stunned by an entrance. (Cited in *Sunday Telegraph Magazine* 1996)[6]

> I've seen a woman get nearly beaten to death by her husband. I know what misogyny is . . . I want people to be afraid of the women I dress. (Quoted in *Vogue USA* October 1997: 435)

In the *Dante* show in particular, the chilly elegance of the models, with their accessories of shaved feathers, antlers and thorns, combined with McQueen's razor-sharp cutting techniques to produce an image tinged equally with desire and dread, an image intended, like the Medusa's head emblazoned on a shield, to act as a talisman to protect its bearer in an uncertain world. Medusa-like, McQueen's woman was designed to petrify her audience, dressing if not actually to repel or disgust, at least to keep men at a distance, rather than to attract them.

The representation of female sexuality as terror has a long history (Tseëlon 1995) in which the power of female display, or allure, is pictured as terrifying, sometimes deathly: Mary Ann Doane, in her book on the cinematic femme fatale, argued that women's power over men, their power to enchant and allure, was also a castration threat (Doane 1991). And Freud, in his brief essay 'Medusa's Head', of 1922, wrote 'we read in Rabelais of how the devil took to flight when the woman showed him her vulva' (Freud 1955: 274). Hence the ambivalence of most representations of the femme fatale, who comes to a sticky end, and who is frequently an articulation of male fears about the social and sexual mobility of women in transitional periods (Doane 1991: 2).

Yet McQueen's images of a woman so powerfully sexual that no one would dare to lay hands on her, a woman who used her sexuality as a sword rather than a shield, also drew on an earlier, and more dissident, representation than the fin-de-siècle vamp or her early twentieth-century cinematic successor. Both in the cruelty of McQueen's cut, and in the choice and styling of his catwalk models, he recalled, rather, the great female libertines of the Marquis de Sade, with their repertoires of savage dominance and mastery. Sade's dangerous female libertines were superwomen so exceptional that they were almost beyond gender; their power to terrify lay precisely in the distance between their purely biological femininity and their transgender actions. McQueen's first ready-to-wear collection for the house of Givenchy, shown in March 1997, featured extraordinarily tall models, whose long coats and micro-minis emphasized their height, which was further augmented by especially tall wigs and high stiletto heels. These terrifyingly tall amazons stalked the runway. The bruised and battered models of the earlier collections had given way, by approximately 1997, to a regiment of superwomen. McQueen, like Sade, was fascinated by a dialectical relationship between victim and aggressor, and the parade of women he created on the catwalk resembled Sade's aggressors rather than their victims. They were far removed from, say, the parodic humour of Thierry Mugler's use of actual drag-queens as models, for example in his spring-summer 1992 collection where he used the female impersonator Ru Paul as a model. McQueen's runway suggested a world without men, not because men were absent from it (for they were not), but because it was a world in which gender was unsettled by women who were both hyperfeminine and yet, in some respects, terrifyingly male.

In his collections of this period McQueen began to evidence a fascination with the dynamics of power, in particular with a dialectical relationship between predator and prey, between victim and aggressor. In *Dante* Stella Tennant modelled with a hooded and tethered bird of prey on her wrist; in *Eclect Dissect*

McQueen came onto the runway for his end-of-show bow with a tethered bird of prey on his. In his visual imagination there operated an economy very like that of double entry bookkeeping: every instance of goodness was balanced by one of cruelty, every gesture of dominance also sketched a gesture of sub-servience. As his shows progressed the victimized model gave way to a more powerful image, as prey became predator. In *It's a Jungle Out There*, shown in February 1997 in London's Borough Market, McQueen meditated on the theme of the Thomson's Gazelle and its terrible vulnerability to predators. He used the idea of animal instincts in the natural world as metaphor for the dog-eats-dog nature of the urban jungle, staging the show against a forty foot-high screen of corrugated iron drilled with imitation bullet holes and surrounded by wrecked cars, adding dry ice and crimson lighting for drama. In a television interview he said,

> The whole show feeling was about the Thomson's Gazelle. It's a poor little critter
> – the markings are lovely, it's got these dark eyes, the white and black with the tan
> markings on the side, the horns – but it is the food chain of Africa. As soon as it's
> born it's dead, I mean you're lucky if it lasts a few months, and that's how I see
> human life, in the same way. You know, we can all be discarded quite easily...
> you're there, you're gone, it's a jungle out there! (in *Cutting Up Rough* 1997).

Yet the design and styling of a hide jacket with pointed shoulders from which a pair of twisting gazelle horns stood up, worn by a model whose metallic contact lenses made her look like an alien, subverted the fatal passivity of the Thomson's Gazelle. Though the animal was referred to in the model's dramatic black and white face make-up, the horns, and the hide jacket, McQueen repositioned its parts and added the huge shoulders and metallic contact lenses to create a woman more like Rider Hagard's *She*: predatory, scary, powerful, and only half human. These were the characteristics of McQueen's femme fatale, a figure who suggested the terrifying power of women rather than their soft vulnerability.

Angela Carter's *The Sadeian Woman*, first published in 1979 by the feminist press Virago, was a late twentieth-century interpretation of the problems Sade raised about the culturally determined nature of women. Carter wrote that Sade's heroines healed themselves of their socially inflicted wounds through sexual violence, for 'a repressive society turns all eroticism into violence' (Carter 1979: 26). Sade, she wrote, 'cuts up the bodies of women and reassembles them in the shapes of his own delirium' (1979: 26). Four women – the ruthless and self-serving Juliette, the aristocratic man-hater Clairwil, the microbiologist, poisoner and magician Durand, and the voluptuary Princess Borghese – are merely four examples of what Carter (1979: 25) called 'a museum of woman-monsters' that Sade conjured up because, she wrote, 'a free woman in an unfree society will be a monster' (1979: 27).

McQueen created his own 'museum of woman-monsters' in his second couture collection for Givenchy, *Eclect Dissect,* shown in July 1997. In thinking up the theme of the show his art director Simon Costin combined, in a single collage, the late Victorian costumes McQueen was currently looking at with a series of animated skeletons and muscle men from the sixteenth-century anatomical plates of Andreas Vesalius; the cut of some of the dresses in the collection was influenced by the figures from these anatomical plates in which the skeletons vogue, modelling their own bodies. The concept behind the collection was a paragraph written by Costin who dreamed up a fictional fin-de-siècle surgeon and collector who travelled the world collecting exotic objects, textiles and women which he subsequently cut up and reassembled in his laboratory. The 'scenario' of the catwalk show staged the return of these gruesomely murdered women who came back to haunt the living. It was shown in a Paris medical school, swathed with blood-red velvet curtains and decorated with medical specimens. The models impersonated the ghosts of the long-dead women, dressed in the exotica collected by their murderer on his foreign journeys. Spanish lace, Burmese necklaces, Japanese kimonos and Russian folk dresses were jumbled up with the art of the taxidermist: stuffed animals and birds, and animals' skulls. The models, tall and imposing, were not, however, victims but vengeful ghosts. One strode out in an outfit which fused Madam Butterfly kitsch with an imposing dominatrix look: the Japanese obi became a corset, the kimono a tight, Western skirt, in a late twentieth-century interpretation of Mirabeau's turn-of-the-century text, *The Torture Garden.* The analogy between the doctor and the designer as anatomist was clear. McQueen himself could be seen as a kind of anatomist, dissecting and flaying conventional fashion to show us the death's head beneath the surface, and, particularly, the link between eroticism and death which permeated so much of the fashion imagery of the 1990s.

Carter made the case for Sade as a 'terrorist of the imagination', a 'sexual guerrilla', who revealed that everyday social, economic and political relations were mirrored in sexual relations. In Sade's writings, the cruelty of statesmen, princes and popes exceeded that of all other men. Yet his great women were even more cruel still, as they used their sexuality in an act of vengeance in a world which otherwise condemned them to a life of passive endurance – a life of victimization without power or autonomy, like that of Sade's virtuous Justine. So although the pornographer as terrorist may not think of himself as a friend of women, he is always their unconscious ally because he approaches some kind of emblematic truth about gender relations and power.

Carter described Sade's late eighteenth-century writing as being at the threshold of the modern period, looking simultaneously backward to the ancient régime and forward to a revolutionary future. A hundred years later, at the beginning of the twentieth century, the French poet and critic Guillaume Apollinaire equated Sade's undoubtedly monstrous Juliette with the New Woman, writing – admiringly – that Juliette was the woman whose advent Sade, at the beginning of the nineteenth century, could only anticipate (1979: 75). Yet Carter herself qualified her original assertion that Sade's women were free women. In his darkly mechanistic world women were *either* sacrificial victims *or* ritual murderesses, but in either case always overseen by men, a world in which every instance of freedom was balanced by one of repression. This dialectical structure can be mapped onto McQueen's visually plotted universe in which victims mutated into amazons, a shield became a sword, the woman's body an emblematic Medusa's head.

Yet Sade's female libertines, or McQueen's amazonian models, cannot be classified simply as New Women for a new age, for the woman as aggressor is no freer from the trammels of gender relations than her dialectical sister, the woman as victim. If one is a pawn and the other a queen, free to go where she will, nevertheless there is always a king elsewhere on the board, a lord of the game (1979: 80). Sade's free-wheeling Juliette was as locked into a dialectic of gender, power and sexual violence, even as she transcended them, as the enslaved and miserable Justine.

Yet Sade's pornographic narratives were also a critique of the nature and exercise of power, in particular of political oppression, in his own time and, like McQueen's, his vision was singularly dark. Carter wrote that, for Sade, 'all tenderness is false . . . all beds are minefields' (1979: 25). Similarly, for McQueen, there could be no sanctified view of history, culture or politics. The past was neither picturesque nor romantic. Such views merely served to mask vicious realities, and a desire to strip history of its romance defined McQueen's imagery. Whereas a designer such as John Galliano romanticized history and culture, McQueen made it harsh and painful to watch, as in the *Highland Rape* collection.[6] In building McQueen's 'yob' reputation, journalists stressed his working-class upbringing, his education in a sink school in East London, and his taxi-driver father, but underemphasized the fact that his mother was a local historian and former lecturer. As a child, he was taken with her to St Catherine's House where she researched the McQueen family origins, discovering that they had been Spitalfields Huguenots, a fact which influenced McQueen's choice of venue for the *Dante* collection, Hawksmoor's Christchurch, Spitalfields. McQueen's mother recounted how, while she researched the family origins, her young son investigated the story of Jack the Ripper, a theme which subsequently informed his graduate collection (Rumbold 1996).

The violence of McQueen's vision was fuelled by 'a desire to strip romance to the truth' (Hume 1993) as he saw it, just as the violence of Sade's writing was fed by his own political disaffection, his disappointed Utopianism. Amongst the chilly femmes fatales of McQueen's *Dante* collection, with its male models styled to look like Los Angeles gang youths, were jackets photo-printed with images of Don McCullen's war photographs. The collection was about religion as the cause of war throughout history. It was staged on a candle-lit cross-shaped runway, against a backdrop of flashing, back-lit, stained-glass windows, and had a soundtrack of Victorian church music which, as the show started, was drowned out by the sound of gunfire, and then by a hard-core club track. Against this backdrop, the harshness of McQueen's images of women shifted and began to resignify.

Beyond the surface cruelty which patterned both Sade and McQueen's work lay a deeper structural connection which united these apparently disparate figures in the same tradition. The darkness of McQueen's view of history and culture echoed that of Sade's utopian, yet despairing, political idealism. Over half of the extraordinarily violent and pornographic *Philosophy in the Boudoir* consists of a political treatise entitled *Just one more effort, Frenchmen, if you would become republicans*. This treatise was extracted from its pornographic context and reprinted as a pamphlet in the revolution of 1848 by the followers of the utopian Saint Simon. Sade's books, inventorized at his death, included the complete works of Rousseau and Voltaire; yet his pornographic vision renounced both reason and enlightenment in favour of a view of the world as fundamentally driven by relations of power. For Sade, freedom only existed in opposition to, and was defined by, tyranny. Propelled by this seemingly Manichean dualism, Sade's contradictions extended to his sexual choices and his political ideals equally. Despite the extreme cruelty of his sexual writings he claimed the smell of blood from the guillotine made him feel sick. Although a supporter of the revolution he was opposed to the death penalty and, as a judge during the Terror, was briefly imprisoned on the charge of 'moderatism' (Carter 1979: 32).

It is Sade's nihilism which makes him modern, as well as the proximity of sex and politics in his sensibility. Both Sade's and McQueen's worlds are post-Edenic. Each paints a picture of a tragic universe, an alienated world of Baudelaire's 'modernity' in which 'sexuality becomes the ruination of harmonious, "centred" love. There has arisen in the modern period a literature of a sexuality that is not about love, happiness or duty but about trauma, otherness and unspeakable truth' (Rajchman 1986: 47). This literature is not new: it runs from Sade through Baudelaire to Genet and Bataille, and is now 200 years old. What was new, however, at the close of the twentieth century, was that these ideas found expression in the work of a fashion designer, perhaps for the first time since the inception of this literature, the late eighteenth-century, which is also the period of post-Revolutionary French fashions *à la victime* in which, for example, women wore a red ribbon round the neck in reference to the cut of the guillotine. In a fashion plate of 1798 these scarlet *croisures à la victime* have moved down from the neck to traverse the bodice to signify that their wearer would sacrifice everything for her lover (Ribeiro 1988: 124). As in many of McQueen's designs today, political trauma has become eroticized; Terror bleeds into Eros.

Sade's books have been banned to the general public for the best part of 200 years; they are in print now, as they were at the time of the French Revolution, both periods of instability and oscillation, between revolutionary freedom and state or corporate oppression. If, in Carter's (Carter 1979: 9) phrase, 'our flesh arrives to us out of history' (her more poetic formulation of Foucault's concept of sexuality as historically determined), perhaps such fashions gesture towards moments of cultural trauma which we can only just begin to describe.

Notes

1. In fact this review was not of McQueen's first but of his second collection, *Nihilism*, shown at the Bluebird Garage in London in October 1993. In her article Hume's tone was shocked but not disapproving, and she went on to equate McQueen's work, in its significance, with that of Vivienne Westwood in the 1970s and Comme des Garçons in the 1980s.

2. For example, 'I don't like frilly, fancy dresses. Women can look beautiful and wear something well without looking fragile' (McQueen, quoted in Jennifer Scruby, 'The Eccentric Englishman', *Elle American*, July 1996); of the type of model chosen for McQueen shows, his assistant Katy England said, 'They must be able to carry off the clothes, as well as being beautiful. Some of the really young girls are gorgeous, but are not ready to do McQueen yet, they just haven't got enough attitude. We need strong, ballsy girls' (Katy England in Melanie Rickey, 'England's Glory', *The Independent* Tabloid, Friday 28/2/97: 4)

3. McQueen was referring here to his sixth show after graduation, *The Hunger*, shown in October 1995.

4. Menkes cited McQueen's comment on this collection that 'it's not so much about death, but the awareness that it is there'.

5. For example: Jeffrey Deitch, *Post-Human*, Musee d'Art Contemporain, Pully/Lausanne 1992, Museo d'Arte Contemporanea, Turin 1992, Desle Foundation for Contemporary Art, Athens 1992–3, Deichtorhallen Hamburg 1993; Mike Kelley, *The Uncanny*, Gemeentmuseum, Arnhem 1993; *Abject Art: Repulsion and Desire in American Art*, Whitney Museum of American Art, New York 1992–3; Venice Biennale, Italy 1994; *Elective Affinities*, Tate Gallery, Liverpool 1993; Stuart Morgan,

Rites of Passage, Tate Gallery, London 1995; *L'Informe: mode d'emploi*, Centre Georges Pompidou, Paris 1996. *The Quick and the Dead: Artists and Anatomy*, Royal College of Art, London, Warwick Arts Centre, Coventry & Leeds City Art Gallery, UK 1997–8. And the exhibition *L'amour Fou: Photography & Surrealism* at the Corcoran Gallery of Art, Washington DC in 1985 and then at the Hayward Gallery, London in 1986 was an important predecessor.

6. In relation to the *Highland Rape* collection McQueen commented that he wanted men to think, when a woman came into the room, not 'cor I'd love to screw her' but 'she looks amazing but I couldn't go near her.'

References

Allen, V. M. (1983), *The Femme Fatale: Erotic Icon*, Whitson, Troy, NY.

Baudrillard, J. (1990), *Fatal Strategies*, Semiotexte, New York.

Bronfen, E. (1992), *Over Her Dead Body: Death, Femininity and the Aesthetic*, Manchester University Press, Manchester.

Buci-Glucksmann, C. (1994), *Baroque Reason: the aesthetics of modernity*, trans. Patrick Camiller, Sage Publications, London, Thousand Oaks, New Delhi.

Carter, A. (1979), *The Sadeian Woman: An Exercise in Cultural History*, Virago, London.

Cutting Up Rough (series: The Works, producer: Teresa Smith, series editor: Michael Poole), BBC2, broadcast 20.7.97.

Dijkstra, B. (1986), *Idols of Perversity: Fantasies of Feminine Evil in Fin-de-siècle Culture*, Oxford University Press, New York & Oxford.

Doane, M. A. (1991), *Femmes Fatales: Feminism, Film Theory, Psychoanalysis*, Routledge, New York & London.

Freud, S. (1955), 'Medusa's Head', *Standard Edition* (ed. Strachey, J.), Hogarth Press, London.

Heath, A. (1995), 'Bad Boys Inc', *The Face*, vol.2. no.79, April, p. 102.

Hoare, S. (1996), 'God Save McQueen', *Harpers Bazaar*, USA, June, pp. 30 & 148.

Hume, M. (1993), 'McQueen's Theatre of Cruelty', *The Independent*, Thursday 21 October, p. 29.

Hume, M. (1996), 'Scissorhands', *Harpers & Queens*, August, p. 82.

Krauss, R. (1986), 'Corpus delicti', in Krauss, R. & Livingston, J. *L'amour fou: photography & surrealism*, Abbeville Press, New York, & Arts Council of Great Britain, London.

Lorna V. (1997), 'All Hail McQueen', *Time Out*, 24 September–1 October, p. 26.

Marcus, T. (1998), 'I am the resurrection', *i-D*, 179, September, p. 148.

Menkes, S. (1996), 'The Macabre and the Poetic', *International Herald Tribune*, 5 March, p. 10.

Rajchman, J. (1986), 'Lacan and the Ethics of Modernity', *Representations*, 15, Summer, pp. 42–56.

Ribeiro, A. (1988), *Fashion in the French Revolution*, B.T. Batsford Ltd., London.

Rumbold, J. (1996), 'Alexander the Great', *Vogue UK*, July, catwalk report supplement.

Showalter, E. (1991), *Sexual Anarchy: Gender and Culture at the Fin-de-siècle*, Bloomsbury, London.

Sunday Telegraph Magazine, 22 September 1996.

Tseëlon, E. (1995), *The Masque of Femininity: The Presentation of Woman in Everyday Life*, Sage, London, Thousand Oaks, New Delhi.

Vogue USA, October 1997, p. 435.

Webb, P. (1985), *Hans Bellmer*, London: Quartet Books.

Women's Wear Daily, 1995. Tuesday, 14 March, p. 10.

Fashioning the Queer Self[1]

Ruth Holliday

In this chapter I examine material from video diaries which were recorded by a number of people in 'queer communities[2].' I am interested in the ways in which identities are performed, especially in relation to clothing and fashion. I aim to explore the similarities and differences in respondents' accounts, and want to chart their *experiences* of identity. In so doing I hope to illustrate some key aspects of theoretical debates about identity, whilst also considering how far people's experiences of their own identities mirror the fractured selves currently described by academics (for example Hall 1996) or the theoretical insights of notions of performativity in relation to identity (Butler 1990); are identities outside the academy experienced as more fixed and less complex than these writings suggest?

In particular, I want to focus on the notion of 'comfort'. Throughout the diarists' accounts, this term is used to justify a number of identity positions and personal stylizations. Some of these extracts are included in this chapter, but *many* others are not. I am interested in why this particular expression is used, and I try to unpack some of the different meanings surrounding it; the term has many connotations, some of which I explore here. I am also interested in some of the *effects* of the word, and want to explore the extent to which notions of comfort work to articulate individualizing discourses of identity which preclude strong political identity positions (a question especially resonant in a post-identity-politics climate).

Identities on Camera

My research involved giving respondents camcorders and asking them to make 'video diaries'. In the brief for these, respondents were asked to demonstrate (visually) and talk about the ways in which they managed or presented their identities in different settings in their everyday lives. The participants were asked to dress in the clothes they would wear in each situation, describing them in detail and explaining why they thought these self-presentation strategies were appropriate. This technique was designed to make sure that participants were as explicit as possible about the presentation of their identities in different spaces. Theoretical themes were then developed as they arose from the data, according to the significance that respondents afforded them and the frequency with which issues arose across all of the respondents' accounts.

I would like to stress at the outset the importance of the video diaries in capturing the performativities of identity in ways which are qualitatively different from other sociological research methods. In one sense, the self-representation is more 'complete' than the audio-taped interview, which only provides aural data. The visual dimension of the construction and display of identity is obviously more easily gleaned through this method. In addition, video diaries have a common currency, largely due to their recent extended television coverage (in the UK at least), which makes them a familiar form to respondents. In theory (if not necessarily in practice) video diaries afford respondents the potential for a greater degree of reflexivity than other methods, through the processes of watching, re-recording and editing their diaries before submission, and because each diarist has at least one month in which to create their diary. Regardless of the 'accuracy' or 'realism' of the diaries, then, they do at least afford more potential than other more traditional research methods for the respondents more fully to represent themselves (for more on this, see Holliday 2000). For example, Gill[3] says about the process:

> Why am I telling you all these things about myself? Well, I think that if you asked me I'd tell you, but you're going to tell other people; um, because I think that it's important and I think I've got things to say . . . The least favourite bit of my body is this little bit in here, because I've got a fat bit there, and a front-on picture of my belly, although I let a bit of that be shown earlier and viewed that to see if I was going to let it stay in.

This implies that making a video diary can be a reflexive and even empowering process, since it offers the subject greater 'editorial control' over the material she chooses to disclose – and because she feels she has 'important' things to say that are here given a space to be said.

I would now like briefly to discuss the location of this chapter in relation to other writings in the field and the particular approach which I intend to adopt. Because of the nature of the video diaries and the significance of identity presentations, it is important that I briefly review some of the relevant literature on consumption, fashion and dress.

Fashioning the Self

A huge volume of literature is developing on consumption and its meaning, especially focused around fashion and dress (see other chapters in this volume). Academic writings on fashion have frequently emphasized the communicative meanings of the consumption and display of fashion and dress. However, Colin Campbell (1996) is especially critical of certain postmodern writers (Baudrillard is implied) who attribute too much importance to the symbolic meaning of products (and clothes) and too little to the meaning of actions. He shows the ways in which postmodern writers, who stress the playfulness of identity – the ways in which identities might be taken up and thrown off at will – inevitably position consumption and display as a set of rational, unconstrained choices. Whilst there is some validity in this argument, he proceeds to adopt an opposite polemic, where *individuals* or *consumers* function almost unconsciously within a constrained set of choices, based on previous shopping experiences. However, it is his homogenizing and feminizing assumptions about 'individuals' involved in consuming fashion that are the most troubling:

> a woman holds up a dress and says, 'this won't suit me, I am too small; it would look good on a taller woman', or, another will say, 'round necklines don't suit me', or 'I can't wear yellow, it doesn't suit my complexion.' (Campbell, 1996: 102)

Using this framework effectively erases the social, rendering fashion a question of individual taste or 'personal identity', and leaving little room for discussion of the visible manifestations of social identities via dress. Even in Cambell's example it is clear that a discourse of *style* is at work, a discourse which dictates what garment colours go with which complexion and at what age one must stop wearing V-necks and start wearing round-necked clothes. Furthermore, in my research it is clear that fashion's communicative role in the production of identities is an important one and must not be overlooked, especially in the context of queer identities (see Holliday 1999).

Having been invisible (or pathologized) for so long in writing, the media, law and culture more generally, as well as being literally invisible on the bodies of subjects, queer identities have been increasingly visible through a number of mechanisms. The politics of visibility as well as the many everyday cues and codes of dress, gesture or conduct are often used to communicate identity to others of the same or different groups. For example, the development of queer styles such as butch and camp (to name but two) have become signifiers of sexuality (Munt 2001; Nestle 1987) and are mapped onto the surface of bodies, not least through clothes. As Rosa Ainley comments: 'Without visual identity there is no presence, and that means no social support networks, and no community' (1995: 122). Thus, Campbell's female consumer whose choice lies in whether it is the red or the blue frock that suits her most is irrelevant to strong social identities, such as those constructed around sexualities, if indeed she is relevant to anyone but Campbell's imaginary shoppers. This issue is echoed in Elizabeth Wilson's (1985: 122) work:

> If . . . the self in all its aspects appears threatened in modern society, then fashion becomes an important – indeed vital – medium in the recreation of the lost self or 'decentred subject' . . . for the individual to lay claim to a particular style may be more than ever a lifeline, a proof that one does at least exist.

Arguably, until the 1990s, fashion itself may have provided the most important signifier in the construction of queer identities in the West. Gay men were marked simply by being *fashionable* against the backdrop of a masculinity (beyond temporary affiliation to specific youth subcultures) largely disinterested in a subject dismissed as the preserve of women. Feminist lesbians, of course, visibly fought fashion as a constraining and feminizing force of capitalism and heteropatriarchy (although fashion has always had a place within femme lesbian and bisexual cultures (see for example, Hemmings 1999; Nestle 1989)). However, the 1990s complicated matters. Androgyny, fashionable many times in history but most recently developed by lesbian and bisexual women, has slipped easily into the mainstream of youth culture more generally. Moreover the media frenzy over 'lesbian chic' (possibly fuelled by panics over the erosion of visible differentiation between straight and queer women) has inspired some (middle-class) lesbians and bi women to reclaim fashion, and to muscle in on some of the 'boyz' fun' organized around the plethora of new clubs and bars. This is to some extent facilitated by a new-found disposable income in the climate of greater opportunities for (middle-class) women.

Furthermore, as Silverman (1986, quoted in Evans and Thornton 1989) explains, postmodern fashion puts quotation marks around the garments it revitalizes, allowing them to be re-read in a space of ironic distance between the wearer and the garment. This opens up a space for 'playing' with fashion which is the antithesis of being its victim, and thus the feminist arguments about the regulation of women's bodies through fashion decline in importance. In addition, Sean Nixon (1996) shows how the recent growth in UK men's magazines such as *FHM* and *GQ* has processed fashion as an acceptable pastime for straight men. Thus, queer markers in the 1990s have become more subtle and sophisticated than the jeans and checked shirts advocated for all gay men in the 1970s, and have moved signification away from generic styles of dress onto the specifics of labels such as, for example, Levis, Adidas, Ted Baker, Versace. That is not to say, though, that these labels, in themselves, can be taken as reliable evidence of sexuality, only that in specific contexts they can hint in a particular direction; thus are the complexities of sexual (and other) identity performances at the start of the millennium.

Reading Identities

With this in mind, it might be expected that queer subjects spend much time considering the particular styles open to them in order to construct particular identity positions based not only around sexuality and gender, but also around class, ethnicity and so on. However, in the video diaries I collected for this study, clothing used to express identity was viewed rather unreflexively. Several of the respondents, when dressing in their 'going out' or 'staying in' clothes, expressed as the primary motivation in their choice of these clothes the ideal of 'comfort' – that they had chosen the clothes that they were wearing because these were the most comfortable. In some cases participants were completely unable to add anything to this motive for buying and wearing these clothes, and here lies the key to the (limited) possibilities of identity performances I hope to explore. For example, there was some attempt to pass over the question of 'labels' of clothing which clearly have social meanings in specific contexts at the time of writing. The clearest instance of this is when Jo explains the purchase of an 'original' Adidas tracksuit top. She expresses the motive for this purchase as being about comfort and liking the look of the white stripes down the sleeves, but later in the diary provides a slightly different interpretation:

> I think I look at other clothes that other people wear and if they look nice and comfortable, then I choose to wear them. I mean I saw a woman in [a gay bar] that had an Adidas top on, and it really suited her, it looked really nice . . . so that's probably why I choose to wear Adidas tops . . . Plus she was damn sexy [laughs].

Thus what Jo initially describes as an acquisition for comfort we now discover to be a highly inconvenient purchase: it had to be an 'original' Adidas garment, only available from particular second-hand shops (on 'retro style' and cultural capital see McRobbie 1994), precipitated by a fleeting flirtation in a highly specific location.

The *social* meaning of this purchase is perhaps reinforced through a quote from Carl. He is about the same age as Jo and also frequents 'trendy' gay bars:

I wear trainers now, rather than boots. Adidas trainers, very important, because they're quite fashionable at the moment and if you're going to be accepted on the scene, you've got to dress right.

On the scene – in queer social space – fashion enunciates identity, then, but this carries a premium; the fact that 'you've got to dress right' highlights the issue of access to capital and credit as crucial determinants of who can wear what, and thus who can be what. This point is made most clearly in the diaries by Andi, a self-styled 'gender nomad':

I don't have the financial security to invest heavily in electrolysis, breast implants, hair stylists and extensive wardrobes. I make the best of what I can come across . . . The last thing I want to look like is some tranny who . . . has either modelled herself on her mother or her aunties . . . Comfort! Comfort and practicality comes out top [for me] every time.

In the most acute sense, then, Andi's lack of financial capital prevents her from becoming her preferred gender. The technologies of transformation are available, but at a price. Furthermore (and I will return to this later) comfort is used as a mark of authenticity, as opposed to 'trannies' (transvestites) who simply copy their aunties or mothers.

The Politics of Comfort

Comfort therefore comes to stand in for authenticity, and thus has clear links with notions of nature and the natural body/self. The naturalizing discourse of comfort incorporates what might be called political and 'subcultural' resonances. In this context, the political can be thought of as discourses emanating from lesbian, gay, bisexual and transgender politics; subcultural, in contrast, refers to everyday experiences and explanations of identity – which may match with the political, but may also contradict it. At one level, then, comfort can be taken to embody *resistance* to the hegemonic discourses of 'proper' feminine or masculine behaviour and attire. In the case of the former, lesbian and bisexual feminism has been quick to point out that it is *culture* which demands femininity (see Butler 1990). If femininity is imposed by patriarchal culture and is socially constructed, then it can be changed or at least resisted. Thus, first- and second-wave feminisms retain a binary system of gender and sex, where gender is implicitly assumed to follow sex. Feminism's rejection of patriarchal claims, then, has been the rejection of traditional femininity, but also a replacement of this with notions of women's *nature*; for example, co-operative and non-hierarchical relationships with other women,

women's connectedness to the Earth and to 'Mother Nature', and so on.[4] This discourse has reproduced itself on the surface of the body as a return to the 'natural body'. As Evans and Thornton explain:

> Looking for an expression of an authentic 'natural' self, however, women based their appearance on the masculine model (short hair, trousers, no make-up) or an infantile model (coloured dungarees and lace-up shoes). The appearance of femininity was seen as some kind of contrivance but the validity of the masculine model went unquestioned. (1989: 12)

In this project, then, appeals to comfort become appeals to the 'nature' of feminism; that is, the rejection of (*unnatural*) femininity.

Butler undoes this particular version of feminism by referring back to de Beauvoir, who famously asserted 'one is not born a woman, but rather one becomes one'. To take this statement to its logical conclusion, there is no guarantee that all those born female will become women nor that those born male won't. In short there is no reason to believe that gender will follow sex or that the binaries of sex and gender will remain as binaries. Thus, in its appeal to nature and comfort, second-wave feminism actually closes down the possibilities of gendered (subject) and sexual (object choice) identities. Appeals to comfort are complicit in the restriction of possible identities through their implicit fixing of 'true' gender to the 'natural' body: what is comfortable for the lesbian could not be comfortable for the 'false' (feminine or trans-gendered) subject and vice versa. It is this restriction, filtering into lesbian and bisexual subjectivity, which stems from an originally emancipatory feminist political project – perhaps as its unintended consequence.

For men, however, the rejection of accepted patterns of masculinity may mean subjecting oneself to exactly the technologies of the body from which feminists have struggled to emancipate women:

> I'm shaving my legs [on camera]. Because I get quite long hair on my legs and gay men don't like that. At least I don't anyway. And I don't feel comfortable with it . . . This is an important part, I s'pose, of me and my identity. In that, I don't feel comfortable being me if I've got quite long hair, because I do get quite long hair, all over really, on my arms and legs and chest. I don't know if you can see [pulls up arm hairs to demonstrate]. And the image at the moment is quite young and fit and smooth. So you feel quite out of it if you're not young and fit and smooth. And as I'm not young and fit, the closest I'm going to get is smooth. I cut my hair really, not shave it; if I ever get a body, as in muscles and stuff, I might get my chest waxed. But at the moment I can't see the point in spending all that money, because I don't show my body, and I'm not going to show my body until I feel comfortable with it. That's one of the problems of being gay I suppose. (Carl)

In this quote the dynamic of comfort is quite clearly contradictory; whilst Carl does not feel 'comfortable' going out on the scene unless he attends to his body, he is quite clearly uncomfortable about having to do it.

Comfort as Inside/Out

Comfort also signifies the comfort one might feel from the degree of fit between the outside of one's body and its inside (the imagined self) – the way in which identity is mapped onto the body. Comfort means in this case that one expresses externally that which one feels inside. In other words, there is a wish to close the gap between performance (acting) and ontology (being), a desire to be self-present to both oneself and others. Comfort in this case derives from being 'recognisably' queer (or in the case of transgendered subjects, recognisably their preferred gender identity) to both oneself and others. For instance, Karen enters a scene in her diary wearing full leathers:

> These are my other dressing up and going out clothes. I think these clothes definitely are about my sexual identity in that they make me feel like a lesbian. And they also make me feel fairly confident as a lesbian as well. Although I quite like dresses in terms of dressing up and going out, I don't feel as confident in dresses as I do in trousers. If I had to choose something to wear I think it would be trousers, as a lesbian.

The leathers she wears, then, make her *feel like a lesbian* and make her *confident as a lesbian*. The fit between outside and inside is more complete when wearing these clothes than in other attire, and this hints at the performative nature of identities. In part this notion is informed by the politics of visibility. As a discursive absence, lesbians and bisexual women must enforce their presence through the communication of signs. This cannot be left to the chance conversation or discovery but must rather be signified (through butch, for instance), where signifiers are fixed to a supposed ontological truth of being.

Here again first and second wave feminist and lesbian politics assert a binary: the binary of being and acting – the self and its performance. For example, Frye (1985, quoted in Fraser 1997: 43) writes:

> being lesbian or being heterosexual are not simply matters of sexual preference or bodily behaviours. They are complex matters of attachment, orientation in the world, vision, habits, or communication and community . . . In my own case, being lesbian is an attitude evolved over perhaps fifteen years . . . It would have been 'inauthentic' to act the lesbian in certain ways too early in that process. It now would be inauthentic not to, in certain ways and certain situations.

Thus, although the binary of acting and being is set up by feminists, there is still an implication that acting *follows* being, and is thus part of it. Mariam Fraser shows how the bisexual woman disrupts this logic in that she is considered *inauthentic*: she acts like a lesbian but is not one. Transgendered women are similarly accused of inauthenticity (see also Zita 1992). This leads Andi in the diaries (and many other transgender subjects) to use a similar logic – that in fact the authentic self is one's very being and that to be comfortable, one's body must reflect this:

> It doesn't matter how much you spend on plastic surgery . . . the best plastic surgeon. It has to be spiritual before it can be physical. You have to be able to prepare your soul, your spirit and your mind. Because without that the rest of it is purely what it is – cosmetic.

As with sex and gender, then, a binary is set up by feminism, only to be fixed as signifier and signified. The binary is really two sides of the same coin, where the cultural mirrors the biological. The essentialism of the recourse (in this case not to the body but to the 'self') is once again reinstated by feminist political logic, so it is unsurprising that the comfort expressed by our diarists locates the comfort of identity in the individual body, reinstating the notion of the expressive individual. The essentializing of comfort through the homology of acting and being prescribes exclusive sexuality. If acting following being represents the authentic, then acts which are not located in the body or identity are clearly inauthentic. Thus, for lesbian feminism, the bisexual and transgendered (among others) are inauthentic copies of the authentic lesbian self.

What is being masked in this manoeuvre is the very *performativity* of that identity – its creation through a discourse of power. The choice of comfortable clothes proposes identity as a 'natural' phenomenon – giving identity an essentialism which therefore assists heterosexuality in retaining a false binary. It covers up the 'construction' of identity and therefore masks its historical roots as a discourse, closing down other potential positions or movements within that discourse. Foucault and Butler are both quick to point out that all discourses, not just hegemonic ones, are located in power; all definitions (identities and representations) are exclusive. As Butler (1991: 13–14) says:

> identity categories tend to be instruments of regulatory regimes, whether as the normalizing categories of oppressive structures or as the rallying points for a liberatory contestation of that very oppression . . . To propose that the invocation of identity is always a risk [of being recolonized under the sign of lesbian] does not imply that resistance to it is always or only symptomatic of a self-inflicted homophobia.

Once identity is understood as performativity divorced from any notion of an essential self or individual truth, multiple identity positions or identity fictions become possible, or at least plausible. Thus, the fixing of comfort to the expressive individual self denies the performativity of identity and thus the transgressive possibilities of the disruption of that performance. Though Butler is quick to point out that performativity is not voluntary or arbitrary, the recognition of identity as performative does offer possibilities for its subversion.

Performing Bodies

The notion of comfort/discomfort was discussed by the diarists in a number of additional contexts. Many respondents, for example, talked about a certain 'discomfort' when going out 'on the scene'. This tended to be expressed as a feeling of being watched or stared at; not being 'cruised' but being in some sense 'evaluated'. In fact Jo said that she sometimes felt more comfortable in 'straight' spaces than in queer ones, and Carl talked at length about wanting to wear clothes that he felt unable to on the scene because he did not have the 'right' body to wear 'skimpy' items of clothing:

> This is what I plan to wear. It's all black which makes me feel comfortable because it slims me down. I feel a bit chubby. Although I quite fancy the blue, which is very clingy and tends to show any lumps and as I've got them I don't think I'll wear that. This is what I want to wear one day. It's my favourite top ever. I've never worn this out yet. It's wonderful. I bought it in the gay part of New York – Greenwich Village. I think that it's really nice, I love this, but I don't actually wear it so far, basically because I don't think I've really got the body for it, so until I feel comfortable wearing that it'll be going back to the wardrobe. But hopefully by the end of this month I'll be able to wear it.

This gaze is not one of desire, then, but rather a disciplinary gaze, a policing of body shapes and styles of dress, which left several of the respondents feeling some kind of inadequacy in what they felt to be 'their own' spaces.

The diarists' accounts make clear the power at work within the so-called 'emancipatory' discourses (and spaces) of queer. This does not imply that the discourses of lesbian and gay culture are as destructive as homophobic ones (it is unlikely that one would get beaten up for poor fashion sense), but they are powerful and do exert disciplinary technologies on the bodies of their subjects. These technologies in turn produce performativities of sexual identities which locate their performance precisely in the idea of the biological or psychological self. As Lauren Berlant (1997: 17) summarizes:

[Poststructuralist theorists] . . . have shown how sexuality is the modern form of self-intelligibility: I am my identity; my identity is fundamentally sexual; and my practices reflect that (and if they don't, they require submission to sexual science, self-help, or other kinds of laws).

However, identity strategies can be very complex in terms of their different locations at the point of the subject. Any queer subject is frequently inter-pellated by a number of discursive subject positions and these different locations can be difficult to reconcile (see Mercer 1994). For example, Karen struggles with issues around sadomasochism (SM):

I think these clothes give very clear messages about the kind of dyke people see that I am when I wear my leathers . . . That's another reason why I like wearing these types of clothes. I think for me, that's sometimes quite difficult for me being a Black woman . . . because there are massive issues around power and SM. I've had many, many debates with other Black lesbians about that . . . whether it's just another form of slavery . . . especially as my partner's white and I'm a bottom.[5] But I know what I like and I know I feel comfortable in it and in control.

This brings me to another point about the empirical material presented here: the link between the comfort of the outside of the body with the 'naturalness' and authenticity of the inside (the 'self') prioritizes the individual over the social – 'I know what I like' rather than conforming to regulatory (social) discourses. Individuality is here stressed in opposition to the 'uniform of queer'. The misrecognition of oneself as an individual, in opposition to fashion and subculture, denies the place of the social in the construction of identity positions. In Jo's case, for example, her choice of tracksuit top is clearly one of *social* meaning. The desire to purchase and wear this top is the result of a social interaction in a queer location. Her inspiration in her choice of dress, far from deriving from within herself (as she suggests), comes from a kind of *queer aesthetic* with which she identifies. This queer aesthetic is always social; outside of the social it has no meaning. Within the social it signifies her comfort, physical but also aesthetic – comfort in reflecting her identity, but also in being able to 'express' it. Thus, although the popular discourse of LGBT cultures locate sexuality within the individual, the social is always important in its development.

The Body as Social Text

Identity is spread over the surface of the body, constructed as the outward text of the inner ethics of the self. As Elizabeth Grosz explains, drawing on Derrida's notion of the signature:

the paradoxical and divided position of the subject in and beyond the text, involves the necessary and irreducible trace of the one within the other, the implication of the text's outside with its inside, and of its inside with establishing its borders and thus the outside, in short, its fundamentally folded, 'invaginated' character (1995: 20).

Thus, the inscription on the body of the text of a subject's identity is an individual inscription which also at once signs the subject as a product of other texts. In the sense in which the body is a text, identity is always inscribed socially, although this will have differing manifestations as the body's author attempts to inscribe proprietorial meaning. In this sense, then, the queer body is the signature of queer textuality. It is not static or constant, but is shifting, like the signature, never manifesting itself twice in identical ways, yet at the same time carrying the mark of both its author and the texts which produce it. Card's (1985, quoted in Fraser 1997: 213) outline of Aristotle's notion of 'family resemblance' is useful here. The term resemblance can be applied to anything which is called by the same name but does not 'possess any one characteristic in common'.

Elspeth Probyn: sees this thing which Card describes as family resemblance as an ensemble of images which are written on the body, using the Deleuzean notion of productive desire:

> The similarity of bodies, is a matter not of similar origins but rather is compelled by a similarity of desire to arrange one's body, to queer oneself through movement. As I see the configuration of my body as image on her body, I also can feel the configuration of hers on mine. However, this is not a constant or immediate fact; it has to be made, to be configured through the desire to conjoin images (1995: 15).

This configuration is not total, however. Not all lesbians desire all lesbians (or look like all lesbians), rather it is the social configuration in conjunction with the individual signature mapped onto the body, or parts of the body, which marks out individual desires; something in the interplay, as Probyn puts it, between bodies and representations. Thus, queer identities are constructed 'family resemblances' not mapped onto the body in identical ways; they might be more or less subtle, they are mediated by the materiality of bodies, by the interplay of other identities and by the appropriateness of dress codes for particular spaces. This is the strength of the family resemblance – its versatility; it is not a uniform through which all its members are unequivocally marked for all audiences.

But still, this is only half (or less) of the story – a story is created not only by writers, but by readers. Any bodily text can convey its intended meaning only if its readers decode it in the way the author requires. 'Family resemblances' can only be spotted by those who 'know' the 'family'. Meaning is constructed by readers as well as writers of texts, and therefore there are infinite possibilities for the queer body to be misread. A short anecdote one diarist told illustrates this point exactly. He was at college, arriving late one day:

> I walked in and this bunch of girls were going 'Martin's gay, Martin's gay' – Martin is this straight guy in our class. And Martin says, 'Yes, and for all you know Steve [the respondent] could be my lover'. And the girls said, 'Oh, don't be stupid, we *know* Steve isn't gay, you're the one who's gay because you're obsessed with your appearance, always looking in the mirror'. So I said '*Au contraire!*', and gave them my big 'I am gay' speech, because I've worked hard for this reputation and I'm not about to lose it. And they said 'Oh Steve, you're so funny, you're such a wit and a wag, I've told my parents all about you!' . . . They wouldn't believe me!

This causes Steve amusement, but also dismay. There is an extreme discomfort in being read against one's signature (the reputation which he has worked hard for). The misreading of cultural codes by his (straight) audience invokes a reaction where Steve attempts to refix the meaning of his bodily text, supplementing it with the intertextuality of gay political and ontological discourses. When this too is misread, the discomfort of the lack of homology between his self and his body leaves Steve bemused.

Identity meaning is disrupted by its multiplicity. Discomfort in this case, then, derives from the momentary dislocation of the essentialist narrative: *if I am gay, then I am comfortable dressing gay, and therefore others will recognise that I am gay*. Expression of identity follows identity, which follows biology. Comfort follows from being a writerly rather than readerly text, although what is written may be highly context-specific. The disruption of this 'natural' flow of essentialistic discourse leads to a hyperperformativity of sexuality (the 'I am gay' speech; the momentary power of the confessional which is subsequently reinterpreted or ignored) which at once threatens exposure of identity itself as performative through the conflation of the binary of acting and being.[6]

This problem is particularly acute for many transgendered people who feel they are read in opposition to their preferred gender identity. The discomfort of this reading leads many to undergo transsexual surgery, a very painful and risky undertaking that frequently leaves patients disabled (see Whittle 2001). But this surgery is only granted after a period of 'living as' one's preferred gender and convincing a psychiatrist of the sincerity of the case. Thus, for many transsexuals, the hyperperformativity of one's preferred gender (and more specifically, medicalized definitions of gender dysphoria) is a necessary part of the change process (see Stone 1991).

Conclusion

Identity may be thought through on a number of levels. Different spaces of performativity afford subjects more or less critical distance from the performances of identity in which they engage, using a combination of political and subcultural discourses. However, rejection of hegemonic discourses may be expressed as individuality, rather than the social 'other' in which one is implicated. Subjects are likely to be less critical of such technologies which operate on the 'scene', reducing ontological contradictions and negative experiences of regulatory regimens to individual faults such as 'bitchiness'.

Traditional political discourses of sex, gender and sexuality are ill-equipped to explain and examine the micro-powerplays which take place in all spheres of the creation of the queer subject. Instead these discourses set up false binaries which offer the subject little explanatory proficiency in negotiating the everyday technologies of the self. Thus the subject often resorts to the cultural discourses of essentialism, prevalent in queer culture, in order to negotiate a position. The fixity of such positions, combined with the unworkability of standard political discourses, often seem to leave the subject disempowered, unable to explain or put into a cogent political context the ontological experiences which contradict these discourses.

Comfort for the diarists is ultimately produced in the harmony of self-explanations and self-presentations. This is the degree of fit between one's *account* of/for oneself and one's self *expression*, the harmony of the inside and outside of one's body; in other words, the desire to become a writerly text. Where some disjuncture appears between these discourses, discomfort is produced. Not having enough resemblance to one's 'family' can for instance be disconcerting. Prevailing cultural and political discourses offer such harmonies only through fixity and conformity, in the alignment of the self with hegemonic (or subcultural) discourses (which we might describe, in the Foucauldian sense, as 'knowing thyself'). This fixity or definition, as Butler points out, is always at the expense of exclusion and a 'haunted' subjectivity – the ghost of the excluded 'other' or 'otherness' which serves as a constant reminder of what one could become. What a poststructuralist politics provides, then, is a shift from 'knowing thyself' to 'taking care of the self', the comfort of the alignment of the political to the body of the subject rather than vice versa.

To elaborate on this I would like to make use of Freud's (1914) concept of narcissism, and especially the narcissistic gaze, to introduce a *social* theory of identity performance. Unlike popular notions of narcissism, defined as self-love, Freud's position is that narcissism is not about desire for one's own reflection but for what the self would like to be – an idealized self. In another manoeuvre, one does not simply have desire for an object (the idealized self) but also an identification *with* the object – a desire to be it *and* to be desired by it. Thus, narcissistic desire is both desire *for* and desire *to be* one's idealized self (Lewis and Rolley 1997; Probyn 1995). If one maps this framework onto the social, then, queer subjects both desire the objects of their gaze (others whom one identifies with an idealized version of oneself) and want to be their desired object, to be objectified by them. This scenario explains how shared cultural codes, of dress and adornment in particular, circulate in queer subcultures. That is not to say, of course, that all lesbians desire all lesbians (Probyn 1995), but that specific items of clothing and jewellery, or haircuts or body modifications, come to have currency in specific queer subcultures (it explains very neatly Jo's motivation for the purchase of her Adidas top). Finally, an important point to note here is that dressing up to go out on the scene is not simply a process of identifying oneself as a passive sexual object, but rather the double movement of having and being, creating an idealized self in the gaze of the other (object of one's desire). This explains one of the most fundamental and pleasurable *activities* of the scene: to look and be looked at (Bech 1997). As Lewis and Rolley (1997: 299) conclude (in relation to fashion magazines – but I feel the argument holds in this context):

> The importance of dress as a signifier of sexual identity, and of looking as a social, identifying and *sexualised* activity . . . coalesce to provide a supplementary pleasure in the activity of consuming [queer culture] . . . 'looking like what you are' in terms of self-presentation is crucial for a recognisable [queer] identity and structurally central to the theorisation of marginal identities.

The comfort of identity is thus far from an individual or individualizing state within queer culture. Rather it is always social, though its *discourse* may sometimes carry the rhetoric of individualism. Fashioning the queer self is a practice located at the intersection of these imperatives.

Notes

1. The support of the Economic and Social Research Council (ESRC) is gratefully acknowledged. The work was funded by ESRC award number R000236657. I would also like to thank David Bell, Jon Binnie, Azzedine Haddour, Harriette Marshall, Rolland Munro, Mark Jayne, John O'Neill, and Graham Thompson for their helpful comments on earlier drafts of this chapter.
2. Queer Communities here refers to a coalition of 'non-straight' subjects including lesbians, bisexuals, gay men and transgendered people.
3. The names of the diarists have been changed for this chapter.

4. But, of course, this is a very white, Western notion of woman, which in its romant-icism of nature excludes women who might envisage their emancipation in escape from such a connection.

5. A 'bottom' is the submissive partner in sadomasochistic sex.

6. See Butler (1997) on gay speech in the military – 'I am gay' becomes a perform-ative rather than constative (descriptive) speech act.

References

Ainley, R. (1995), *What Is She Like: Lesbian identities from the 1950s to the 1990s,* London: Cassell.

Bech, H. (1997), *When Men Meet: Homosexuality and modernity,* Cambridge: Polity.

Berlant, L. (1997), *The Queen of America goes to Washington City: Essays on sex and citizenship,* Durham: Duke University Press.

Butler, J. (1990), *Gender Trouble: Feminism and the subversion of identity,* New York: Routledge.

Butler, J. (1991), 'Imitation and gender insubordination', in Fuss, D. (ed.), *Inside/ Out: Lesbian theories, gay theories,* New York: Routledge.

Butler, J. (1993), *Bodies That Matter: On the discursive limits of sex,* New York, Routledge.

Butler, J. (1997), *Excitable Speech: A politics of the performative,* New York: Routledge.

Campbell, C. (1995), 'The sociology of consumption', in Miller, D. (ed.), *Acknowledging Consumption,* London: Routledge.

Campbell, C. (1996), 'The meaning of objects and the meaning of actions', *Journal of Material Culture,* 1 (1): 93–105.

Evans, C. and Thornton, M. (1989), *Women and Fashion: A new look,* London: Quartet.

Foucault, M. (1979), *The History of Sexuality Volume One: An introduction,* Harmondsworth: Penguin.

Foucault, M. (1986), *The History of Sexuality Volume Three: The care of the self,* Harmondsworth: Penguin.

Fraser, M. (1997) 'Lose your face' in Bi Academic Intervention (eds), *The Bisexual Imaginary: Representation, identity and desire,* London: Cassell.

Freud, S. (1914), 'On narcissism: an introduction', in J. Strachey (ed./trans.), *Standard Edition of the Complete Psychological Works of Sigmund Freud,* London: Hogarth Press, vol. 14.

Frye, M. (1985) 'History and responsibility', *Hypatia,* 8 (3): 215–17.

Graham, Paula (1995), 'Girl's camp? The politics of parody', in Wilton, T. (ed.), *Immortal Invisible: Lesbians and the moving image,* London: Routledge

Grosz, E. (1995), *Space, Time and Perversion,* New York: Routledge.

Hall, S. (1996), 'Who needs identity'? in Hall, S. and du Gay, P. (eds) *Questions of*

Cultural Identity, London: Sage.

Holliday, R. (1999), 'The comfort of identity', *Sexualities* 2 (4): 475–91.

Holliday, R. (2000), 'We've been framed: visualising methodology', *Sociological Review* 48 (4): 503–21.

Lewis, R. and K. Rolly (1997), '(A)dressing the dyke: lesbian looks and lesbians looking', in Nava, M., Blake, A., MacRury, I. and Richards, B. (eds), *Buy This Book: Studies in advertising and consumption,* London: Routledge.

McRobbie, A. (1994), *Postmodernism and Popular Culture,* London: Routledge.

Mercer, K. (1994), *Welcome to the Jungle: New positions in black cultural studies,* London: Routledge.

Munt, S. (2001), 'The Butch Body', in Ruth Holliday and John Hassard (eds), *Contested Bodies,* London: Routledge.

Nestle, J. (1987), *A Restricted Country: Essays and Short Stories,* London: Sheba.

Nestle, J. (1989), 'The fem question', in Vance, C. (ed.), *Pleasure and Danger: Exploring female sexuality,* London: Pandora.

Nixon, S. (1996), *Hard Looks: Masculinities, the visual and practices of consumption,* London: UCL Press.

Probyn, E. (1993), *Sexing The Self: Gendered positions in cultural studies,* London: Routledge.

Probyn, E. (1995), 'Queer belongings: the politics of departure', in Elizabeth Grosz and Elspeth Probyn (eds), *Sexy Bodies: The strange carnalities of feminism,* London: Routledge.

Silverman, K. (1986), 'Fragments of a fashionable discourse', in Modleski, T. (ed.), *Studies in Entertainment,* Bloomington: Indiana University Press.

Stone, S. (1991), 'The empire strikes back: a posttransexual manifesto', in Epstein, J. and Straub, K. (eds), *Body Guards: The cultural politics of gender ambiguity,* New York: Routledge.

Whittle, S. (2001), 'The trans-cyberian mail way', in Holliday, R. and Hassard, J. (eds), *Contested Bodies,* London: Routledge.

Wilson, E. (1985), *Adorned in Dreams: Fashion and modernity*, London: Virago.

Zita, J. (1992), 'Male lesbians and the postmodernist body', *Hypatia* 7 (4): 106–27.

Dress, Gender and the Public Display of Skin

Joanne B. Eicher

Why is it that at balls and parties, when man comes dressed in his usual style, *fashion requires woman to display her person, to bare her arms and neck?* Why must she attract man's admiration? Why must she secure his physical love? The only object of a woman's life is marriage, and the shortest way to a man's favor is through his passions; and woman has studied well all the little arts and mysteries by which she can stimulate him to the pursuit. Every part of a woman's dress has been faithfully conned by some French courtesan to produce this effect. Innocent girls who follow the fashion are wholly ignorant of its philosophy. Woman's attire is an ever-varying incentive to man's imagination – a direct and powerful appeal to his passional nature. (Elizabeth Cady Stanton 1857 as quoted in Russell 1892, italics added).

Elizabeth Cady Stanton, champion of women's rights in the United States, wrote the above extract in a letter read at an 1857 Dress Reform Association convention held in Canastota, New York, a year after the Association had been established. Her comments about the 'display of skin' by many Euro-American women in public places continues to be a compelling argument to feminists as we enter the third millennium. My own interest in dress and gender stems from a perspective of the critical role of dress (defined broadly as supplementing and modifying the body), in constructing and identifying gender (Eicher and Roach-Higgins 1992). Roach-Higgins and I provided examples of primarily EuroAmerican male and female differences in dress in relationship to how much of the shape and contours of the body are revealed. For example, a man's 'white-collar worker's biological presence is diminished by the shape and volume of his business suit that masks his body contours' (Eicher and Roach-Higgins 1992: 20). Even though women's business dress, including uniforms, generally follow this pattern, often more of their bodies are exposed as when they wear short skirts or have an open neckline. In this paper, I compare the gendered display of skin in formal public places for EuroAmericans with the Kalabari of Nigeria. These two cases illustrate the power of dress as a nonverbal communication system of both personal and sociocultural identity in three major settings that I distinguish as public, private, and secret (Eicher, 1981; Eicher and Miller, 1994). These settings apply equally to men and women in daily life as they dress to appear in public arenas of work and leisure as well as in more private arenas within circles of family and friends and finally in the most intimate and secluded arenas of the bedroom and bath. In this paper, I concentrate only on gendered dress for formal, public occasions.

I begin by examining the dress and the display of skin among the Kalabari people among whom I have lived and conducted research since 1980. For the Kalabari, the amount of skin appropriate for display by men and women interrelates with the construction of gender roles and a hierarchy of dress that parallels sociopolitical status for men and sociobiological status for women. Several scholars, both Kalabari and non-Kalabari, have described and analyzed the hierarchy of dress among the Kalabari (Daly, 1984; Daly, Eicher and Erekosima 1986; Eicher 1997; Eicher and Erekosima 1992, 1993, 1996; Erekosima 1989; Erekosima and Eicher 1980, 1994; Iyalla 1968; Michelman 1987, 1992; Michelman and Eicher 1995; Michelman and Erekosima 1992).

The gender codes of Kalabari men's and women's dress arise both from current practices and gender hierarchies that stem from their oral traditions and written documents. Their oral histories concern early trading and fishing practices and way of life before European contact. The written documents begin with Portuguese sea merchants at the end of the fifteenth century. These include accounts by European explorers, traders, and missionaries along with recently written accounts by Kalabari themselves. The gender hierarchies for men and women differ and relate to their social worlds. Men controlled the commercial aspects of trading and women controlled domestic affairs. Possibly the activity of fishing was a collaborative venture, although little written documentation exists in regard to this activity. Their rich cultural life and analysis of their worldview has been extensively documented (Ereks 1973; Erekosima 1989; Horton, 1960; 1962; 1969; 1975).

Expectations differ for men and women in public for covering their bodies for both formal ceremonies and everyday occasions. Figure 12.1 illustrates Kalabari men's dress as it corresponds to the four acknowledged ranks of sociopolitical status beginning at the lowest rank (Erekosima 1982; 1989). First, the shirt called *etibo* along with a wrapper or trousers, is worn by the *asawo* (the young men that matter). Second, the *woko*, an upper garment also worn with wrapper or trousers, is appropriate for the *opu asawo* (gentlemen of substance). Third, a specific ankle-length gown known as *doni*, with a shirt and wrapper underneath is dress for the *alapu* (the chiefs) whereas, the fourth example of *ebu*, or ankle-length gown of Indian madras with matching wrapper

Figure 12.1 Kalabari men's dress categories (left to right): Etibo, Woko, Doni, Ebu and Attigra.

underneath is reserved for the *amanyanabo* (the king). In addition to these four ranked outfits, a full-length gown called *attigra* with specific accessories is designated as ceremonial apparel for display by men of achievement or prominence at key events in Kalabari life. In each of these examples of dress, men in public are fully covered from head to toe with only their face, neck, hands and sometimes lower arms (when wearing *etibo* and *woko*) exposed. The apparel of boys and youths is not categorized or included in the ranking system for males, but for the twentieth century has consisted of Western-style clothing found in many places throughout the world for school-age children. Prior to that, unclad bodies for tiny boys and one-piece shirt-like garments or short pants and a shirt were appropriate for older boys.

Figure 12.2 illustrates the expected dress of Kalabari women. In contrast to men, the ranking for women's dress begins with childhood and physical maturation, ending with the expected status of marriage and the birth of a child (Daly 1984; Iyalla 1968). First, the dress of small girls is known as *ekuta de* (bead display), for they are bedecked with strings of beads around their necks and hips. Second, the prepubescent girl wears a small piece of cloth covering her pubic area for the stage known as *bite pakri iwain*.[1] Third, a 'half length' of cloth (*konju fina*) worn as a wrapper from waist to mid-thigh is prescribed for the young nubile woman and fourth, a full-length wrapper from waist to ankle, known as *bite sara* is appropriate for the fully adult woman, assumed to be married. Paralleling the men, women also have an additional type of

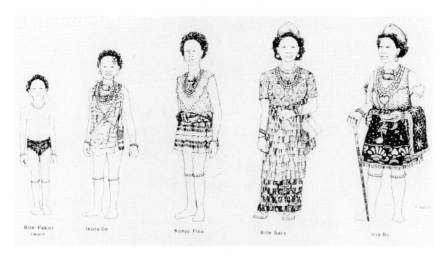

Figure 12.2 Kalabari women's dress categories (from Daly, M.C., Kalabari Female
Appearance and the Tradition of Iria, unpublished dissertation,
University of Minnesota, 1984: 48).

outfit of special-occasion apparel. This ensemble is used by a woman who has
borne a child and gone through a sequestering period after the baby's birth.
The period of time 'celebrates the period of transition in the female life cycle
from late childhood through childbirth' (Daly 1984) and is known as *iria*. The
woman is called an *iriabo* (a person who has gone through *iria*), and she wears
a knee-length wrapper, beads, a hat, and other special accessories. During the
twentieth century, both young and teenage girls, like boys and youths, have
worn Western-style clothing on a daily basis at school and at home, often school
uniforms. Prior to universal primary education, both young boys and girls wore
little or no clothing until old enough to wrap a piece of cloth around them.

For everyday public situations, adult women cover both upper and lower
body. However, for ceremonial occasions, a specific type of dress is an important
part of the *iria* tradition. Dress for the stages of womanhood involves a display
of skin not found in the dress of males. As described above, young girls in
public ceremonies cover their pubic area with beads, and as they approach the
time of menses, add a small piece of cloth over the pubis. After the menarche,
they wear a knee-length wrapper. (Boys of equivalent ages do not participate
in ceremonial occasions, except for family funerals.) According to extant photographs from the late 1880s and through the mid-1900s, young girls commonly
exposed their upper torsos and later, their developed breasts as a sign of
beauty, eligibility for marriage, and finally as accomplishment of motherhood.

However, by the end of the twentieth century, as a result of knowing about Western standards of modesty through television and print media, most women cover their breasts, but when involved in special public ceremonies may expose their shoulders, back, calves, and feet.

The vertical and linear lines of dress for men who are formally responsible for power and economic decisions in the arena of Kalabari life contrast sharply with the horizontal lines of dress for women. Because women are seen as the bearers of children, they are also thought to be formally responsible for the reproduction and continuation of Kalabari society (Daly, Eicher and Erekosima 1986: 51; Michelman 1987; Michelman and Erekosima 1992). Dress is related to these responsibilities, for the vertical lines found in the gowns and wrappers emphasize the hat and head of men, the location of decision-making (Erekosima 1989). The horizontal lines of women's wrappers and blouses emphasize the roundness of the fertile or potentially fertile woman. As Daly (1999) discovered in her daily contacts with both Kalabari men and women who talked about Kalabari body ideals as well as commenting on Daly's own body and manner of dressing, a Kalabari woman prides herself on being full-bodied. The ideal Kalabari woman's figure:

> is substantial and thick or 'plumpy' as stated by Kalabari informants. Traditional Kalabari beauty emphasizes well developed breasts and buttocks. 'To be up to a woman,' is to be fat; fat in this context refers to well-developed breasts and buttocks. (Daly 1984: 61)

The Kalabari are clear about what it means for a woman to have an ideal body shape and they use the term 'coming out' for a woman who is developing properly. When a woman gains weight or her breasts, abdomen and buttocks become more pronounced, the Kalabari remark, 'Ah, but you're coming out' (Daly 1984: 93). Finally, when a woman has been sequestered, pampered by her husband and her own family with fattening foods, soothing baths, and extensive childcare for the newborn, she is expected to display herself to the community as properly fattened:

> One proverb states that 'the iria bo (sic) who does not fatten, her buttocks is plenty of cloths,' showing that an iria bo (sic) who does not become sufficiently large will wear more wrappers to give the illusion of greater size. (Daly 1984: 120)

Being properly fattened also means having ample body contours which includes a thick waist. Daly (1999) states that during fieldwork she was asked why she cinched her waist and realized she was being asked about wearing a belt. The woman asking her the question explained that:

Figure 12.3 Kalabari woman at Briggs compound in Abonnema, in 1903, dressed as Iriabo.

a real Kalabari woman breathes easy, because she has a 'thick waist', a waist that is nearly the dimensions of her buttocks. Having a thick waist suggests that a woman has born children and consequently contributes to the wife's or husband's lineage group, one of the significant contributions that women can make to their ancestors. (Daly 1999: 344–5)

Figures 12.4 and 12.5, two photographs of three seated males and three seated females at a public ceremony, provide one illustration of the gender differences in dress. These photographs were taken during a seventeen-day centenary celebration in 1984 in the city of Buguma, Nigeria, which marked the migration from an early place of settlement, the island of Elem Ama, to a new location, the island of Buguma. The particular event was the feasting of the chiefs, when the community honoured the chieftaincy elite. The three men in Figure 12.4 are chiefs in full regalia, heavily robed, bejewelled, and with hats. Figure 12.5 shows two women on the left in the foreground who were going through the ritual of *iria* along with an older woman on the right, dressed similarly to function as a lead dancer of the women in the ceremonies. Each woman also wears a hat and coral, but their clothing consists of textiles that in this instance cover their breasts, leaving shoulders and arms bare. Their wrappers (not completely visible in the photograph) extend from their waist

Figure 12.4 Kalabari chiefs in full regalia, heavily robed, bejewelled with hats at the 17-day Bugama Centenary celebration in 1984.

Figure 12.5 These Kalabari women (in forefront) dressed as Iriabo with coral hats and necklaces with bare shoulders, at 17-day Bugama Cenetary celebration.

to their knees and their knees, calves, ankles, and feet were left bare for display and dancing. When in a seated position, each woman modestly covers her lap and legs with Indian madras cloth, a textile especially treasured among the Kalabari (Eicher and Erekosima 1987; 1996; Evenson 1991; 1994; Petgrave 1992). Using the madras textile guards against exposing her private parts because her wrapper is short, is a part of Kalabari decorum.

The display of skin among the Kalabari relates to their values placed on gendered dress for public appearances. These include community celebrations such as the Buguma Centenary of 1984, the large 1991 masquerade festival known as *Owuarusun* (Parade of the Water Spirits), and kin funerals where the extended family, friends, and acquaintances gather from the community at large. Kalabari adult males appear in public for everyday or ceremonial purposes with the upper and lower body as well as the head, and usually the feet, covered. Although a man may choose to dress casually with only a wrapper around his waist and a bare chest within the confines of his compound, he will not leave his domestic space with his chest bare or legs uncovered. Such dress is appropriate only for personal, secluded spaces within the house and its grounds, such as when arising in the morning, preparing for or going to and coming from the bath, or for relaxation at day's end. Bare feet for men, as for women, are appropriate in public when dancing, in order that well-executed dance steps can be appreciated by onlookers. Otherwise, men wear shoes, although dress etiquette decrees they be worn without socks.

In sharp contrast, the bare shoulders, breasts, and legs of a Kalabari woman may be displayed when she is dressed to participate in any part of an *iria* ceremony, even though these parts of an adult woman's body are not visible when she is dressed for everyday activities. However, an *iriabo* during her ceremonial walk through the town to visit her in-laws, friends and her own kin and to attend the church service for showing thanksgiving after the birth of her child and her subsequent sequestering (Daly 1984) may leave her breasts uncovered. Thus, presentation of gendered, ceremonial dress differs markedly for Kalabari men and women.

Dress and the body can be analyzed according to the symbolic interaction framework of appearance and the self as proposed by Gregory Stone (1962). Critical to his framework are the concepts of program, review, validation, and challenge. Prior to Stone's article on appearance and the self, symbolic inter-actionists concentrated on the verbal exchange of symbols, ignoring the visual cues of dress or the influence of nonverbal communication on the interaction process between and among individuals. The concepts of program and review refer to the impressions of an individual given to others through appearance (the program). The resulting assessment (the review) of the individual's program by those viewing him or her, implies a response of approval or disapproval (whether verbally or through body language). Stone proposes that when the program and review coincide, the self is validated, for what the individual intends to convey about personal and social identity through appearance is matched by the assessment of those who are reviewing the individual through dress. Thus, the matching of program and review validate the individual's proposal of identity. The program of an individual includes all aspects of dress that announce the identity of an individual to others, and a *gendered program* of dress implies that individuals dress to project their interpretation of their gendered self. The review of the gendered self results in the conclusion by others that the individuals viewed are men or women and the self is validated. Stone concludes that when program and review do not coincide, the self is challenged, and his article implies that individuals will change their programs when challenged in order to be validated. (As an aside, we might question whether this indeed is true for all individuals, as the case can be more complex when some individuals, as might often be said of contemporary youth, wish to defy the 'rules' of expectations for dress and wilfully dress in fashions contrary to the expectations of some of their reviewers, such as their parents, or even youth with different value systems than theirs.)

In the Kalabari example, the gendered body for men and women is presented through the program of dress, and the self is validated when the program is reviewed as individuals intended. For the Kalabari, the prominent historical role of men in economic and political structure of their society has been emphasized through the progression and transition from young-men-that-matter (*asawo*) to gentlemen-of-substance (*opu asawo*) to chiefs (*alapu*), culminating in the top position of the king (*amanyanabo*) and their corresponding ensembles. Men's positions begin with adulthood accompanied by titles as indicated in parentheses and an appropriate outfit with a name. Women's positions begin as little girls and progress through their sociobiological maturation to adulthood and motherhood. Women's positions have only two major titles, that of women (*ereme* with little girls being called *ere etubo* which means 'little woman') and *iriabo* (a woman who is going through *iria*), but each of the stages of dress has its own name.

Significantly, the names for men's ensembles refer to the top garment worn by men. In contrast, the names for women's ensembles refer to the bottom items or garments that cover the genitalia, the reproductive body site. Thus, differences in strategic body coverage and the amount of skin display for men and women correlate with the Kalabari construction of gender for men and women. In each of the Kalabari categories for dress, gender, and age, Stone's concepts of program and review coincide which results in validation of the gendered self. When I dressed in a wrapper and blouse in the Kalabari manner for a special occasion during my eight research trips to the Kalabari area, I was usually greeted with the phrase, 'Ah, a real Kalabari woman!' Daly had similar responses to dressing in Kalabari apparel (1999). The only challenge to the program of Kalabari women and dress that I witnessed during fieldwork was through an unwitting 'violation of the rules' by a visitor. For example, one young American woman photographing the Centenary Celebration in Buguma in 1984 who wore khaki pants and a casual blouse was chided by onlookers who told her that she was not properly dressed. Indeed, in the 1980s, few Nigerian women wore trousers or jeans. By the early 1990s, young women and teenagers were seen wearing such apparel in towns and cities in southern Nigeria. However, in Buguma, the expectation was that adult Kalabari women would wear a wrapper and blouse or a dress (a 'frock' as a skirted, one-piece garment is often called) for church or Kalabari cultural events.

Although feminists may protest the seemingly simplistic analysis of Kalabari differences in dress in relationship to gendered dress, these differences in display of skin for men and women are not peculiar to Kalabari culture. Such differences between men's and women's dress in exposure of body surface to public view have long existed in EuroAmerican culture and expectations for body coverage and exposure of skin for gendered dress in many public situations appear similar to those of the Kalabari. As examples, I will use formal dress for American weddings and occasions such as the annual Miss America Pageant and Hollywood Academy Awards ceremony. I have watched the latter two events annually for at least the last ten years to observe the dress of men and women involved. Men usually dress in suits or similar ensembles that cover their torsos from neck to feet (often tuxedos). In contrast, women choose gowns that display various parts of their bodies. For the business suit, the formal suit known in the United States as 'tails', or for the tuxedo, the shapes of men's bodies are hidden from view. They wear layers of clothing: underwear, shirt, jacket, trousers, socks, and shoes covering their bodies from the neck down with only their heads and hands exposed. Women, on the other hand, select from a wide range of types of dress that allows either covering up or showing off their bodies in various ways. A dress may be designed to cling to a body and/or to display cleavage, bare shoulders, a bared back, or a glimpse of leg and thigh through a slit skirt.

In the United States, invitations often indicate appropriate dress for a formal occasion by only stipulating (or at least suggesting) appropriate male attire with phrases such as 'White Tie' or 'Black Tie.' This indicates that a specific men's ensemble of coat style, trousers, shirt and accessories is preferred wear. Women subsequently define their dress according to current fashion to fit with the injunction for male dress. Depending on current fashions in silhouette and other details such as skirt length, this usually means that women often choose an appropriate gown, or in contemporary times, a 'dressy' trouser ensemble. If we use Stone's concepts of program and review to analyze these examples of gendered dress for EuroAmerican men and women, validation of the gendered self occurs when the program and review of the program coincide in the presentation of these examples of appropriate dress for such mainstream occasions. I recognize that there may be subcultural exceptions to these examples such as the dress of lesbians and gays along with various youth examples.

Featherstone's (1991: 171) useful analysis of the body in EuroAmerican consumer culture expands Stone's concept of program for the body. Featherstone claims the emphasis on body maintenance and appearance has two basic categories of the inner and outer body:

The inner body refers to the concern with the health and optimum functioning of the body which demands maintenance and repair in the face of disease, abuse and the deterioration accompanying the aging process. The outer body refers to appearance as well as the movement and control of the body within social space . . . [including] appearance, preservation of self and management of impressions.

Appearance, preservation of self, and management of impressions in both Kalabari and American terms relates to gendered dress and the sexed body, a term I borrow from Judith Okley (1996). Obviously, both men and women have sexed bodies and gendered dress in every society. Men's gendered dress in both Kalabari and EuroAmerican ceremonies covers the body fully with minimal skin display. In both cases, men's dress does not visibly display a sexed body. Instead, they minimize and mask the outlines of their bodies and bare only their faces and hands (occasionally the neck and in the case of Kalabari men, their feet when they wear no shoes and their ankles when they wear shoes with no socks). In downplaying the sexed body, men's dress indicates power and social standing. (An exception in Europe and America to men downplaying the sexed body is when they wear athletic attire in public places, such as swimming trunks on the beach. Other exceptions include dress for informal occasions where tight jeans, trousers or shorts with a bare chest, or an open shirt that shows a bare chest.) In contrast to the often exposed bodies of women, the fully-dressed and covered bodies of Kalabari and EuroAmerican men in public support Malcolm Young's observation that: 'Men's bodies and their sexuality are taken for granted whereas women's bodies are extensively defined and sexual and social meanings are imposed upon them' (1992: 271).

Certainly, the sexed bodies of both Kalabari and EuroAmerican women are extensively defined with sexual and social meanings imposed on them. In each case, women display more skin when dressed for formal, public occasions. However, there the similarity ends. For the Kalabari woman, the sexed body for public display emphasizes being round and plump with a definite implication of fecundity. As I have watched women being dressed for special occasions, as *iriabo* mourners in a funeral, they are dressed with layers of textiles underneath the top wrapper in order to appear pregnant. In contrast, the sexed body of a woman in EuroAmerican terms clearly does not emphasize a body shape that hints of pregnancy or maternity. Instead, a slim body shape implies, as Featherstone suggests above, control through exercise and diet. As a matter of fact, women who are not slim but also not pregnant have a horror of being considered pregnant. In one well-known example, Jean Nidetch, founder of Weight Watchers International®, disclosed that she decided to tackle her own 'weight problem' when an acquaintance asked her if she was pregnant, and she was not.

EuroAmerican women's dress for formal occasions, as in the case of the Miss America contest and weddings, ideally emphasizes a slim body with no hint of pregnancy. Women who are not slim attempt to look as slender as possible, implying virginity in contrast to Kalabari women's appearance of being fecund. I find Sherry Ortner's (1996: 75–8) discussion and elaboration of Margaret Mead's (1930) idea of the 'sacred maid' complex from Samoa useful in analyzing the slim EuroAmerican body. The sacred maid (*taupo*) position 'is one of responsibility and honor' and she is expected to remain virginal until marriage. A significant requirement of the Miss America Pageant has been that the contestants are single (interpreted as never married). Such a requirement implies that each contestant is a virgin, for they are additionally required to declare that they have never had a child or had an abortion. Certainly the gowns they wear in the pageant activities follow the display of skin and slim-bodied patterns that I have suggested is common in public for formal EuroAmerican events. Following the 1999 Miss America Pageant, its Executive Director recommended that the contestants would simply be required to prove that they are not married or the mother of a child at the time of the pageant. The controversy over this recommendation was so great that the Executive Director was asked to leave his $250,000-a-year job. A thoughtful columnist commented, however, that the rules were not changed because:

> The ideal woman is someone who's young, beautiful, sexy and available to men because she's unattached and unencumbered by children. She is a virtual virgin, if not an actual one . . .
>
> The pageant is the embodiment of a male sexual fantasy that's been embraced by millions of romance-seeking women whose real lives don't fit the fantasy one bit. It doesn't matter if a Miss America contestant has had sex with a score of guys, or if she has a steady, live-in boyfriend or a fiancé. She's supposed to project an image of sexuality combined with sexual purity, whether she's sexually pure or not. Nothing could dispel the chastity myth more abruptly than a marriage license (even a defunct one) or a child. (McCarthy, 1999)

She concludes by saying that the pageant should raise its rules to reflect the changes in American society, acknowledging that many young women in their twenties have had a sex life which may have included pregnancy and an abortion.

Similarly, although we know that many young EuroAmerican women at marriage are not virginal, the white wedding dress has been used as the symbol of virginity. (A personal anecdote stresses the power of this symbolism. A young man and woman who had been living together and were to be married within the month were my dinner guests. As the bride-to-be described many of the details of the upcoming formal wedding, she mentioned the colour of her wedding gown, and I asked rather incidentally how she happened to select ivory as the colour. She said her mother, who didn't approve of her living with her fiancé before marriage, wouldn't allow her to wear 'bridal white' because she was 'spoiled'.) In elaborating upon the example of the wedding dress, even though white is said to represent virginity, many formal wedding gowns call attention to the sexed body of the bride. They are frequently designed with a slim waist, deep frontal décolletage, display of bare neck, shoulders, and sometimes back. For example the Fall, 1999 issue of *Bride's*, a magazine from the publishers of *Vogue*, *Glamour* and *Mademoiselle*, featured (both in advertisements and editorial features) 271 women as brides (as indicated by the colour white and the formality of their gowns), 73 women as bridesmaids (as indicated by colours other than white of their gowns) and 13 women as 'mother of the bride' (as determined by woman's age the and design of the gown). In addition, 33 men, assumed to be 'grooms', were shown in advertisements and editorials. In all cases, the men wore some type of suit with a shirt and shoes that covered them from neck to feet. In the case of the brides, 239 had décolletage, 269 an exposed neck, 257 exposed arms, 235 exposed shoulders and 149 an exposed back. Of the 73 bridesmaids, 71 exposed their arms, 68 their shoulders, 60 their back and 52 had décolletage. For the women who appeared to be older, whether falling into the categories of older brides or mothers of the bride or groom, much less of the body was exposed with only one showing off her arms and ten displaying some décolletage.

Beauty contests around the world provide still another example of the sexed body as influenced by EuroAmerican customs of dress for women. Women parade in close-fitting bathing suits and evening gowns with ample skin exposure, but certainly not an ample waistline. The late Diana, Princess of Wales was a prototype of the EuroAmerican body. Her display of a slim body in a myriad of styles of dress and skin exposure caused photographers from around the world to capture her persona in formal and everyday dress. She wore ballgowns with décolletage and bare shoulders and short-skirted dresses and suits with her long, lean legs on view. Even since her death, books continue to document her fashion sense that typifies the EuroAmerican values for a woman's body and appearance (e.g. Graham and Blanchard 1998).

Each of these EuroAmerican cases provide examples of young women portrayed as the 'sacred maid' with the assumption of virginity in contrast to the procreative role or 'abundant mother' in Kalabari terms with the assumption of fecundity. Slenderness is not a desirable feature for an *iriabo*. Although both Kalabari and EuroAmerican women display a sexed body through their dress, and through the display of skin, the message in Kalabari terms clearly conveys that dress changes as biological change occurs, acknowledging maturation through the reproductive cycle. In EuroAmerican examples, the message is not one of fecundity, but instead the connection to reproduction is ignored. In fact, although apparel specially designed as maternity wear has been developed for pregnant women (Bailey, 1992), women often delay wearing such clothes and pride themselves on looking slim as long as possible before beginning 'to show'. Susan Bordo (1993: 208) has written extensively on the issue of the slender body in American society and suggests that slim women's bodies symbolize neutralization of women as women are pushing into more areas of work that once were solely the domain of men:

Today, it is required of female desire, loose in the male world, to be normalized according to the professional (and male) standards of that world; female bodies, accordingly, must be stripped of all psychic resonances with maternal power.

Her analysis fits well in making a comparison between the Kalabari and Euro-American examples of gendered dress and the sexed body.

Recently in social science and literary criticism circles, concern with the topic of the body has burgeoned, but little attention has been paid to analyzing gender, the sexed body, and dress. One exception is Elizabeth Wilson (1992) who conjectures that the early writing by costume historians and theorists relating sexuality (I suggest substituting the term 'sexed body') to dress and fashion was undoubtedly overstated. For example, she cites Laver whose theory of fashion claimed that shifting erogenous zones of the female body arise in regard to fashions in dress in order to keep men from becoming sexually bored. She asserts that his analysis views sexuality and dress from the point of view of men in relationship to women with no attempt to explain women's perspective of their own dress (Wilson 1992: 12). In addition, we might note that Laver's theory does not include the assessment by women of men's dress. She insists that feminist writing about dress 'has incorporated something of an implied reaction against the idea that women's dress is only about sexual allure . . . Instead there has been more emphasis on all other social meanings of dress' (Wilson 1992: 12). She concludes, that 'clearly sex and dress are closely related' (Wilson 1992: 12), reinforcing Ernest Crawley's statement that 'The great bifurcation of dress is sexual' (1918/1931: 54). Both of these observations apply equally to Kalabari dress of men and women where the display of skin relates to the social construction of gender in Kalabari life.

In conclusion, consider why the images of a man in an off-the-shoulder dress shirt or a lounge suit with an exposed midriff as shown in Figures 12.6 and 12.7 are humorous. Would an equivalent example of Kalabari men's dress that shows bare shoulders result in laughter among Kalabari readers? In each case, something would seem amiss in regard to determining whether program and review coincide in validation of the gendered self through dress. I suggest that although there first appeared to be similarities of display of skin in dress between Kalabari and EuroAmerican women and men, deeply held values about fecundity and virginity within each society provide a contrast between the examples of the women's dress. In contrast to the examples of women's dress, there are parallels in dress of both Kalabari and EuroAmerican men. Dress of the sexed body reinforces the social construction of gender and provides a useful affirmation of Stone's (1962) concepts of program, review, validation and challenge.

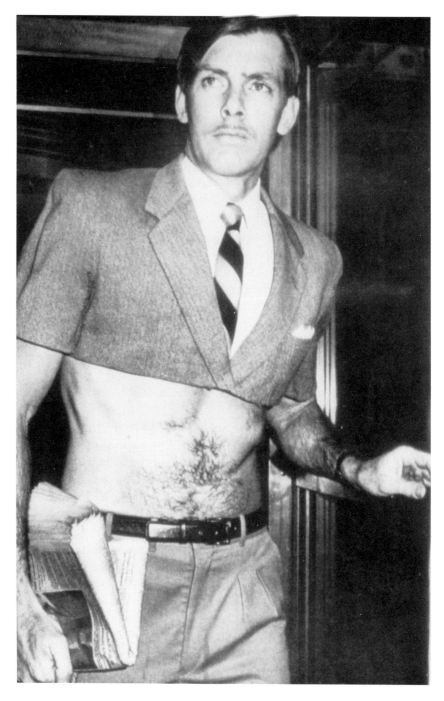

Figure 12.6 'Half-Suit' from Philip Garner's Better Living Catalogue (photographer James Hamilton, 1982: 30).

Figure 12.7 'The Off-Shoulder Shirt' from Philip Garner's Better Living Catalogue (photographer James Hamilton, 1982: 30).

Notes

1. The names used in Figure 12.2 are reversed from those I use: mine are drawn from Ilyalla (1968) and my fieldwork sources. Thus, the discrepancy may be accounted for by noting that little girls infrequently wear these two ensembles, only at times of celebration. In the 1980s and 1990s the difference in dressing little girls for the first two stages was minimal. I saw few little girls, if any, who wore only beads.

References

Bailey, R. (1992) 'Clothes Encounters of the Gynecological Kind: Medical Mandates and Maternity Modes', in R. Barnes and J. B. Eicher (eds), *Dress and Gender: Making amd Meaning*. Oxford: Berg.

Bordo, S. (1993), *Unbearable Weight: Feminism, Western Culture, and the Body*, Berkeley: University of California Press.

Crawley, A. E. (1931), *Dress, Drinks, and Drums*, London: Methuen and Co. Ltd. Reprinted from Crawley, A.E. (1918), 'Dress' in *Encyclopedia of Religion and Ethics*, Charles Scribners and Sons: 40–72.

Daly, M. C. (l984), *Kalabari Female Appearance and the Tradition of Iria*, Unpublished Ph.D. dissertation, Minneapolis: University of Minnesota.

Daly, M. C. (1999), 'Ah, A Real Kalabari Woman!: Reflexivity and the Conceptualization of Appearance', *Fashion Theory 3* (3): 343–61.

Daly, M. C., Eicher, J.B., and Erekosima, T.V. (1986, May), 'Male and Female Artistry in Kalabari Dress', *African Arts 19* (3): 48–51, 83.

Eicher, J.B. (1981), 'Influences of Changing Resources on Clothing, Textiles and the Quality of Life: Dressing for Reality, Fun, and Fantasy', *Combined Proceedings, Association of Clothing Professors of Textiles and Clothing*: 36–41.

Eicher, J.B. (1997), 'Social Change and Dress Among the Kalabari of Nigeria', in N. Johnson and C.L. Wang (eds), *Changing Rural Social Systems: Adaptation and Survival* (Festschrift for J.A. Beegle), East Lansing: Michigan State University Press.

Eicher, J.B. and Erekosima, T.V. (1987), 'Kalabari Funerals: Celebration and Display', *African Arts 21* (1): 38–45, 87.

Eicher, J.B. and Erekosima, T.V. (1992), 'Textile, Trade and Masquerade among the Kalabari of Nigeria', 9th Triennial Symposium of African Arts, 21–25 April, Iowa City, IA.

Eicher, J.B. and Erekosima, T.V. (1993), 'Taste and 19th Century Patterns of Textile Use Among the Kalabari of Nigeria', paper presented at a conference on 'Cloth, The World Economy and the Artisan: Textile Manufacturing and Marketing in South Asia and Africa, 1780–1950', Dartmouth College, Hanover, New Hampshire.

Eicher, J.B. and Erekosima, T.V. (1996), 'Indian Textiles in Kalabari Funerals', *Asian Art and Culture*. Washington, DC: Smithsonian Institution Press; 68–79.

Eicher, J.B. and Miller, K.A. (1994, Oct.), 'Dress and the Public, Private and Secret Self: Revisiting the Model', unpublished paper presented at International Textiles and Apparel Association, Minneapolis, MN.

Eicher, J.B. and Roach Higgins, M.E. (1992), 'Definition and Classification of Dress: Implications for the Study of Dress and Gender', in R. Barnes and J.B. Eicher (eds), *Dress and Gender: Making and Meaning in Cultural Context*, Oxford and Providence: Berg Publishers: 2–28.

Erekosima, T.V. (1982), 'The Use of Apparel and Accessories for Expressing Status in Nigerian Societies: The Kalabari Case Studied as an Education Technology', paper presented at the African Studies Association annual meeting.

Erekosima, T.V. (1989), *Analysis of a Learning Resource for Political Integration Applicable to Nigerian Secondary School Social Studies: The Case of Kalabari Men's Traditional Dress*, unpublished Ph.D. dissertation, Washington, D.C.: Catholic University of America.

Erekosima, T.V. and Eicher, J.B. (1980, 15 Oct.), *Kalabari Men's Dress: A Sophisticated African Response to Culture Contact*, paper presented at African Studies Association, Philadelphia.

Erekosima, T.V. and Eicher, J.B. (1994), 'The Aesthetics of Men's Dress of the Kalabari of Nigeria', in DeLong, M. and Fiore, A. M. (eds), *Aesthetics of Textiles and Clothing: Advancing Multi-Disciplinary Perspectives*. International Textiles and Apparel Association Special Publication on Aesthetics #7, Monument, CO: ITAA.

Ereks (Erekosima) T. V. (1973), 'Kalabari Categories of the Self: A Philosophical Extrapolation in Cultural Dynamism', *Oduma* (October) *Vol. 1* (1): 21–7.

Evenson, S. L. (1991), 'The Manufacture of Madras in South India and Its Export to West Africa: A Case Study', unpublished master's thesis, St Paul, MN: University of Minnesota.

Evenson, S. L. (1994), *A History of Indian Madras Manufacture and Trade: Shifting Patterns of Exchange*, unpublished Ph.D. dissertation, Minneapolis: University of Minnesota.

Featherstone, M. (1991), 'The Body in Consumer Culture', in Featherstone, M., Hepworth, M. and Turner, B. (eds), *The Body: Social Process and Cultural Theory*, London and Thousand Oaks, CA: Sage Publications: 170–96.

Graham, T. and Blanchard, T. (1998), *Dressing Diana*, London: Weidenfield and Nicolson; Princeton, NJ: Benford Books.

Horton, R. (1960), 'The Gods as Guests: An Aspect of Kalabari Religious Life', *Nigeria Magazine*, Lagos, Nigeria.

Horton, R. (1962), 'The Kalabari World-View', *Africa 32*: 197–220.

Horton, R. (1966), 'Igbo: An Ordeal for Aristocrats', *Nigeria Magazine 90*: 168–83.

Horton, R. (1969), 'From Fishing Village to City–State: A Social History of New Calabar', *Man in Africa*, London: Tavistock.

Horton, R. (1975), 'Ekineba: A Forgotten Myth', *Oduma 2* (2): 33–6.

Iyalla, Bliss (1968), 'Womanhood in the Kalabari', *Nigeria Magazine 98*: 216–24.

McCarthy, S. (1999), 'Pageant Should Change Its Rules to Fit the Times', *Star Tribune*, September 21, A13.

Mead, M. (1930), The Social Organization of Manu'a. Bernice P. Bishop Museum Bulletin 76. Honolulu: Bishop Museum.

Michelman, S.O. (1987), 'Kalabari Female and Male Aesthetics: A Comparative Visual Analysis', unpublished master's thesis, Minneapolis: University of Minnesota.

Michelman, S.O. (1992), *Dress in Kalabari Women's Organizations,* unpublished Ph.D. dissertation, Minneapolis: University of Minnesota.

Michelman, S.O. and Eicher, J.B. (1995), 'Dress and Gender in Kalabari Women's Societies', *Clothing and Textiles Research Journal 13* (2): 121–30.

Michelman, S.O. and Erekosima, T.V. (1992), 'Kalabari Dress in Nigeria: Visual Analysis and Gender Implications', in R. Barnes and J.B. Eicher (eds), *Dress and Gender: Making and Meaning in Cultural Context,* Oxford and Providence: Berg Publishers; 164–82.

Okley, J. (1996), 'Women Readers: Other Utopias and Own Bodily Knowledge', in McClancy, J. and McDonaugh, C. (eds), *Popularizing Anthropology,* London and New York: Routledge.

Ortner, S. (1996), *Making Gender: The Politica and Erotics of Culture,* Boston: Beacon Press.

Petgrave, M. D. (1992), 'Indian Madras in Kalabari Culture', unpublished master's Plan B paper, Minneapolis: University of Minnesota.

Roach-Higgins, M.E. and Eicher, J.B. (1992), 'Dress and Identity', *Clothing and Textiles Research Journal 10* (4): 1–8.

Russell, F.E. (1892), 'A Brief Survey of the American Dress Reform Movements of the Past, with Views of Representative Women', *Arena* 33, (Aug): 325–39.

Stone, G.P. (1962), 'Appearance and the Self', in Arnold Rose (ed.), *Human Behavior and the Social Processes: An Interactionist Approach,* New York: Houghton Mifflin Co.

Wilson, E. (1992), 'Fashion and the Postmodern Body', in Elizabeth Wilson and Juliet Ash (eds), *Chic Thrills: A Fashion Reader,* Berkeley and Los Angeles: University of California Press.

Young, M. (1992), 'Dress and Modes of Address: Structural Forms for Policewoman', in R. Barnes and J.B. Eicher (eds), *Dress and Gender: Making and Meaning in Cultural Context.* Oxford and Providence: Berg Publishers.

Index